THESAURUS

of the

SENSES

THESAURUS

of the

SENSES

LINDA HART

*The universe is full of magical things
patiently waiting for our wits to grow sharper.*

—Eden Phillpotts, *A Shadow Passes*

SEE
WELL

HEAR
WELL

TOUCH
WELL

TASTE
WELL

SMELL
WELL

How to Use This Thesaurus

Thesaurus of the Senses is an instrument for your writing success. Whether you are seeking just the right word or need a bit of inspiration, this reference tool can guide your literary travels.

Connect with the Senses. Use the words and exercises in this book to connect with one of your most valuable assets as a writer: your ability to engage physically and emotionally with the world through your senses. Grounding yourself in the senses and seeking out new ways to become aware of sensory experiences can help you connect with readers and find your writing voice.

Expand your perspective. Broaden your viewpoint by using all of your senses to build vibrant descriptions. Browse the different facets of each sense in the book to find rich complexities that will engage readers. Consider shapes, textures, aromas, colors, facial expressions, flavors, and sounds in your word choices. Add spark and zing to your work during the editing process.

Get inspired. Rummage through the word list for inspiration and encouragement. Delight in the *fiery, frothy, furrowed,* and *fluttering* words—all collected in one place. Use your favorite words as writing prompts to launch your next story or poem.

Find the apt word. Explore the word and subject indexes in the back to locate more relevant and related words for your writing tasks. Discover new associations and connections.

Published by Four Cats Publishing LLC

Cover design and illustrations by Tonya Foreman

Printed in the United States of America

ISBN-10: 0988839970
ISBN-13: 978-0-9888399-7-7

To order additional copies, contact Four Cats Publishing LLC,
www.fourcatspublishing.com

Contents

Introduction

Certain words rattle the ground beneath you. They startle, intoxicate, beckon, electrify. They reverberate with excitement and shimmer with emotion. They poke you in the rib cage and entice your tongue. They arouse the senses. These special words, collected like jewels by wordsmiths and poets, in journals and notebooks or on scraps of paper for later use, enliven writing with their astonishing beauty and power. They instill in readers a sense of place rooted in the physical world, and they command attention and respect.

Thesaurus of the Senses is a collection of some of the best English sensory words, curated for their whimsy, grandeur, and resonance. Unlike ordinary thesauri that contain all manner of words—the mesmerizing as well as the mundane—this thesaurus contains the gems of the literary world. Here writers will find excellent company among the *careening, clanging, unflinching, splendorous,* and *velvety* words that add depth, inspiration, and spice to their work.

This collection is intended as a resource for writers, poets, teachers, students, storytellers, and word lovers alike who want to bring sparkle to their writing or who simply want to delight in the rich kinship of language. The words in this thesaurus are often simple and unpretentious. They are not esoteric oddities or corporate "power words," even though they are powerful. Their use is not meant to help win TV game shows or stump dinner companions. Yet these words can stop readers in their tracks with their passion and panache.

Organized loosely by each of the five senses—see, hear, touch, taste, smell—as well as subcategories of the main qualities and dimensions of those senses, this book offers tools to build vivid descriptions and bring rhythm and crackle to writing. These words can also serve as writing prompts to discover hidden connections and unleash creativity.

Rather than an exhaustive collection of words, shades of meaning, and precise definitions, it is a collection of loosely related words intended to spark imagination, serendipity, and association by highlighting the breadth and interconnections of sensory experiences.

Not surprisingly, the largest collection of words is the seeing words—*glisten*, *bedraggled*, *willowy*. Visual words have special impact because they can provide the first, and sometimes the fullest, impression to a reader. They are especially useful for sketching the physical outlines and unspoken emotional texture of a scene quickly through which readers can envision the rest of the story.

Acoustic words add to the music, pace, and rhythm of a work, particularly when combined with crisp dialogue and action. When used sparingly and to great effect, hearing words provide force, surprise, tone, lilt, melody—and a bit of drama.

Tactile words bring immediacy and presence to writing because, like something *prickly*, *frothy*, or *clammy* touching your skin, they cannot be ignored. Like a marinade, they also combine well with other sensory words such as those describing taste and smell.

INTRODUCTION

Taste words, though sometimes overlooked as descriptors unless actual food is involved, can be very tempting, even tantalizing, in writing. Some readers will find it impossible to read through the list of taste words without salivating.

And, smells. Ah, smells! Smells offer a primal and direct connection to memory, pleasure, and revulsion. Along with tastes, scents can captivate our senses, turning a simple walk in a forest or bakery into an emotional and sensual extravagance. From floral to peppery words, the smell list is not exhaustive, but readers can get a whiff of some of its more pungent odors.

Finally, each of our senses is not experienced in isolation. The miracle of our combined senses is how they blend and trigger thoughts and emotions to create meaningful impressions of the world—sometimes a profound kinesthetic and even synesthetic experience.

And on the edge of our five senses is an inexplicable, unnamed sixth sense: our deep insight into and connection with the unknown. Many words in this thesaurus cannot be pinned down to one particular sense or quality. They glimmer in that unfathomable space between the sensory and mystical worlds—a poetic and spiritual wonder.

From the weighty to the wispy, senses are how we perceive and understand the world and how readers come to know an imagined world. When we are acutely attuned, our senses catapult us directly into creative realms. They intermingle to add color, shape, sound, depth, texture, taste, and aroma to our experiences. I invite you to explore the exquisite and intricate world of sensory words and let them infuse your writing with their magic.

Connecting *with the* Senses: Exercises

These exercises are meant to ground you in the senses so that you can more easily connect with and describe your experiences. While doing these exercises, it is handy to have a writing journal or recorder nearby so you can capture your thoughts and feelings more easily.

1. Has something you've seen or heard brought you to tears? How about something you've smelled? Or tasted? Describe your experiences.

2. Of the five senses, what is your strongest sense? What is your weakest or most underdeveloped sense? To pique your weakest sense, write down five intense sensations or experiences that would enliven that sense. What words or descriptions come to mind to describe those heightened experiences?

3. Words carry emotion, melody, and rhythm—sometimes contrary to their actual meaning. Listen to the following words and write about the types of music, sensations, and feelings they convey or evoke: *cataclysmic, resplendent, muddled, precipitous, swirling, cacophony, succulent.*

4. Sensory experiences are both qualitative and quantitative. Quantitatively, they can range from barely perceptible to overwhelmingly intense. Qualitatively, they can range from rich and riveting to dull and bland. In addition, sometimes sensory experiences are a curious mixture of opposites—discordant and harmonious, enticing and repulsive, sweet and sour, etc. Pick a few sensory words and for each word explore its similar and opposite states and the layers of complexity within it.

5. Wherever you are right now, stop to listen. See if you can isolate each separate sound in your space. Write down all sounds that you can identify.

6. Write a five-sentence poem using each of the five senses in a separate line. In the next line, write about a sixth sense you've experienced. In the following lines of the poem, write how the senses you wrote about are connected to each other.

7. Pick a large object in your environment and picture it very small; pick a small object and see it suddenly gigantic.

8. Look at various things and people through different objects such as a vase, colored glass, mirror, magnifying glass, long tube, etc. What do you notice about your perception and reaction to these transformations?

9. Find an exotic fruit or vegetable that you have never tasted before and write about your first experience of tasting it. What places, emotions, and memories does eating it invoke?

10. Describe how you feel when you unexpectedly get caught in a rainstorm, windstorm, or snowstorm.

11. Describe what you are feeling right now using only a whisper.

12. Take a walk outside at your normal pace. Now decrease your pace by half. Now by half again. Continue decreasing your pace by half until you are no longer moving. Describe your sensations and observations at each stage of the process. Now try this exercise walking backwards.

13. Politely eavesdrop on a conversation and listen to the kinds of words and expressions the people use. What tone and volume do they use? Is one person dominating the conversation? How do the others respond? What words describe their interaction? See if you can imagine and describe their facial expressions and gestures without looking at them.

14. The five basic elements of water, earth, fire, air, and space drive our senses. Pick one of these elements and describe your physical and emotional connections to it. Then explore different combinations of these elements, such as water/fire, fire/air, earth/water, etc., and their dynamic effect on you.

15. Describe an outdoor scene using only your sense of smell or taste. What emotions and memories do these smells and tastes trigger?

16. Stimulate your senses by visiting a coffee shop that sells

whole beans that you can smell. Or sniff different kinds of spices in a spice store or soaps in a bath store. What are your favorite and least favorite smells? Are you surprised by how complex the smells are?

17. Build a poem or some prose using the following instructions:

- Begin with a physical object and describe in separate lines what the object looks, sounds, feels, tastes, and smells like.
- What are the object's strengths and weaknesses?
- Describe what is true about the object.
- What is unknowable, indescribable, or hidden about the object?
- Have a character interact with the object and tell you what it means to him/her.
- What would happen if the object became lost or destroyed?
- How can the object be transformed into something else?

18. Make sounds vocally or using your body or an object that express your mood. What words come to mind as you make these sounds?

19. In synesthesia, one sense can trigger another. For example, a sound can trigger certain colors, or certain words can trigger specific tastes or smells. Have you ever had experiences like these? During your day, observe how your senses overlap, bend, and expand. See if you can extend your awareness of your sensory experiences beyond your normal perception. Can you hear grass, smell sunlight, taste wind, etc.?

20. Sometimes one sense magnifies our other senses and emotions, for example, sounds that help us see better or smells that expand our taste. Find other examples. Can smell help us hear something better? Can taste enliven how we see or hear something?

21. When we are intensely using one of our senses, we sometimes block out the other senses, for example, closing our eyes when we experience an intense sound, taste, smell, or touch. What are examples you have experienced?

22. Write about a character and describe how he or she fully senses the world and how others sense him or her.

23. Smells are sometimes difficult to describe and are often based on what something smells like (flowers, gasoline, skunk, etc.) instead of their actual essence. English words for describing smells are surprisingly limited. However, some languages have richer vocabularies describing for smells. For example, the Jahai language of the inhabitants of the Malay Peninsula has a smell word that translates into "to have a bloody smell which attracts tigers." What new, richer ways can you describe smells that you encounter or imagine?

24. Have a companion pick a half dozen foods or condiments and offer them to you to taste one at a time while you keep your eyes closed. How accurately can you describe these tastes?

25. Describe these experiences: riding with a caravan of mules

down a Grand Canyon trail, playing in a bell choir in an echo chamber, licking a lizard's skin, driving a spacecraft near Saturn's rings, singing with a pack of coyotes, lighting the torch at the Olympics, using only your sense of smell to imagine where an old book has been, becoming a river.

SEE

We eat light, drink it in through our skins... Seeing is a very sensuous act—there's a sweet deliciousness to feeling yourself see something.
—James Turrell, American artist

LIGHT *and* DARK - COLORS *and* HUES - SIZES *and*
AMOUNTS - SPACE, LOCATION, *or* POSITION -
SHAPES *and* STRUCTURES - TEXTURES, DESIGNS,
and PATTERNS - FACIAL EXPRESSIONS - MOTION -
DISTINCTIVE QUALITY *or* IMPRESSION -
GENERAL APPEARANCE - VISION *and* SIGHT

Seeing is a faulty sense. Anyone who has ever fallen victim to a magic trick knows that vision is not always trustworthy. It can be a slight of hand. We can haplessly plunge through optical trapdoors or fail to recognize blind spots. Our expectations and beliefs can lead us down blind alleys or into hallucinatory flights of fancy. We see only what we want to see. Or turn a blind eye. Our sight can deceive us, mesmerize us, haunt us.

On the other hand, we can perceive and interpret a phenomenal amount of information in just one glance—patterns, shapes, colors, movements, impressions—and from there accurately assess our surroundings. We can also have exceptional vision beyond sight—a beholder of beauty and possessor of insight, of the unseen and the invisible. We can read between the lines, visualize the impossible, and imagine in our mind's eye elaborate worlds of our own making. We can also display visual virtuosity in the form of extraordinary foresight or hindsight. Or vividly recall an event using photographic memory.

Our world relies heavily on visual impressions, in mass media, advertising, film, art, sports, fashion, music, etc. Some images leave an indelible mark upon us, providing lifelong inspiration or conversely leaving us scarred. As our dominate sense, sight allows us continually record rich visual tapestries and unspoken messages around us. We can visually play back pleasant memories and envision our future from many vantage points. In addition, our eyes can perceive intangible, elusive qualities in people and situations such as allure, charisma, and *je ne sais quoi*, a certain indescribable something.

We constantly project an image of ourselves onto the world. We see and are seen. Yet, the mystery of sight is that we never truly get an accurate glimpse of ourselves as others see us. Though we carry a mental picture of ourselves, and an idealized vision, we remain always behind the mirror, looking out.

In this section, set your sights on words showcasing the many dimensions of visual perception—size, shape, color, design, etc.—that combine into the marvel of seeing. This section also includes words that describe facial expressions—human visuals to which we are acutely attuned—and multifaceted words that reflect a distinctive visual quality or impression.

LIGHT *and* DARK

ablaze
burning, fiery, flaming, glowing, aglow, shimmering, bright, shining

aglow
glowing, shimmering, radiant, ablaze, luminous, luminescent, fiery, bright, shining, flaming

angelic
celestial, ethereal, shining, heavenly, radiant, glorious, luminous, divine

aura
brightness, glow, halo, ambiance, mood, atmosphere

beam, beaming
luster, rocket, spark, gleaming, flaring, glaring, blazing, scorching, flaming, luminous, lucid, brilliant, radiant

blackened
dark, heavy, shadowy, inky, darkened, dimmed, shaded

blaze, blazing
rocket, luster, wildfire, flaring, glaring, beaming, flaming, gleaming, scorching, spark, burst

bright
illuminated, ablaze, burning, aura, shining, glowing, aglow, flashy, shimmering, scintillating, dazzling

brilliant
lucid, bright, illustrious, radiant, vivid, dazzling, golden, luminous, sparkling, lustrous, bold

burning
fiery, smoking, blackened, flaming, ablaze, glowing, aglow, bright, shining

candescent
bright, illuminated, shining, glowing, dazzling, luminescent

celestial
angelic, ethereal, shining, divine, glowing, astral, starlike, luminous, stellar

clarify, clarified
sheer, crystalline, refined, purified, illuminate, elucidate

crystalline
clarified, clear, translucent, glassy, sparkling, lucid, pure

crystallize
clarify, refine, purify, materialize, coalesce

dappled
speckled, spotted, filtered, stippled, blotchy, mottled, flecked

dark, darkly
heavy, shadowy, black, inky, glowering, scowling, sullen, dense, murky, shady, clouded, curtained, sulky, gloomy, morose, moody, brooding

dazzle, dazzling
shining, lively, brilliant, spellbinding, hypnotic, radiant, sparkling, flickering, glimmering, glinting, glistening, glittering, shimmering, twinkling

enlighten, enlightening
illuminate, brighten, shining, glowing, clarify, elucidate

ethereal
angelic, celestial, shining, unearthly, volatile, changeable, heavenly, ephemeral, divine, airy

fiery
flaming, glowing, aglow, ablaze, burning, bright, shining, inflamed, impassioned, passionate

SEE: LIGHT and DARK

flame
> spark, flare, blaze, scorch, gleam, luster, rocket

flaming
> burning, bright, shining, fiery, glowing, aglow, ablaze, shimmering

flare, flaring
> glare, blaze, flame, gleam, luster, scorch, rocket, spark, flicker, sparkle, beam

flash, flashy, flashing
> flamboyant, bright, colorful, elaborate, eye-catching, splashy, vivid, dashing, shimmering, showy

flick, flicker
> flare, spark, glare, glint, shimmer, twinkle, sparkle, blink, dazzle, glimmer, glisten, glitter, flitter, pulse

glassy
> glazed, filmy, glossy, luster, mirrored, gleaming, sleek

gleam, gleaming
> flare, glare, beam, blaze, flame, luster, sparkle, glimmer, glint, glow

glimmer, glimmering
> glint, gleam, glisten, sparkle, twinkle, inkling, flicker, shimmer

glint, glinting
> sparkle, flash, flicker, flare, shine, glare, shimmer, glimmer

glisten, glistening
> glimmer, glint, gleam, sparkle, twinkle, shimmer, glitter

glitter, glittering
> showy, flashy, frilly, glimmer, shimmer, glisten, sparkle

glossy
> shiny, sheen, sleek, glassy, iridescent, opalescent, pearly, gleaming, glaze, slick

glow, glowing
> illuminated, ablaze, shimmering, burning, bright, shining, fiery, flaming, aglow, glimmering

heavy
> shadowy, black, inky, dense, murky, shady, clouded, curtained, gloomy, moody, brooding

illuminate, illuminated
> bright, shining, glowing, clarify, enlighten, spotlight

illumine
> illuminate, brighten, flash, light, irradiate, clarify, gleam

illustrious
> dazzling, shining, lively, brilliant, spellbinding, hypnotic, radiant, esteemed, eminent, preeminent, renowned, magical, splendorous, wondrous, resplendent

inky
> heavy, shadowy, black, dark, pitch-black, dense, murky, shady

lackluster
> dull, dim, vapid, drab, colorless, bland, flat, dreary

lightning
> spark, flash, charge, bolt, thunderbolt

lucid
> beaming, bright, brilliant, crystal-clear, incandescent, luminous, gleaming

luminous
> lucid, beaming, bright, brilliant, shining, radiant, glowing, incandescent

luster
> gleam, spark, radiance, flare, glare, blaze, flame, sheen, sparkle, beam, gloss

lustrous
glamorous, alluring, beaming, dazzling, enchanting, shining, radiant, luminous, magnetic, stunning, gleaming, polished

mirrored
reflecting, shiny, shimmering, glassy, glossy, shining

murky
shadowy, black, inky, dense, shady, clouded, brooding, moody

nebulous
shadowy, foggy, hazy, obscure, dim, fuzzy, faint

opaque
cloudy, shaded, murky, hazy, muddied, foggy, blurry

radiant, radiance
stunning, shining, sparkling, splendorous, brilliant, luminous

ray
beam, spark, glimmer, flicker

reflecting
mirrored, shiny, shimmering, glassy, flashing

resplendent
splendorous, dazzling, shining, brilliant, sublime, glimmering, spellbinding, radiant

searchlight
beacon, torch, lamplight, moonlight, firelight, lantern, flame, flash

shadowy
heavy, black, brooding, murky, shady, clouded, curtained, gloomy, moody, dense, inky

shady
heavy, shadowy, black, sullen, murky, clouded, curtained, gloomy, moody, brooding, dense, inky

sheen
 glossy, shiny, slick, sleek, glassy, polish, gloss, shine, gleam, glint

shimmer, shimmering
 glowing, aglow, shining, flaming, shiny, ablaze, bright, glimmering, flickering

shine, shiny
 bright, illuminated, glowing, polished, refined, mirrored, reflecting, glaze, sheen

spark
 flame, gleam, scorch, rocket, flare, glare, beam, blaze, torch

sparkle, sparkling
 dazzling, flickering, glimmering, glinting, glistening, glittering, shimmering, twinkling, effervescent, vivacious

torch
 beacon, searchlight, lamplight, moonlight, firelight, lantern

twinkle, twinkling
 shimmering, glistening, glittering, flickering, sparkling, blinking, dazzling, glimmering, glinting

Colors *and* Hues

abloom
 bright, flowery, showy, blossomy, blooming

alabaster
 ivory, pale, fair, translucent, creamy

amber
 honey-yellow, yellow-orange, golden

apricot
 peach, light-orange, orange-yellow

aquamarine
   blue-green, sea-green

ashen
   pale, sickly, dreary, ghostly, pallid, sallow, colorless, anemic, bland, gray, faded, colorless, peaked, ghastly, pasty, gaunt

auburn
   light-brown, coppery, reddish-brown, tawny

azure
   sky-blue, cyan, cerulean, aquamarine, turquoise

beige
   tawny, hazel, nut-brown, walnut

black, blackened
   dark, heavy, raven, jet-black, sable, ebony, pitch-black, shadowy, inky

blanched
   pale, white, faded, washed out, clammy, ashen, pallid, pasty

bland
   colorless, ashen, anemic, pale, dreary, faded, lifeless, pallid, sallow

blood-red
   crimson, ruddy, flame-red, fiery, cherry-red, port-wine, scarlet, maroon, ruby

bloom, blooming
   abloom, bright, flowery, showy, blossomy, rosy, blush

blossomy, blossoming
   flowery, showy, abloom, blooming, radiant

blush, blushing
   rosy, blooming, radiant, reddened, vibrant

brindle
> beige, hazel, nut-brown, walnut, russet, coppery, tawny, flecked, multicolored, rusty

bronze
> yellowish-brown, metallic, copper, brass, rust, chestnut, tanned

carmine
> ruby, cherry, cherry-red, ruddy, scarlet, crimson, flame-red

cerulean
> sky-blue, azure, cyan, deep-blue, aquamarine

chalky
> dusty, pale, ashen, snowy, silvery, frosty, milky, powdery

charcoal
> dark gray, gray, gray-black

chartreuse
> pale green, green-yellow, lemon-lime

cherry, cherry-red
> scarlet, ruby, crimson, ruddy, inflamed, flame-red, fiery, port-wine, maroon

colorless
> ashen, anemic, bland, insipid, dreary, faded, lifeless, pallid, sallow, pale

copper, coppery
> rusty, tawny, russet, bronze, metallic, chestnut, auburn

coral
> pinkish-red, pinkish orange, salmon

crimson
> ruby, ruddy, flame-red, fiery, cherry-red, port-wine, scarlet, blood-red, maroon

dingy
>   drab, grungy, shabby, discolored, faded, dreary, muddy, colorless, dull

discolored
>   stained, tarnished, faded, yellowed, blemished, dingy

drab
>   dingy, dull, grungy, shabby, faded, lackluster, gray

drained
>   colorless, faded, bleary, empty, void, pale, dim, faint

dreary
>   bleak, grim, colorless, ashen, bland, pale, faded, drab, pallid, sallow, dull

dull
>   bland, faded, colorless, drab, gray, faint, washed-out, pale, ashen, blanched, bleached, pallid, sallow

ebony
>   dark, heavy, shadowy, raven, jet-black, sable, pitch-black, charcoal, onyx, inky

emerald
>   green, verdant, foliaged, grassy, leafy, mossy, forest, jade

faded
>   drab, gray, faint, washed-out, pale, blanched, withered, bleached, colorless, ashen, bland, dreary, colorless, pallid, sallow, yellowed

flamboyant
>   bright, colorful, flowery, bold, elaborate, showy, flashy, garish, splashy, ornate, dashing

flame-red
>   crimson, ruddy, fiery, cherry-red, scarlet, maroon

flashy
flamboyant, bright, colorful, bold, elaborate, eye-catching, splashy, garish, dashing, brazen, showy

floral
flowery, abloom, showy, blossomy, blooming, verdant

florid
adorned, flowery, fanciful, frilly, blooming, lush, rosy, ornate

flowery
floral, florid, adorned, fanciful, frilly, lush, rosy, ornate, abloom, resplendent, showy, blossomy, blooming

foliaged
grassy, leafy, verdant, vernal, lush, green, emerald

frosty
snowy, silvery, chalky, fleecy, milky, icy

ghostly
ashen, pale, pallid, sallow, shadowy

ginger, gingered
reddish-yellow, saffron, golden

gold, golden
brilliant, dazzling, flaxen, glorious, saffron, shining, shimmering, glistening

grassy
vernal, lush, mossy, verdant, green, emerald, foliaged, leafy

gray
pallid, faded, silvery, ashen, pale, steel-gray, charcoal

hazel
tawny, beige, drab, nut-brown, walnut, chestnut

heavy
dark, dense, murky, blackened, gray

hoary
snowy, silvery, frosty, gray, graying, gray-haired

hue
shade, tint, wash, stain, blush, varnish, tinge, tone

hued
imbued, colored, stained, tinted, dyed, tinged, shaded

imbued
dyed, tinted, hued, colored, stained, saturated, tinged

indigo
purplish-blue, dark-blue, violet, violet-blue, aquamarine, azure, purplish

infused, infusion
tincture, dye, tint, immersion

inky
dark, heavy, shadowy, raven, jet-black, sable, ebony, pitch-black, onyx, murky

insipid
monochrome, lifeless, unimaginative, dull, banal, colorless, dreary, spiritless, vapid

iridescent
opalescent, pearly, soft-hued, moire, glossy, opaline

ivory
cream, creamy-white, off-white, alabaster, fair, pale

jade
blue-green, light-green, emerald, forest, moss

jet-black
dark, heavy, shadowy, inky, raven, sable, ebony, pitch-black, black

kaleidoscope, kaleidoscopic
multicolored, psychedelic, vivid, chromatic, colorful

khaki
brownish-yellow, sandy, camel, biscuit, tan, taupe

lavender
purple-blue, mauve, lilac, violet

leafy
emerald, green, verdant, grassy, lush, foliaged, meadowy, mossy

lilac
light-purple, pale purple, violet, pink, mauve

lurid
gaudy, bright, blinding, intense, vivid, glaring, shocking, flaming, loud, garish

lush
green, verdant, florid, flowery, blooming, rosy, emerald, foliaged, grassy, botanical, leafy

magenta
purplish-red, rose, fuchsia, purple, plum, mulberry

mahogany
reddish-brown, maroon, cherry, brick, bronze, russet, amber, auburn

maroon
brownish-red, mahogany, cherry, ruby, scarlet

milky
turbid, cloudy, thick, opaque, murky, muddy

mousy
   brown, grayish-brown, dull, lackluster, drab, plain, colorless

navy
   dark-blue, blue-black

ochre
   golden-yellow, gold, yellow-brown, golden

olive
   green, grayish-green, muddy green, sage

opalescent
   iridescent, pearly, subtle, soft-hued, moire, glossy, opaline

pale
   ashen, gray, ghostly, pallid, sallow, blanched, faded, faint, dim

pallid, pallor
   pale, bland, dreary, faded, lifeless, ashen, ghostly, sallow, colorless, anemic, pasty, gray, gaunt

pastel
   pale, light, soft, muted, soft-hued

pasty
   ashen, pale, ghostly, bland, dreary, faded, wan, sallow, colorless, anemic, gray

peaked
   ashen, pale, sickly, gray, ghostly, pallid, sallow, colorless, anemic, dreary, faded

pearly
   opalescent, iridescent, lustrous, frosted, milky, ivory

periwinkle
   mauve, lavender, lilac, purple, violet

pewter
gray, tin, gun-metal, silver

pitch-black
dark, heavy, shadowy, inky, raven, jet-black, sable, ebony, black

plum
deep purple, reddish-purple, magenta

raven
dark, heavy, shadowy, inky, jet-black, sable, ebony, pitch-black, onyx

rose
deep-red, pinkish red, blush, maroon, red-violet, magenta

rosy
florid, flowery, blooming, blushing, coral, peach, pinkish

ruby
carmine, cherry, cherry-red, fiery, ruddy, scarlet, crimson, flame-red, blood-red

ruddy
scarlet, crimson, flaming, maroon, flame-red, fiery, cherry-red, port-wine, ruby

russet
tawny, coppery, bronze, chestnut, auburn

rust, rusty
tawny, russet, coppery, bronze

sable
dark, heavy, shadowy, inky, raven, jet-black, ebony, pitch-black

saffron
golden, orange-yellow, bright, creamy, gold

sallow
ashen, pale, gray, ghostly, pallid, colorless, bland, dreary, faded

salmon
pinkish-orange, pale pink, coral, terra cotta, apricot

sandy
light-brown, walnut, yellowish-brown, khaki

scarlet
ruby, carmine, crimson, flame-red, cherry, ruddy, fiery, cherry-red, maroon, blood-red

sepia
reddish-brown, amber, drab, coffee, monochrome, tawny, amber, chestnut

shade
cast, hint, shadow, streak, tinge, stain, hue

sienna
reddish-brown, yellow-brown, rust

silver, silvered, silvery
hoary, snowy, frosty, gray, frosted, metallic, grayish-white, shiny, mirrored

sky-blue
cyan, azure, cerulean, bright blue

slate
blue-gray, azure, purple-gray, purple-blue, pewter, charcoal

snowy
silvery, frosty, fleecy, milky, icy

stained
hued, tinted, dyed, imbued, discolored, splattered

steel-blue
  bluish gray, metallic, pewter

taupe
  grayish-brown, gray-brown, khaki, camel, cream

tawny
  beige, hazel, nut-brown, walnut, rusty, russet, coppery, brindle, drab

teal
  blue-green, cyan, turquoise

terra cotta
  brownish-red, brownish-orange, salmon

tincture
  dye, tint, infusion, extract, pigment, stain

tinted
  stained, dyed, imbued, colored, hued

translucent
  clear, crystalline, luminous, transparent, sheer

transparent
  translucent, clear, luminous, glassy, sheer

turbid
  cloudy, thick, milky, opaque, murky, muddy, obscure, sludgy

turquoise
  blue-green, sky-blue, cyan, teal

vapid
  dull, colorless, lifeless, bland, insipid

verdant
  grassy, leafy, green, emerald, foliaged, meadow, lush, mossy

violet
> indigo, purple-blue, lilac, lavender

vivid
> vibrant, rich, striking, dazzling, glaring, deep, intense, bold, bright, colorful

walnut
> tawny, beige, drab, hazel, nut-brown, khaki, camel

SIZES *and* AMOUNTS

abound, abounding
> plentiful, abundant, bountiful, copious, flourishing, swarming, profuse, teeming, thriving, bristling, bursting, ample, overflowing

abundant
> rich, profuse, fruitful, copious, bountiful, teeming, lavish, plentiful, abounding, ample, flourishing, thriving, generous

aerial
> elevated, atmospheric, majestic, visionary, panoramic, lofty, flying

ample
> plentiful, abounding, abundant, bountiful, copious, teeming

ascendant
> rising, preeminent, momentous, stellar, towering, transcendent, grand

balloon, ballooning
> inflated, overblown, swollen, swelling, bulging, skyrocketing, mounting, soaring

bare
> meager, gaunt, scant, skimpy, spare, vacant, barren, empty, void, blank

behemoth
> monstrosity, enormous, colossal, gargantuan, gigantic, mammoth, giant

booming
> flourishing, bounding, teeming, thriving, swarming, bristling, mushrooming, bursting, overflowing, burgeoning, vigorous

bottomless
> yawning, gaping, cavernous, immense, plunging, vast, endless, unfathomable

boundless
> limitless, infinite, innumerable, measureless, unbridled, eternal, unbounded, unrestrained, immeasurable, vast

bountiful
> abundant, fruitful, copious, teeming, lavish, plentiful, abounding, ample, flourishing, profuse, thriving, prolific

brimming
> overflowing, abundant, teeming, copious, bristling, gushing, awash, swarming

burgeoning
> flourishing, booming, abounding, teeming, thriving, swarming, bristling, bursting, overflowing, vigorous

cavernous
> gaping, yawning, immense, spacious, mammoth, echoing, hollow

colossal
> gigantic, massive, enormous, immense, gargantuan, mammoth, grandiose, majestic, titanic, monumental, towering, behemoth, vast

commanding
> sweeping, powerful, expansive, decisive, imposing, lofty, superior, impressive, soaring

compact
concise, condensed, crammed, tight, dense, compressed, succinct

compressed
compact, condensed, crammed, dense, squeezed, constricted, abbreviated, dense

condensed
concise, truncated, compact, concentrated, succinct

copious
abundant, profuse, fruitful, bountiful, plentiful, abounding, ample, rampant, swarming, teeming, bristling, bursting, exuberant, flourishing, overflowing

deepening
expanding, intensifying, heightening, magnifying, mounting

diffuse
sparse, scanty, scarce, spotty, sporadic, thin, scattered, strewn

diminutive
tiny, miniscule, minute, microscopic, teeny, petite, miniature

dinky
meager, paltry, piffling, puny, dainty, petit, miniature, trifling, trivial

elephantine
colossal, gigantic, immense, mammoth, monstrous, humongous, towering, massive

elevated
highfalutin, majestic, lofty, aerial, superlative, colossal, grandiose, noble, visionary

enormous
colossal, gigantic, massive, immense, vast, towering, gargantuan, mammoth, behemoth

exhaustive
sweeping, far-reaching, expansive, intensive, full-blown, extensive, wide-ranging

exorbitant
extravagant, enormous, inflated, inordinate, outrageous, excessive, preposterous, steep

expansive, expanding
sweeping, extensive, roomy, voluminous, spacious, panoramic, vast, far-reaching, gathering

gaping
yawning, cavernous, immense, enormous, vast, gigantic, colossal, wide

gargantuan
massive, towering, mammoth, colossal, enormous, behemoth, immense, prodigious, staggering, astounding

gigantic
behemoth, titanic, colossal, massive, enormous, immense, vast, towering, monumental, whopping

hair's breadth
tiny, narrow, by a whisker, miniscule, slight

immense
enormous, towering, colossal, gigantic, massive, gaping, yawning, cavernous, vast

infinite
boundless, innumerable, unending, measureless, limitless, eternal, everlasting, perpetual, untold, incalculable, inexhaustible

infinitesimal
minute, miniscule, meager, negligible, imperceptible, insignificant, tiny

inflated
>   extravagant, enormous, exorbitant, overblown, ballooning, excessive, bloated, exaggerated

innumerable
>   limitless, boundless, infinite, measureless, countless, incalculable, untold

insurmountable
>   impossible, overwhelming, overpowering, hopeless, unassailable, devastating

limitless
>   inexhaustible, boundless, incalculable, infinite, innumerable, unending, measureless, ceaseless, perpetual

mammoth
>   gargantuan, colossal, enormous, massive, towering, staggering, prodigious, immense

massive
>   colossal, enormous, immense, towering, gargantuan, mammoth, vast

meager
>   scant, skimpy, spare, trifling, infinitesimal, sparse, paltry, measly

measly
>   paltry, piffling, puny, quibbling, superficial, stingy, trivial

miniscule
>   tiny, minute, microscopic, insignificant, slight, hair's breadth

momentous
>   crucial, pivotal, earth-shattering, eventful, preeminent, ascendant, stellar, towering, transcendent, grand, seminal

monumental
>   titanic, colossal, gigantic, immense, massive, towering, vast

overflowing
cascading, torrential, rushing, swarming, abounding, bristling, bursting, abundant

oversized
cumbersome, unwieldy, ungainly, bulky, eclipsing, ballooning, protruding, expanding

paltry
miserly, piffling, puny, quibbling, superficial, stingy, trivial, measly

panoramic
sweeping, commanding, expansive, aerial, vast, comprehensive, far-reaching

petty
trivial, dinky, paltry, piffling, superficial, measly, trifling

piffling
quibbling, superficial, petty, dinky, paltry, puny, measly, trivial, trifling

plunging
plummeting, nose-diving, yawning, sinking, tumbling, descending, dipping

precipitous
steep, abrupt, headlong, dizzying, sharp, sheer, swift

prodigious
gargantuan, mammoth, colossal, massive, towering, immense, staggering, astounding, enormous, behemoth

profuse
bountiful, teeming, abundant, copious, lavish

puny
trivial, measly, petty, dinky, paltry, trifling, quibbling, superficial

roomy
    voluminous, spacious, expansive, vast, extensive, generous, sizable, ample

scant, scanty
    meager, skimpy, spare, spindly, paltry, sparse, insufficient, stingy, bare

seismic
    huge, earth-scattering, enormous, colossal, massive, mammoth, tectonic, tumultuous, profound, weighty

spacious
    roomy, voluminous, expansive, vast, sweeping, ample, sizable, extensive

spare
    scant, unadorned, stark, fine, thin, confined, meager, bare, slight

sprawling
    spreading, stretched, extended, scattered, rambling, draping

steep
    precipitous, abrupt, headlong, sheer, sharp, elevated, extreme

swarming
    abounding, bristling, bursting, copious, flourishing, overflowing, brimming, thriving, booming, prospering, teeming, vigorous

sweeping
    far-reaching, expansive, commanding, vast, spacious, panoramic, exhaustive

tectonic
    earth-scattering, enormous, massive, seismic, momentous, weighty

teeming
    plentiful, thriving, prospering, swarming, vigorous, abundant, profuse, fruitful, copious, bountiful, lavish, roaring

titanic
colossal, gigantic, immense, massive, monumental, towering, vast, herculean, elephantine

towering
enormous, immense, vast, colossal, gigantic, massive, gargantuan, mammoth, preeminent, momentous, grand, ascendant, stellar, transcendent, titanic, behemoth

unfathomable
immeasurable, inscrutable, incomprehensible, mystifying, deep, unplumbed, boundless

ungainly
cumbersome, oversized, bulky, clumsy, unwieldy, awkward

vast
massive, enormous, voluminous, spacious, expansive, colossal, gigantic, immense, towering

vanishing
evanescent, ephemeral, melting, fleeting, ethereal, transient, fading

voluminous
roomy, spacious, expansive, billowing, vast, copious, swelling, massive, ample

yawning
gaping, cavernous, immense, bottomless, plunging, echoing

SPACE, LOCATION, *or* POSITION

abandoned
isolated, disjointed, detached, estranged, alienated, godforsaken, remote, stranded, sealed off, separated, rootless, secluded, vacant, barren, empty

abyss
    gulf, cavern, chasm, pit, gorge, schism, fissure, crevasse, void

aligned
    symmetrical, proportional, even, uniform, balanced, centered, geometrical

askance
    skewed, unbalanced, crooked, lopsided, uneven, misaligned, awry, askew, oblique, sidelong, twisted, slanted

askew
    crooked, unbalanced, skewed, lopsided, uneven, awry, cockeyed, askance, oblique, sidelong, tilted

barren
    desolate, empty, dreary, forlorn, godforsaken, void, abandoned, deserted, remote, gaunt, stark, vacant, bare

blockaded
    confined, constricted, enclosed, trapped, barricaded, caged

caged
    enclosed, trapped, cramped, blockaded, confined, constricted

canyon
    gulch, gulf, chasm, gorge, ravine, gully, valley

cavern
    gulf, chasm, abyss, gorge, ravine, gully, cave

chasm
    gulf, cavern, abyss, gorge, rift, schism, void

cloistered
    sheltered, confined, enclosed, curtained

confined
    caged, enclosed, cramped, blockaded, constricted

constricted
caged, confined, enclosed, tightened, hampered

crammed
cramped, wedged, compact, tight, squeezed

cramped
blockaded, caged, confined, constricted, enclosed, crammed

crevasse
abyss, gorge, fissure, void, gulf, cavern, chasm, cleft

disconnected
isolated, stranded, secluded, detached, separated, alienated

discrete
distinct, separate, disconnected, detached

distant
forbidding, guarded, impassive, remote, stern, unapproachable, uninviting

distinct
discrete, pronounced, clear, refined, separate, precise

encased
confined, constricted, caged, enclosed, wrapped, sheathed, covered

enclosed
cramped, blockaded, caged, confined, constricted, encased, embedded

estranged
disjointed, detached, alienated, abandoned, isolated, remote, stranded, sealed off, separated

faraway
far-flung, remote, outlying, far-off, afar, yonder, obscure, distant

far-flung
> exotic, remote, distant, outlandish, far-reaching, widespread

gorge
> gulf, cavern, chasm, rupture, abyss, schism

gulf
> cavern, chasm, rupture, abyss, gorge, schism

isolated
> remote, stranded, sealed off, secluded, abandoned, disjointed, detached, estranged, alienated

jammed
> obstructed, cemented, compressed, seized, immobilized, blocked

oblique, obliquely
> tangential, sidelong, askew, pitching, crooked, leaning, slanting, sloped, awry

peripheral
> sideways, tangential, outlying, incidental, remote, oblique, sidelong

precipice
> cliff, brink, bluff, crag, steep, drop, steer

remote
> abandoned, isolated, exotic, far-flung, distant, secluded, detached, stranded, separated

schism
> gulf, cavern, chasm, rupture, abyss, gorge, rift

secluded
> remote, stranded, separated, abandoned, isolated, disjointed, detached

sheltered
> cloistered, enclosed, curtained, protected, insulated, sequestered

sidelong
> oblique, askance, indirect, backhanded

skewed
> unbalanced, crooked, lopsided, uneven, misaligned, awry, askew, askance, oblique, sidelong, twisted, slanted

stranded
> estranged, secluded, isolated, alienated, disjointed, detached, remote, sealed off

tangential
> peripheral, sideways, outlying, incidental, remote, oblique, sidelong

vacant
> abandoned, bare, barren, empty, deserted, void

void
> vacuum, abyss, gulf, cavern, nothingness

SHAPES *and* STRUCTURES

aerodynamic
> sleek, elegant, smooth, fluid, streamlined

airy
> gauzy, delicate, fine-spun, gossamer, lacy, dainty, willowy, wispy, fragile

amalgamation
> blend, mixture, fusion, combination, synthesis

amorphous
> nebulous, blurry, formless, fuzzy, shapeless, murky, vague

angular
> forked, bent, bony, rawboned, jagged, pointed, forked

anomalous
   irregular, twisted, peculiar, deviating, incongruous, divergent

asymmetrical
   unbalanced, crooked, lopsided, misaligned, skewed, askance, uneven

atrophied
   wasting, emaciated, shrinking, withering, disintegrating

ballooning
   swelling, swollen, inflated, bursting, bloated, enlarged, expanding, distended

barbed
   spiny, prickly, thorny, spiky, spiked, sharp

battered
   crumbling, ravaged, dilapidated, decaying, rickety, deteriorated, aged, ramshackle, beat-up

bifurcated
   forked, divided, branched, divergent, split

billow, billowy
   fluffy, puffy, rippling, swirling, streaming, ballooning, spewing, rolling, undulating, wavy

bloated
   swollen, bulging, distended, turgid, inflated, puffy, engorged

bony
   gangly, lanky, spindly, gawky, scrawny, angular, rawboned, skinny, lean

branched, branching
   twiggy, gawky, reedy, spidery, twisting, snaking, bifurcated, forked, split

brawny
> burly, hefty, stocky, robust, full-bodied, hearty, muscular, sinewy, steely, rugged, sturdy

breakable
> flimsy, brittle, fragile, rickety, shaky, willowy, frail, wobbly, delicate, weak

brittle
> rickety, splintering, shaky, flimsy, fragile, breakable

bulbous
> bulging, swollen, distended, rotund, round, globular, orbed, curved

bulging
> puffy, distended, swollen, turgid, inflated, bloated, protruding

bulky
> clunky, heavy, hefty, unwieldy, awkward, cumbersome, ungainly, oversized

burly
> hefty, stocky, brawny, fleshy, beefy, weighty, meaty, portly

byzantine
> intricate, complex, convoluted, serpentine, tangled, knotty, elaborate

chunky
> paunchy, rotund, plump, bulbous, round, pudgy, stout, stocky, portly

clunky
> bulky, awkward, heavy, hefty, unwieldy, leaden

coiled
> twisted, bent, looped, curled, spiraled, corkscrew, helical

concave
curved, recessed, hollow, sunken, indented

contorted
twisted, disfigured, distorted, deformed, gnarled, misshapen, crooked, marred, warped

contoured
curved, shaped, smoothed, outlined, formed, molded

convoluted
tangled, complicated, elaborate, snaking, intricate, serpentine

corrugated
grooved, ridged, fluted, creased, puckered

cracked
crumble, fracture, chipped, fissured, rupture, gaping, cratered, dented, splintered, shattered

craggy
steep, rough, rugged, weathered, ragged

crater
hollow, gaping, crack, abyss, cavern, pit

creased
grooved, ridged, fluted, puckered, corrugated, pleated, rumbled, folded, wrinkled

crooked
contorted, warped, lopsided, uneven, misaligned, skewed, twisted, misshapen, tortuous, winding, meandering, slanted, distorted, gnarled

crumbling
battered, dilapidated, rickety, decaying, aged, deteriorated, eroded, collapsing, disintegrating

cumbersome
unwieldy, awkward, blundering, lumbering, ungainly, oversized, bulky

curly
wavy, rippled, kinked, swirled, spiralled, looped

curved, curvaceous
winding, wavy, circuitous, meandering, twisting

curvy
shapely, curvaceous, curving, voluptuous, bending, twisting, corkscrew, wavy

dangling
slack, baggy, drooping, floppy, limp, hanging

deformed
contorted, twisted, disfigured, distorted, grotesque, misshapen, gnarled, marred, warped

delicate
intricate, fine, exquisite, dainty, gauzy, airy, fine-spun, gossamer, lacy, sheer, willowy, wispy, threadlike

dense
heavy, dark, weighty, ponderous, opaque, packed, impenetrable

dented
hollow, cracked, sunken, marred, concave, gouged, indented

deviating
twisted, anomalous, divergent, circuitous, tortuous, meandering, winding

dilapidated
decrepit, shabby, rickety, battered, decaying, aged, deteriorated, ruined, disheveled

disfigured
 misshapen, crooked, contorted, twisted, distorted, deformed, gnarled, warped, marred

disjointed
 disconnected, alienated, isolated, detached, separated, fragmented, jumbled

dislocated
 disordered, distorted, disarray, displaced, jumbled

distended
 bloated, inflated, engorged, swollen, bulging, puffy

distorted
 contorted, twisted, disfigured, deformed, crooked, awry, warped, misshapen, marred

doughy
 flabby, fleshy, mushy, pasty, thick, chunky, paunchy

drooping, droopy
 dangling, slack, baggy, floppy, limp, wilted

elliptical, ellipsoidal
 oblong, oval, elongated, ellipse

faceted
 multi-sided, complex, multi-stranded, multi-dimensional

feeble
 flaccid, limp, weak, frail, flimsy, failing, decrepit

fine
 narrow, precise, thin, slender, slight, spare, tenuous, fragile, flimsy, exquisite, fine-spun

flabby
 flaccid, floppy, slack, sagging, doughy, fleshy, mushy, paunchy

flaccid
feeble, limp, droopy, weak, flabby, floppy, flimsy

flattened
compressed, crushed, compact, squashed, pressed

fleshy
heavy, weighty, brawny, meaty, paunchy, plump, jowly, doughy, flabby, mushy, pasty, thick, burly

flexible
fluid, flowing, resilient, stretchy, adaptable, pliable, supple, elastic, bendable

flimsy
brittle, fragile, breakable, rickety, shaky, willowy, frail, wobbly, wispy, floppy

floppy
flabby, flaccid, flimsy, malleable, slack, baggy, dangling, drooping, limp

fluid
flexible, flowing, liquid, watery, shifting, molten, runny, changeable

fluted
grooved, creased, corrugated, wrinkled, furrowed, puckered, ridged

forked
bifurcated, branching, pronged, split, divided

formless
amorphous, nascent, unformed, nebulous, chaotic, shapeless

fragile
flimsy, brittle, shaky, willowy, frail, breakable, rickety, wobbly, wispy

fragmented
uneven, choppy, frayed, spotty, erratic, haphazard, splintered, broken

frail
shaky, willowy, wobbly, fragile, flimsy, brittle, breakable, rickety, wispy

full-bodied
robust, dynamic, hearty, sturdy, vibrant, vigorous, zestful

fused, fusion
mixture, synthesis, amalgamation, melding, mingling, integration, blended

gangly
bony, lanky, spindly, gawky, scrawny, long-legged, leggy, skinny

gashed
jagged, spiky, serrated, rough, ragged, gouged, lacerated, split, ripped

gawky
gangly, bony, lanky, spindly, scrawny, twiggy, reedy, scraggly

geometrical
symmetrical, proportional, aligned, balanced

globular
spherical, rounded, bulbous, orb, circular

gnarled
disfigured, contorted, distorted, knotty, twisted, knobby, crooked, misshapen, deformed, marred, warped

grooved
corrugated, ridged, fluted, creased, puckered, crimped, sculpted, carved

gutted
destroyed, demolished, wrecked, ransacked, ravaged, decimated, looted, stripped, ruined

heavy, heavy-set
fleshy, weighty, brawny, meaty, paunchy, plump, dense, stocky, stout, portly, burly

hefty
bulky, clunky, heavy, portly, chunky, massive, weighty

hollow
sunken, concave, deep-set, recessed, vacant, empty

impenetrable
impervious, indestructible, persistent, resistant, dense, bulletproof, unyielding

impervious
indestructible, impenetrable, persistent, resistant, unyielding, inflexible, refractory, immune, watertight

inflexible
taut, intractable, stiff, unbending, unyielding, hardened, tough, rigid

intractable
unbending, unmanageable, inflexible, obstructive, stiff, unyielding

jagged
spiky, serrated, rough, angular, broken, forked, gashed, ragged, saw-toothed

knobby
bumpy, gnarled, rough, lumpy

knotty
elaborate, twisted, gnarled, thorny, tangled, convoluted

lanky
gawky, scrawny, gangly, bony, spindly, twiggy, reedy

lean
angular, slender, lanky, wiry, sinewy, brawny, ropy

leggy
shapely, overgrown, stringy, bony, spindly

limp
drooping, floppy, flaccid, slack, baggy, dangling

lithe
sinuous, flexible, supple, willowy, graceful, pliable

lopsided
unbalanced, crooked, uneven, misaligned, skewed, asymmetrical, askew, tilted

malleable
pliable, flexible, supple, moldable, yielding, elastic, workable, springy, bendable

marred
gnarled, warped, misshapen, disfigured, contorted, deformed

matted
rumpled, crinkled, tousled, knotted, tangled, flattened

misaligned
unbalanced, crooked, lopsided, uneven, skewed, askew, irregular, awry

misshapen
contorted, warped, twisted, buckled, skewed, crooked, disfigured, deformed, distorted, gnarled, marred

muscular
robust, brawny, full-bodied, hearty, sinewy, rugged, strapping

mushy
doughy, squishy, flabby, fleshy, pasty, thick, spongy

narrow
fine, precise, thin, slender, slight, spare, slim, tight, hair's breadth

nebulous
formless, amorphous, fuzzy, chaotic, shapeless, hazy, ambiguous, shadowy

papery
lacy, slinky, wispy, airy, delicate, dainty, gauzy, willowy

paunchy
rotund, plump, bulbous, round, chunky, stout, stocky, portly, meaty, doughy, fleshy, heavy, burly

perforated
riddled, punctured, pitted, punched, pierced

pliable
flexible, supple, malleable, elastic, limber, lithe, willowy

plump
paunchy, fleshy, heavy, weighty, burly, brawny, meaty, chunky, beefy

pointed, pointy
jagged, spiny, thorny, barbed, spiked, edged

puffy
inflated, swollen, bulging, bloated, distended, enlarged

punctured
riddled, perforated, torn, ripped, pierced, ruptured

ragged
jagged, spiky, serrated, rough, angular, forked, gashed, slipshod, tattered, torn, shredded, scraggly, scruffy, ratty

rambling

twisting, winding, meandering, tortuous, sprawling, disconnected, circuitous, serpentine, roundabout

ramshackle

tottering, rickety, shifting, wobbly, flimsy, shabby, tumbledown, dilapidated, crumbling, shaky

ravaged

blighted, corrosive, devastated, disintegrating, haggard, plagued, ruinous, wasted, wrecked

rawboned

angular, bony, gaunt, scrawny, gawky, skinny, lanky

reedy

twiggy, branching, gawky, lanky, gangly, leggy

resilient

adaptable, flexible, mobile, changeable, responsive, pliable, sturdy, supple, durable

rickety

dilapidated, decrepit, shabby, flimsy, brittle, fragile, breakable, battered, decaying, deteriorated, shaky, wobbly, tottering, aged, ramshackle, tumbledown

riddled

perforated, punctured, saturated, pierced, peppered, pelted, marred

ridged

grooved, fluted, creased, puckered, corrugated, ribbed, toothed, jagged

rigid

immobile, immovable, stagnant, unmoving, changeless, stiff, unyielding

robust
> brawny, dynamic, full-bodied, hearty, muscular, sinewy, staunch, rugged, sturdy, vibrant, vigorous

ropy
> wiry, lean, sinewy, stringy, thready, fibrous

rotund
> plump, bulbous, round, chunky, paunchy, stout, portly

rough-hewn
> chiseled, angular, rawboned, sharp, coarse, unrefined, unfinished, unpolished

rounded
> spherical, globular, bulbous, orb, circular

rubbery
> malleable, elastic, pliable, spongy, springy, stretchy

rugged
> rough, resistant, robust, durable, sturdy, enduring, craggy, steep, hearty, muscular

rutted
> rough, craggy, rugged, irregular, grooved, knobby, bumpy, uneven, choppy

scraggly
> scrawny, gawky, bedraggled, ragged, shoddy, unkempt, disheveled, frayed, frazzled, threadbare

scrawny
> spindly, gangly, bony, lanky, gawky, scraggly, rawboned, ragged, meager, stunted

sculpted
> chiseled, shaped, carved, molded

serpentine
  snaking, meandering, convoluted, circuitous, twisted, winding, wavy, curvaceous

serrated
  jagged, spiky, ragged, toothed, notched, saw-toothed

shaky
  flimsy, wobbly, fragile, breakable, rickety, ramshackle, tottering, unsteady

shallow
  empty, flimsy, superficial, flat, hollow

shapely
  leggy, curvy, curvaceous, buxom, graceful, balanced, elegant

silhouette
  contour, outline, shadow, etching, profile

sinewy
  muscular, burly, robust, brawny, full-bodied, hearty, sturdy

sinuous
  billowy, flexible, supple, lithe, curving, coiling, twisting

skew, skewed
  unbalanced, crooked, lopsided, uneven, misaligned, awry, askew, distorted, slanted

skimpy
  scant, spare, spindly, meager, thin, paltry, skinny

skinny
  wiry, lean, sinewy, ropy, thread, gawky, bony

slack
  baggy, dangling, drooping, floppy, limp, lax

sleek
> elegant, smooth, fluid, streamlined, aerodynamic

slender
> thin, slight, spare, narrow, fine, precise, lean, slim

slight
> narrow, fine, precise, thin, slender, spare

slinky
> supple, willowy, sinuous, smooth, sleek

snaking
> serpentine, circuitous, curvaceous, meandering, twisted, twisting, winding, wavy, convoluted

spidery
> webby, twiggy, branching, angular

spiked, spiky
> jagged, serrated, angular, forked, gashed, ragged, spiny, prickly, thorny, barbed, pointy

spindly
> gangly, bony, lanky, gawky, scrawny, leggy, bare, gaunt

spiny
> prickly, thorny, barbed, spiky, pointed, sharp

spiral, spiralled
> coiled, twisted, bent, looped, curled, rolled, curved, arched, furled

splintering, splintered
> fragmented, fractured, disintegrating, frayed, crumbling, shattered, broken, disconnected

springy
> fluid, stretchy, elastic, supple, flexible, rubbery

SEE: SHAPES *and* STRUCTURES

statuesque
> majestic, shapely, stately, elegant, towering

stiff
> inflexible, unbending, recalcitrant, rigid, wooden

stocky
> brawny, burly, hefty, sturdy, chunky, stubby, squat

stout
> rotund, plump, burly, round, chunky, paunchy, portly

streamlined
> sleek, elegant, smooth, fluid, aerodynamic, refined

stretchy
> elastic, springy, supple, bouncy, pliable, malleable

strewn
> dispersed, scattered, unleashed, flung, tossed, littered

stringy
> fibrous, flossy, wiry, sinewy, ropy, thread, gangly, leggy

sturdy
> robust, hearty, muscular, rugged, vibrant, unyielding, durable

sunken
> hollow, gaping, cracked, dented, submerged, indented, recessed, concave

supple
> sinuous, muscular, flexible, lithe, pliable, resilient, bendable, elastic, stretchy

swollen
> bulging, bursting, distended, bloated, inflated, puffy, engorged, turgid

symmetrical
proportional, even, aligned, uniform, balanced

tattered
ripped, torn, shredded, shabby, ragged, ratty, holey, threadbare

tenuous
fragile, slender, fine, delicate, thin, shaky, airy, flimsy

thicket
grove, clump, underbrush, shrub, tangle

thorny
spiny, prickly, barbed, spiky, pointy

thready
wiry, lean, sinewy, coarse, brawny, ropy, stringy

toothed
serrated, notched, ragged, ridged, saw-toothed

tortuous
crooked, twisting, winding, meandering, snaking, convoluted, curving

turgid
distended, bulged, inflated, puffy, swollen, engorged, bloated

twiggy
branching, lean, gawky, lanky, leggy, reedy, spidery, tenuous

twisted, twisting
coiled, bent, looped, curled, spiraled, crooked, tortuous, winding, entangled, intertwined, contorted, deformed, distorted, gnarled, convoluted, meandering, rambling

unbroken
continuous, constant, unified, sound, solid, whole

uneven
asymmetrical, disproportional, misaligned, lopsided, irregular, crooked, askew

ungainly
cumbersome, oversized, bulky, clumsy, unwieldy, awkward

uniform
even, constant, steady, unbroken, consistent, smooth, symmetrical

unwieldy
awkward, ungainly, cumbersome, oversized, massive, burdensome, bulky

voluptuous
curvaceous, shapely, curvy, buxom

warped
deformed, distorted, gnarled, misshapen, disfigured, contorted, crooked, marred, twisted

wavy
meandering, serpentine, snaking, winding, circuitous, curvaceous, curvy, undulating, rippled, curved

webbed
interwoven, intertwined, entangled, twisted, braided, enlaced, fretted, interlaced, woven

whorl, whorled
spiraled, curled, looped, ringed, coiled, twisted, helical, eddy, whirlpool, corkscrew

willowy
delicate, dainty, wispy, airy, graceful, lithe, lacy, papery, slinky

winding
curvaceous, meandering, serpentine, snaky, twisted, circuitous, wavy, convoluted

wiry
> lean, sinewy, coarse, brawny, ropy, stringy, thready, wavy

wispy
> airy, brittle, delicate, dainty, gauzy, lacy, papery, slinky, willowy

withered
> decaying, gaunt, haggard, emaciated, shriveled, wrinkled, wizened

wizened
> shriveled, creased, withered, shrunken, gnarled, wrinkled

wobbly
> ambling, doddering, faltering, tottering, oscillating, toppling, rickety, bobbling, capsizing, tumbling, careening

Textures, Designs, *and* Patterns

adorn, adorned
> decorate, embellish, festoon, garnish, wreathe, elaborate, flowery, fanciful, frilly, lush, ornate, luxuriant, lavish, resplendent, beaded, fancy, ornamented, trimmed, bejeweled

beaded
> jeweled, adorned, bejeweled, embellished, festooned, ornamented

bejeweled
> jeweled, embellished, festooned, adorned, beaded, ornamented, trimmed, bespangled, studded, spangled

bespangled
> spangled, embellished, studded, bejeweled, glittering, adorned, glimmering, sprinkled, trimmed, sequinned

blotched, blotchy
> marked, patchy, uneven, tarnished, besmirched, blemished, spotty, smudged, tainted, fragmented

burnish, burnished
buff, finish, glaze, gloss, luster, polish, shine, varnish, wax, patina

bushy
woolly, hairy, unruly, thick, shaggy, disheveled, scruffy, scrubby

checkered
patterned, multicolored, decorative, motley, quilted, patchwork

coating, coated
patina, burnish, wear, finish, glaze, veneer, polish, shine, gloss

corroded
tarnished, damaged, rusted, eroded, deteriorated, rotted, worn

cottony
silky, fine-spun, satiny, sleek, velvety, plush, delicate, fluffy

craggy
weathered, weather-beaten, rugged, rough, stony, rocky

creased
crinkled, weathered, wrinkled, craggy, rumpled, shriveled, pleated

crinkled
wrinkled, scrunched, creased, shriveled, rumpled, ruffled

dainty
delicate, intricate, fine, exquisite, wispy, airy, gauzy, lacy, papery, slinky, willowy

decorated, decorative
adorned, embellished, festooned, garnished, wreathe, gilded, ornamental

delicate
intricate, fine, exquisite, dainty, gauzy, airy, fine-spun, gossamer, lacy, sheer, willowy, wispy, threadlike

dense
> heavy, dark, weighty, thick, opaque, compressed, solid

dog-eared
> threadbare, worn, crumbling, rickety, battered, run-down, ragged, ramshackle, scruffy, ratty

durable
> sturdy, enduring, indestructible, impervious, persistent, resistant, rugged, unchanging, vital

earthen, earthy
> hearty, clay, muddy, natural, rocky, stony

elaborate
> extravagant, showy, intricate, ornate, embellished, adorned, frilly, grandiose, flowery, fanciful, resplendent

embellished
> adorned, decorated, festooned, garnished, wreathed, luxuriant, lavish, resplendent, ornate, adorned, flowery, fanciful, elaborate, fancy, frilly

enlaced
> intertwined, entangled, twisted, braided, fretted, interlaced, woven, interwoven, webbed

eroded
> rusted, corroded, tarnished, oxidized, ravaged, degraded

extravagant
> showy, ornate, flamboyant, flashy, adorned, elaborate, lavish

fanciful
> elaborate, whimsical, extravagant, imaginative, dreamy, adorned, flowery, frilly, lush, ornate, romantic, resplendent, embellished

festoon, festooned
> garnish, wreathe, trim, adorn, decorate, embellish, jewel, ornament

filigree, filigreed
lace, ornamented, lattice, interlaced, lacy

filmy
translucent, fine-spun, fragile, chiffon, gossamer, sheer, dainty, wispy, transparent

fine
narrow, precise, thin, slender, slight, spare, tenuous, fragile

fine-spun
gauzy, airy, delicate, gossamer, lacy, fragile, wispy, filmy

finish
patina, coating, gloss, burnish, glaze, veneer, polish, shine

flecked
freckled, marbled, blotchy, spotted, streaked, checkered

freckled
flecked, spotted, blotchy, checkered, speckled

fretted
enlaced, interlaced, webbed, interwoven, braided, woven, twisted, intertwined, entangled

frilly
fanciful, embellished, fancy, lacy, gossamer, delicate, fine-spun, threadlike, ornate, adorned, flowery, resplendent, elaborate, fine

frothy
effervescent, airy, breezy, bubbling, fizzy, sparkling, sudsy, foamy

furry
hairy, fuzzy, bearded, shaggy, fleecy, downy, woolly

fuzzy
foggy, cloudy, murky, hazy, opaque, muddy, obscured, nebulous, amorphous, blurry, shadowy, furry, hairy, bearded, shaggy

garland
wreathe, twine, lace, ribbon, festoon, laurel, crown

garnish
festoon, wreathe, adorn, decorate, embellish, trim

gauzy
airy, delicate, fine-spun, gossamer, lacy, sheer, filmy, translucent, wispy, dainty, papery

gilded
golden, embellished, decorative, embroidered, festooned, ornate, adorned, luxurious

glaze
glassy, tint, varnish, film, gloss, luster, shine, finish, veneer, polish

gossamer
delicate, fine-spun, lacy, threadlike, sheer, airy, fine, filmy, silky

hairy
fuzzy, bearded, furry, shaggy, woolly, whiskered

insignia
emblem, regalia, badge, symbol, seal, crest

interlaced
entangled, twisted, intertwined, interwoven, woven, braided

intertwined
braided, enlaced, fretted, interlaced, interwoven, entangled, woven, twisted, webbed

interwoven
intertwined, entangled, twisted, braided, enlaced, fretted, woven, interlaced, webbed

intricate
ornate, exquisite, dainty, elaborate, complex, entangled

jagged
> rugged, craggy, weathered, weather-beaten, rough, pitted, irregular, uneven, ridged, spiked

jeweled
> adorned, beaded, bejeweled, embellished, festooned, ornamented, trimmed

lace
> wreathe, garland, twine, ribbon, thread, filigree, mesh, trim, mesh, tie, border

lacy
> dainty, gauzy, papery, slinky, threadlike, frilly, gossamer, fine, delicate, fine-spun

luxuriant, luxurious
> rich, thick, adorned, embellished, festooned, lavish, sumptuous, stately, glorious, majestic

mosaic
> patchwork, collage, pattern, montage, melange, pastiche, medley

mottled
> dappled, spotted, blotchy, speckled, stippled, streaked, checkered, freckled

ornamented
> bejeweled, embellished, jeweled, adorned, beaded, festooned, trimmed, gilded, ornate

ornate
> adorned, flowery, fanciful, elaborate, embellished, fancy, frilly, resplendent

patchy
> uneven, fragmented, choppy, frayed, spotty, haphazard, blotchy, i irregular

pastiche
  mosaic, motif, patchwork, collage, synthesis, montage, melange, medley, blend

patina
  coating, wear, finish, burnish, glaze, veneer, polish, shine, gloss

peppered
  riddled, pelted, stippled, perforated, punctured, saturated

pitted
  rugged, pockmarked, pocked, craggy, weathered, weather-beaten, rough, jagged, uneven

plumage
  feathers, cluster, clump, shock, tuft, strand

plush
  opulent, rich, lavish, luscious, luxuriant, sumptuous, showy, posh, elegant, fancy

pocked, pockmarked
  rugged, pitted, craggy, weathered, weather-beaten, rough, jagged

polish
  patina, glaze, shine, finish, sheen, gloss

polished
  refined, glossy, impeccable, smooth, buffed, burnished, tasteful, shiny

prickly
  spiny, thorny, barbed, spiky, pointy, bristly, knotty

regalia
  insignia, finery, emblem, crown, badge, crest

ribbon
  twine, lace, thread, wreathe, garland

rough
craggy, steep, rugged, irregular, stony, rutted, uneven

rugged
craggy, weathered, weather-beaten, rough, pitted, jagged, bumpy, coarse, worn

rumpled
creased, crinkled, matted, tousled, wrinkled, trampled, flattened

rusted
corroded, tarnished, oxidized, eroded, pitted, decaying

satin, satiny
silky, fine-spun, sleek, velvety, shiny, silken, smooth, glossy

scrawl, scrawled
scribble, hieroglyphics, symbol, stylized, illegible

scribble
scrawl, hieroglyphics, illegible, graffiti

sheer
airy, crystal, gossamer, clarified, translucent, gauzy, chiffon, thin, filmy, see-through

showy
flashy, frilly, glittering, ornate, garish, luxurious, plush, opulent, rich, lavish

shredded
torn, tattered, ragged, chopped, frayed, ripped

shriveled
crinkled, wrinkled, creased, weathered, withered, shrunken

silky
cottony, fine-spun, satin, sleek, velvety, fleecy, silken

sleek
   silky, fine-spun, satin, velvety, glossy, shiny, sheen, slick, glassy

slick, slickness
   glossy, shiny, sheen, sleek, glassy, slippery

slippery
   slick, shiny, glassy, lubricated, slimy, oily, greasy, smooth

spangled
   studded, bejeweled, glittering, adorned, glimmering

spare
   scant, unadorned, stark, fine, precise, thin, bare, gaunt

sparse
   diffuse, scanty, scarce, spotty, sporadic, stark, thin

speckled
   dappled, spotted, blotchy, mottled, stippled, freckled, checkered,
   flecked, studded

spotted
   flecked, dotted, dappled, speckled, splotchy, freckled, sprinkled,
   blotchy, patchy

sprinkled
   spotted, sprayed, peppered, dappled, speckled, dotted, splotchy,
   freckled, flecked, studded

stippled
   speckled, dappled, spotted, blotchy, mottled, dotted, blotted

studded
   flecked, mottled, spotted, variegated, bespangled, bejeweled,
   spangled

tableau
   scene, spectacle, view, montage, melange

See: Textures, Designs, *and* Patterns

tapestry
   fabric, design, regalia, finery, screen, pattern, valance, textile

tarnished
   besmirched, blemished, blotchy, debased, scorched, smudged, tainted, eroded, corroded, rusty

threadbare
   shopworn, tattered, torn, worn, dull, scruffy, dog-eared, ragged

torn
   shredded, holey, tattered, patchy, ragged, threadbare, frayed, ripped

trimmed
   festooned, ornamented, jeweled, adorned, beaded, bejeweled, embellished

unadorned
   natural, stark, spare, unvarnished, stripped, austere, unembellished, pure, plain

variegated
   mottled, checkered, speckled, striped, patchy, flecked, dappled, hued

varnish
   glaze, glassy, tint, film, finish, coat, luster, polish, gloss

velvety
   silky, cottony, fine-spun, satin, sleek, silken

veneer
   finish, glaze, polish, patina, burnish, coating, wear, shine

weathered
   wrinkled, craggy, creased, crinkled, shriveled, scraggy, withered, worn, weather-beaten

withered
    decaying, gaunt, haggard, barren, stark, desolate, emaciated

wizened
    shriveled, creased, withered, shrunken, wilted, gnarled, winkled

worn
    threadbare, shopworn, tattered, torn, dog-eared, frayed, ragged

woven
    interwoven, intertwined, entangled, twisted, braided, enlaced, fretted, interlaced

wreathe
    garland, twine, lace, ribbon, crown, festoon

wrinkled
    rumpled, creased, crinkled, matted, tousled, craggy, shriveled, scraggy, weathered, aged

FACIAL EXPRESSIONS

abashed
    shamefaced, regretful, pitiable, sorrowful, sheepish, mortified, remorseful

affable
    jovial, gleeful, joyous, hearty, light-hearted, congenial, amiable, pleasant, good-humored

agape
    appalled, dismayed, astonished, aghast, wide-eyed, incredulous, awed, open-mouthed

agitated
    disturbed, tumultuous, frenzied, hysterical, flustered, tempestuous, stormy, frantic, turbulent, distracted, disquieted, rattled

SEE: FACIAL EXPRESSIONS

alert
> perceptive, sharp, discerning, vigilant, cogent, penetrating, piercing, watchful, guarded, mindful, observant

amazed
> wide-eyed, astonished, dumbstruck, flabbergasted, astounded, bedazzled, surprised, startled, stupefied, awed

anguished
> distressed, devastated, inconsolable, morose, heart-broken, woeful, bleak, dismal, mournful, grief-stricken, sorrowful

animated
> expressive, vibrant, lively, exuberant, vivacious, passionate, spirited

assured
> self-possessed, calm, composed, balanced, equanimous, poised, unruffled, unflappable

astonished
> flabbergasted, amazed, astounded, awed, bedazzled, wide-eyed, dumbstruck, surprised, startled, stupefied

astounded
> bedazzled, perplexed, wide-eyed, dumbstruck, surprised, startled, stupefied, flabbergasted, amazed, astonished, awed

austere
> stern, unapproachable, uninviting, grave, resolute, strict, taciturn, unbending, staid, cold

awed
> surprised, startled, wide-eyed, bedazzled, astonished, amazed, dumbstruck, astounded, flabbergasted, stupefied

baffled
> puzzled, perplexed, bewildered, confounded, confused, stumped, befuddled, dazed

bedazzled
> wide-eyed, astonished, dumbstruck, dazzled, amazed, astounded, stupefied, stunned, mesmerized, captivated, awed, enchanted

befuddled
> bewildered, flustered, confounded, dazed, agitated, baffled

belligerent
> hostile, menacing, forbidding, unfriendly, threatening, pugnacious

bewildered
> confounded, stunned, baffled, puzzled, perplexed, dazed, rattled, befuddled

bitter
> icy, cold, cutting, dispassionate, distant, impassive, numb, reticent, sharp, stony, detached

blank
> empty, glazed, void, bare, stony, impassive, deadpan

breathless
> headlong, panting, breakneck, dashing, gasping, wheezing

brooding
> sulky, morose, sullen, moody, despondent, languishing, gloomy, dark

cagey
> guarded, cunning, crafty, wary, sneaky, evasive, secretive, cautious, wily

composed
> poised, refined, unruffled, unflappable, self-possessed, assured, balanced, equanimous, placid, calm

contemplative
> wistful, longing, yearning, wishful, thoughtful, pining, musing, nostalgic, ruminating

contemptuous
disdainful, scoffing, scornful, sneering, mocking, derisive, insulting

contorted
twisted, disfigured, distorted, deformed, convulsed, writhing, tortured, wrenched

convulsed, convulsing
twisted, shuddering, contorted, shuddering, writhing, tormented, agitated, unsettled, disturbed, pained

crafty
cagey, cunning, sneaky, evasive, secretive, sly, calculating, devious, scheming

cunning
crafty, cagey, sneaky, guarded, evasive, secretive, canny

deadpan
blank, empty, glazed, void, stony, glassy, vacuous, emotionless

defiant
resistant, stubborn, obstinate, bull-headed, willful, headstrong, rigid

delirious
fierce, deranged, frantic, raving, savage, crazed, manic, unhinged, wild, demented, howling

deranged
raving, savage, wild, fierce, delirious, frantic, howling, demented

despairing
despondent, mournful, melancholy, dispirited, brooding, forlorn, inconsolable

despondent
mournful, inconsolable, despairing, melancholy, forlorn, dispirited, morose, doleful, dejected, disheartened

detached
stoic, impassive, lethargic, withdrawn, stony, callous, dry

dim-witted
foolish, absurd, vacuous, inane, fatuous, empty, vapid

disdainful
contemptuous, haughty, arrogant, pompous, scornful, derisive, indifferent, sneering

dispirited
despondent, inconsolable, despairing, melancholy, forlorn, mournful, teary-eyed

dizzy
woozy, befuddled, unsteady, dazed, witless, whirling, confused, dazed, giddy, groggy

dramatic
stagy, cinematic, histrionic, melodramatic, theatrical, overblown

dreamy
contemplative, languid, meditative, peaceful, romantic, placid, tranquil, whimsical, wide-eyed

droll
quirky, wry, comical, dry, witty, amusing, eccentric

drunken
boozy, carousing, inebriated, sloshed, bumbling

dumbstruck
surprised, startled, amazed, stupefied, wide-eyed, astonished, flabbergasted, bedazzled, perplexed, awed

ecstatic
blissful, exultant, jubilant, rejoicing, euphoric, joyous, triumphant, rapturous, beaming, dreamy, elated, enraptured

elated
> triumphant, exultant, jubilant, rejoicing, ecstatic, joyous, delirious, delighted, enraptured

emotional
> dramatic, hysterical, histrionic, melodramatic, cinematic, moving, sentimental, impassioned, tender, poignant, tearful, weepy, stagy, teary-eyed

empty
> blank, void, vacant, glassy, glazed, deadpan, vacuous, hollow

enigmatic
> mysterious, secretive, perplexing, puzzling, obscure, mystifying, cryptic

equanimous
> poised, composed, assured, balanced, unruffled, unflappable, self-possessed, calm, placid

euphoric
> ecstatic, blissful, exultant, jubilant, rejoicing, elated, enraptured, joyous

evasive
> sneaky, secretive, cagey, guarded, cunning, crafty, deceptive, elusive

exasperated
> aggravated, disturbed, galled, irked, provoked, weary, troubled, vexed, incensed

exhilarated
> sparkling, vivacious, intoxicated, elated, delighted, invigorated, animated, euphoric

expressive
> animated, vibrant, exuberant, vivacious, spirited, lively, colorful, striking, energetic

expressionless
blank, emotionless, deadpan, inscrutable, vacant, impassive, stony, wooden

exuberant
jaunty, cheerful, buoyant, ebullient, exhilarated, elated, animated, lively

ferocious
barbaric, beastly, belligerent, fierce, monstrous, raging, terrifying

fidgety
jittery, flustered, quivering, restless, trembling, twitchy, jumpy, uneasy, shaky

fierce
raging, forceful, wild, howling, savage, ferocious, barbaric, beastly, belligerent, intense

flabbergasted
astonished, dumbstruck, amazed, wide-eyed, bedazzled, perplexed, surprised, startled, awed, stupefied, astounded, gobsmacked

flinty
unyielding, hardened, immovable, steely, unflappable, unbending, stern, stony, rigid

flustered
uneasy, jittery, fidgety, quivering, restless, nervous, shaky, jumpy, trembling, twitchy, turbulent

forlorn
despondent, inconsolable, despairing, melancholy, mournful, dispirited, dejected, hopeless

frantic
agitated, distracted, feverish, tumultuous, turbulent, frenzied, distressed, frenetic, hysterical, panic-stricken, panicky, distraught, wild

fraught
> distraught, frantic, panicky, overwrought, panic-stricken, agitated, overwrought, distressed

frightened
> spooked, disturbed, alarmed, appalled, startled, fearful, terrorized, frozen

frightening
> creepy, spooky, disturbing, appalling, chilling, alarming, hideous, terrifying, eerie, freaky

gaunt
> haggard, withered, somber, hollow, scrawny, emaciated, angular, bony, stark

ghostly
> ashen, pale, spooky, pallid, sallow, eerie, murky

glassy
> vacant, blank, empty, glazed, expressionless, dazed

glazed
> empty, glassy, vacant, blank, vacuous, dazed, dumbfounded

gleeful
> jovial, joyous, blissful, elated, delighted, jubilant, exuberant

gloomy
> dismal, somber, forlorn, sulky, morose, dark, sullen, moody, dour, brooding

glowering
> dark, scowling, sullen, glaring, brooding, gloomy, skulking, angry, frowning

grim
> dreary, forlorn, bleak, forbidding, stony, stern, cold

groggy
> dizzy, woozy, befuddled, unsteady, witless, confused, dazed, giddy, disoriented

guarded
> distant, remote, unapproachable, wary, leery, uninviting, defensive, watchful, alert, cautious, vigilant, cagey, evasive, stern

haggard
> gaunt, withered, stark, exhausted, emaciated, hollow, pale

hardened
> flinty, unyielding, immovable, steely, unflappable, unbending, stern

haughty
> pompous, arrogant, disdainful, contemptuous, scornful

histrionic
> hysterical, cinematic, showy, melodramatic, operatic, dramatic, stagy, theatrical

hostile
> malicious, menacing, belligerent, forbidding, unfriendly, vicious, threatening, pugnacious, cold

hysterical
> frantic, frenetic, frazzled, wild, histrionic, dramatic, melodramatic, inconsolable, tumultuous, frenzied, raging

icy
> frozen, biting, bitter, detached, cold, cutting, dispassionate, distant, frosty, impassive, numb, reticent, sharp, shivery, stony

immovable
> unyielding, hardened, steely, unflappable, unbending, motionless

impassive
> distant, expressionless, remote, stony, icy, frozen, detached, cold, dispassionate, numb, reticent, stoic, stern

inconsolable
hysterical, frantic, despondent, despairing, melancholy, dispirited, wild, mournful

indecipherable
puzzling, enigmatic, inscrutable, cryptic, mystifying, perplexing

inflamed
prickly, festering, crimson, raw, feverish, fiery, flushed, heated, ignited, livid, smoldering

inscrutable
enigmatic, indecipherable, mystifying, incomprehensible, cryptic, puzzling, perplexing

jovial
festive, gleeful, joyous, affable, hearty, light-hearted, delighted

joyous
hearty, light-hearted, jovial, gleeful, affable, elated, ecstatic

jubilant
elated, triumphant, exultant, joyous, gleeful, rapturous, delighted

leery
guarded, wary, apprehensive, cautious, uncertain, suspicious

listless
languid, dull, lumbering, sleepy, poky, lethargic, shuffling, spiritless, slumberous, fatigued

longing
wistful, yearning, wishful, thoughtful, mournful, contemplative, pining, regretful, musing, nostalgic, ruminating, pensive

melancholy
despondent, inconsolable, despairing, mournful, forlorn, gloomy, dispirited, woeful

menacing
intimidating, threatening, hostile, glowering, frightening, ominous, vicious, scowling

moody
sulky, gloomy, morose, dark, sullen, brooding, glowering, dour, melancholy

morose
brooding, moody, sulky, gloomy, dark, sullen, mournful, dour, melancholy

mortified
shamefaced, regretful, pitiable, sorrowful, sheepish, remorseful, abashed, rueful

mournful
forlorn, rueful, musing, nostalgic, gloomy, ruminating, pensive, regretful, despondent, teary-eyed, melancholy

musing
contemplative, pining, nostalgic, wishful, thoughtful, pensive, wistful, longing, yearning, meditative, ruminating

nostalgic
musing, ruminating, wistful, contemplative, longing, yearning, wishful, thoughtful, pensive, pining, regretful

open-mouthed
flabbergasted, astonished, dumbstruck, amazed, wide-eyed, awed, bedazzled, surprised, startled, stupefied, astounded

overwrought
fraught, distraught, frantic, panicky, distressed, uneasy, exhausted

panicky, panicked
frenzied, fraught, distraught, frantic, distressed, overwrought, desperate, panic-stricken

peevish
sullen, petulant, cantankerous, testy, prickly, acrimonious, irritable

penetrating
sharp, discerning, keen, piercing, biting, fierce, discerning, intense

pensive
longing, yearning, wishful, thoughtful, mournful, contemplative, wistful, pining, regretful, musing, nostalgic, ruminating

perplexed
baffled, bewildered, confounded, cryptic, enigmatic, puzzled

piercing
penetrating, perceptive, keen, shrewd, sharp, fierce, intense

pining
longing, yearning, wistful, wishful, thoughtful, musing, pensive, contemplative, nostalgic, ruminating

placid
poised, self-possessed, composed, assured, balanced, equanimous, unruffled, unflappable, tranquil, calm

poised
elegant, graceful, stylish, tasteful, self-possessed, calm, composed, assured, balanced, equanimous, refined, unruffled, unflappable, placid

pugnacious
hostile, aggressive, bullying, menacing, combative, bellicose

puzzled
baffled, perplexed, bewildered, confounded, rattled, confused

puzzling
baffling, cryptic, mysterious, quizzical, enigmatic, perplexing, bewildering, inexplicable, confounding, mystifying

quizzical
> puzzling, enigmatic, bizarre, curious, eccentric, odd, sardonic

raging
> ranting, raucous, raving, ferocious, barbaric, beastly, belligerent, fierce, monstrous

rapturous
> ecstatic, euphoric, blissful, jubilant, elated, triumphant, exultant, joyous, gleeful, rhapsodic

regretful
> yearning, wishful, wistful, longing, thoughtful, pensive, pining, musing, mournful, contemplative, nostalgic, ruminating, rueful, remorseful, sorrowful

rueful
> shamefaced, regretful, pitiable, sorrowful, sheepish, mortified, abashed, remorseful

ruminating
> contemplative, pining, wistful, longing, yearning, wishful, musing, mournful, thoughtful, pensive, nostalgic

sardonic
> scornful, disdainful, mocking, bitter, caustic, sneering, cynical

savage
> howling, raving, wild, fierce, delirious, deranged, frantic, ferocious, vicious

scornful
> disdainful, contemptuous, scoffing, sneering, scowling, withering, rude, haughty

scowling
> glowering, sneering, glaring, moody, surly, gloomy, frowning, sullen

secretive
cagey, guarded, sneaky, evasive, cunning, crafty, wary, enigmatic, furtive

self-possessed
composed, assured, balanced, poised, unruffled, unflappable, equanimous, calm, placid

shamefaced
rueful, regretful, pitiable, sorrowful, sheepish, mortified, abashed, remorseful

sheepish
shamefaced, regretful, pitiable, sorrowful, mortified, abashed, remorseful, rueful

sickly
emaciated, feeble, ashen, pallid, sallow, peaked, languid, peaked, pale, gaunt

sorrowful
shamefaced, regretful, sheepish, mortified, abashed, remorseful, rueful

spiritless
languid, lumbering, sapless, shuffling, slumberous, apathetic, listless

spiteful
edgy, huffy, snappish, testy, bad-tempered, cantankerous, feisty, fractious, ill-tempered

startled
wide-eyed, astonished, dumbstruck, flabbergasted, astounded, bedazzled, perplexed, surprised, stupefied, awed

steadfast
unyielding, adamant, headstrong, inflexible, ironfisted, resolute, rigid, unflinching, unflappable

steely

cold, flinty, unyielding, hardened, immovable, unflappable, stony, unbending, callous, stern, icy

stern

unapproachable, uninviting, staid, austere, grave, stony, taciturn, stern, unbending

stoic

detached, impassive, lethargic, withdrawn, unexpressive, resigned, unemotional, indifferent

stony

icy, frozen, biting, callous, detached, dispassionate, distant, frosty, impassive, numb, reticent, cold, steely

stunned

bewildered, dazed, confused, dumbfounded, astonished, numb, astounded, dismayed, startled, stupefied

sulky

sullen, moody, gloomy, morose, dark, brooding, dour, morose, frowning, sour

sullen

moody, glowering, brooding, scowling, morose, sulky, gloomy, dark

surly

sulky, sullen, sour, scowling, testy, morose, rude, gruff, dour, irritable

teary, teary-eyed

despondent, inconsolable, despairing, melancholy, mournful, tearful, forlorn

tempestuous

tumultuous, agitated, frazzled, frenzied, hysterical, raving, stormy, turbulent, volatile, passionate, fiery

testy
> bad-tempered, cantankerous, cranky, crotchety, crusty, feisty, fractious, ill-tempered, edgy, huffy, irritable, snappish, spiteful

thoughtful
> wistful, longing, yearning, wishful, pensive, contemplative, pining, musing, nostalgic, ruminating

tormented
> agonized, haunted, pained, tortured, twisted, anguished, vexed, distressed

tortured
> tormented, convulsed, haunted, twisted, contorted, disturbed, distressed, pained

tranquil
> languid, meditative, dreamy, hushing, contemplative, peaceful, soothing, placid, calm

transfixed
> mesmerized, hypnotized, enchanted, captivated, engrossed, fascinated, riveted

trembling
> twitchy, turbulent, quivering, jittery, flustered, fluttery, fidgety, restless, shaky, uneasy, nervous, jumpy

unbending
> recalcitrant, inflexible, hostile, willful, flinty, hardened, immovable, steely, unflappable, stiff

uncertain
> ambiguous, dubious, hesitant, doubtful, reluctant, tentative, faltering, vacillating, skeptical

undaunted
> brazen, unblinking, unabashed, bold, fearless, intrepid, unflinching

uneasy
fidgety, restless, quivering, jittery, flustered, shaky, jumpy, twitchy, turbulent, trembling

unflappable
immovable, steely, flinty, unyielding, hardened, unbending, cool, unruffled, unflinching, cool-headed

unflinching
unyielding, adamant, headstrong, fearless, impervious, stern, resolute

unglued
crazed, unmoored, unhinged, unsteady, unstable, unraveled

unhinged
unmoored, unglued, deranged, unstable, demented, unraveled, crazed

unruffled
unflappable, composed, balanced, equanimous, placid, poised, cool-headed, collected, calm

unsteady
dazed, woozy, dizzy, befuddled, giddy, erratic, wobbly, shaky

unyielding
adamant, headstrong, inflexible, steadfast, unflinching, flinty, hardened, immovable, steely, unflappable, unbending

vacuous
inane, fatuous, empty, vapid, foolish, dim-witted, absurd

vapid
lifeless, empty, absurd, vacuous, fatuous, foolish, dim-witted, colorless, inane

vengeful
vindictive, unforgiving, spiteful, hostile, avenging

vindictive
vengeful, unforgiving, spiteful, hateful, malicious, ruthless

wary
guarded, leery, apprehensive, cautious, distrustful, suspicious

weary
exhausted, drained, frazzled, bewildered, fatigued, worn

wide-eyed
perplexed, surprised, startled, stupefied, astonished, dumbstruck, astounded, flabbergasted, amazed, awed, bedazzled

willful
defiant, inflexible, hostile, stiff, unbending, stubborn

wistful
longing, yearning, wishful, thoughtful, pensive, contemplative, pining, regretful, musing, nostalgic, ruminating

withdrawn
stoic, detached, impassive, taciturn, aloof, restrained, distant

woeful
anguished, dismal, sorrowful, heart-broken, miserable, pitiful, morose, bleak

wolfish
feral, barbaric, predatory, greedy, vicious, ferocious

wooden
stilted, awkward, glazed, empty, glassy, vacant, blank, vacuous

woozy
dizzy, befuddled, unsteady, dazed, unstable, tipsy, groggy, confused

wry
mocking, displeased, disgusted, vexed, unimpressed, annoyed

yearning
> musing, nostalgic, wistful, longing, wishful, thoughtful, pensive, mournful, contemplative, pining, regretful, ruminating

Motion

abound, abounding
> plentiful, abundant, bountiful, flourishing, profuse, overflowing, swarming, teeming, thriving, bristling, bursting, copious

amble, ambling
> rambling, dawdling, sauntering, drifting, meandering, strolling

balloon, ballooning
> soar, rocket, distend, surge, swell, billow, spiral, bloat

blunder, blundering
> lurching, lumbering, bungling, bumbling, floundering

bobble, bobbling
> careening, staggering, tottering, toppling, capsizing, plunging, tumbling, wobbling, bungling, floundering

breakneck
> headlong, breathless, dashing, impulsive, plunging, precipitous, rash, reckless, heedless

brim, brimming
> overflowing, abundant, teeming, copious, bristling, gushing

bristle, bristling
> overflowing, boiling, seething, fuming, ruffled, flaring, infuriated, raging

bubble, bubbling
> churning, burbling, boiling, seeping, trickling, fizzing, percolating, foaming, frothing

bungle, bungling
botched, blundering, fumbling, bumbling

burst, bursting
cascade, flow, overflow, pour, spout, slosh, spew, spill, waterfall, torrent, rush, plummet, explosive, volcanic, swarming, abounding, copious, overflowing, gushing

capsize, capsized
toppling, bobbling, careening, tottering, plunging, tumbling, wobbling, upended

careen, careening
swaying, tilting, pitching, tottering, toppling, bobbling, plunging, tumbling, wobbling, lurching

cascade, cascading
flow, burst, overflow, pour, spout, slosh, spew, spill, waterfall, rush, torrent, plummet

cataclysm, cataclysmic
upheaval, catastrophe, apocalyptic, disastrous, calamitous, ruinous

chaotic, chaos
random, erratic, disarray, pandemonium, confused, disordered, frantic, frenetic, tumultuous, haphazard, clamorous, frenzied, hysterical, raucous, stormy, tempestuous, turbulent

choppy
patchy, uneven, fragmented, frayed, wobbly, erratic, haphazard, hitching, jolting, halting, jarring

circuitous
serpentine, twisted, winding, convoluted, meandering, snaking, rambling, wavy, circular

clumsy
bungling, bumbling, blundering, gawkish, ungainly, awkward

convulse, convulsing
jerking, thrashing, twisting, shuddering, writhing, agitated

disarray
chaos, pandemonium, confusion, turmoil, disorder

dodder, doddering
ambling, faltering, oscillating, tottering, shaking, quivering, shifting, shuffling, swaying, staggering

ebb, ebbing
dwindling, receding, waning, subsiding, diminishing, shrinking, slackening, fading

explosive
bursting, edgy, passionate, volcanic, volatile, changeable, impulsive, mercurial

falter, faltering
floundering, wobbling, tottering, ambling, doddering, oscillating, stumbling, shifting, lurching

fidget, fidgety
quivering, restless, jittery, flustered, fluttery, trembling, twitchy, jumpy, turbulent, uneasy, shaky

fleeting
vanishing, evanescent, ephemeral, melting, ethereal, transient, fading, short-lived

flitter, flittering
flit, fling, quiver, pulse, flicker, dart, swoop, ripple

float, floating
buoyant, fluid, effervescent, bouncy, ebullient, springy, airy, breezy, drifting, hovering

flourish, flourishing
thriving, swarming, bristling, bursting, overflowing, teeming

flow, flowing
cascade, burst, overflow, pour, spout, slosh, spew, spill, waterfall, torrent, rush, plummet

fluttery, fluttering
flustered, fidgety, quivering, jumpy, turbulent, restless, trembling, jittery, twitchy, shaky

frenetic
frenzied, chaotic, frantic, hysterical, manic, uproarious, furious, wild, obsessive

frenzy, frenzied
chaotic, frantic, frenetic, hysterical, manic, crazed, tumultuous, agitated, turbulent, wild

fumble, fumbling
awkward, blundering, bungling, stumbling, grappling, groping, floundering, bumbling, clumsy

gyrate, gyrating
lurching, pitching, reeling, swirling, throbbing, twirling, whirling, undulating

halting
choppy, hitching, jolting, jarring, stumbling, faltering, bumbling, vacillating

haphazard
chaotic, aimless, careless, irregular, random, erratic, reckless, disordered

headlong
breathless, breakneck, dashing, impulsive, plunging, precipitous, rash, reckless, heedless

heedless
rash, reckless, careless, headlong, impulsive, aimless

hitching
choppy, jolting, halting, jarring, stumbling, glitchy, sputtering

immobile
crippled, incapacitated, paralyzed, rigid, stagnant, unmoving

incapacitated
crippled, immobile, paralyzed, debilitated, impaired

jammed
blocked, cemented, compressed, seized up, immobilized, frozen, obstructed, clogged

jarring
jolting, choppy, hitching, grating, halting, disturbing, clashing, grinding

jittery
shaky, trembling, twitchy, jumpy, flustered, fluttery, fidgety, restless, quivering, turbulent, uneasy

jolting
jarring, alarming, choppy, hitching, halting, knocking, shaking, jostling

jumpy
twitchy, turbulent, uneasy, flustered, fluttery, fidgety, quivering, restless, shaky, trembling, jittery

lapping
splashing, swishing, sloshing, licking, swallowing, rolling

lumber, lumbering
plodding, slogging, shuffling, trudging, lurching

lurch, lurching
rolling, careening, gyrating, pitching, reeling, swirling, throbbing, twirling, undulating, whirling

meander, meandering
crooked, twisted, tortuous, winding, snaking, convoluted

oscillate, oscillating
tottering, pitching, vacillating, wobbling, faltering, shifting, seesawing, wavering

overflow, overflowing
cascading, spouting, spewing, spilling, rushing, swarming, abounding, bursting, waterfall, torrent

pandemonium
chaos, disarray, confusion, turmoil, disorder, commotion, bedlam, turbulence

paralyzed
immobilized, stunned, crippled, incapacitated, numb, frozen

plunge, plunging
plummet, hurtle, nosedive, careen, topple, tumble, sink, lunge, pitch

quiver, quivering
flustered, fluttery, jumpy, turbulent, uneasy, jittery, fidgety, restless, shaking, trembling, twitchy

restless
uneasy, quivering, jittery, flustered, fluttery, trembling, twitchy, fidgety, jumpy, shaky

rampant
unrestrained, unbridled, uncontrolled, unrestricted, runaway

rolling
billowy, careening, gyrating, lurching, pitching, reeling, swirling, throbbing, thundering, twirling, undulating, whirling

shuffle, shuffling
dragging, limping, lumbering, stumbling, ambling, scraping

slosh, sloshing
cascading, overflowing, pouring, spouting, spewing, splattering, rushing, spilling

spew, spewing
spout, slosh, spill, cascade, burst, overflow, pour, belch, gush, spit, cascade, expel

spill, spilling
overflow, pour, spout, slosh, spew, cascade, burst, torrent, rush, slop, squirt, disgorge

spiral, spiralling
balloon, soar, rocket, surge, swell, billow, roll, curled, corkscrew

splash, splashing
splatter, dapple, shower, speckle, slosh, sprinkle, splurge, burst, dash, slop

splatter, splattering
splash, splotch, swish, slosh, spew, spill, douse, drench, plunge

sporadic
sparse, diffuse, patchy, spotty, haphazard, fitful, irregular, scattered

spout, spouting
burst, overflow, cascade, flow, spew, spill, waterfall, torrent, rush, pour, slosh, gush, emit, spray, squirt

stagnant
immobile, rigid, unmoving, immovable, static, dormant

stagnate, stagnating
deteriorating, declining, languishing, festering, stalling

stymie, stymied
obstructed, hindered, hampered, thwarted, impeded, confounded, crimped

swarm, swarming
abounding, bursting, copious, flourishing, overflowing, brimming, thriving, prospering, roaring, teeming

swirl, swirling
billowing, careening, gyrating, twirling, undulating, whirling, rolling

taper, tapering
diminishing, dwindling, narrowing, waning, slackening

teeming
plentiful, thriving, prospering, swarming, vigorous, bountiful, abundant, profuse, fruitful, copious, robust

thwart, thwarted
obstructed, hindered, hampered, stymied, impeded, circumvented, foiled

topple, toppling
plunging, tumbling, wobbling, careening, staggering, tottering, bobbling, capsized

torrent
cascade, burst, overflow, spout, spew, waterfall, rush, downpour, deluge

totter, tottering
wobbling, ambling, doddering, faltering, oscillating, shifting, careening, toppling, bobbling, plunging, tumbling

tumble, tumbling
plunging, wobbling careening, staggering, tottering, toppling, bobbling, flopping

tumult, tumultuous
turmoil, havoc, upheaval, mayhem, volatile, agitated, frenzied, hysterical, explosive, tempestuous, turbulent, chaotic

turbulent
stormy, trembling, unstable, jumpy, tumultuous, agitated, chaotic, frenzied, tempestuous

twitchy, twitching
trembling, jumpy, quivering, jittery, flustered, fluttery, fidgety, restless, shaky, turbulent, uneasy

unbridled
boundless, irrepressible, unrestrained, unchecked, uncontrolled, riotous, chaotic

undulate, undulating
rolling, billowing, careening, twirling, whirling, gyrating, pitching, swirling, throbbing

unravel, unraveling
decipher, untangle, unscramble, unwind, disentangle, collapse, decode, untie

unrestrained
unbridled, boundless, excessive, irrepressible, rampant, unchecked

unscramble
decipher, unravel, untangle, decode

unspool
unravel, untangle, unwind, disengage, untwist

untangle
unscramble, unsnarl, decipher, unravel, decode, disentangle

upend, upended
capsized, overturned, inverted, unsettled, pitched, topsy-turvy, cockeyed, jumbled, toppled

volatile
changeable, effervescent, ephemeral, explosive, charged, fluid, mercurial, wavering, erratic, turbulent

volcanic
> explosive, bursting, passionate, fiery, violent, excitable, volatile, turbulent

wane
> ebb, dwindle, recede, taper, fade, slacken, subside, wither, diminish

whirl, whirling
> swirl, twirl, gyrate, flurry, whirlwind, stir, spin, orbit, twist, revolve

DISTINCTIVE QUALITY *or* IMPRESSION

abominable
> atrocious, wretched, vile, despicable, detestable, odious, loathsome

absorbing
> engrossing, enriching, gripping, inspiring, riveting, captivating, compelling, enthralling

absurd
> preposterous, senseless, ridiculous, ludicrous, foolish, outlandish, wacky

abysmal
> woeful, abominable, anguished, bleak, dismal, dreadful, deplorable, pitiful, appalling

airy
> buoyant, effervescent, breezy, exhilarating, frothy, sparkling, lively, vivacious, floating

alchemy
> magic, transformation, sorcery, wizardry

allure, alluring
> enticing, captivating, charming, enchanting, fascinating, seductive, hypnotic, beguiling, arresting, bewitching, engrossing, enthralling, gripping, intriguing, magnetic, mesmerizing, disarming

ambiance
   aura, mood, atmosphere, tone, impression

anomaly
   oddity, aberration, curiosity, peculiarity, deviation, freak

aplomb
   poise, composure, equanimity, elegance, grace, serenity, tact

appalling
   egregious, frightful, outrageous, atrocious, detestable, wretched,
   dreadful, hideous, ghastly

appealing
   alluring, tempting, arousing, captivating, charming, fascinating,
   enchanting, seductive, enticing

arousing
   thrilling, captivating, enchanting, enlivening, gripping, rousing,
   evocative

arresting
   hypnotic, beguiling, alluring, bewitching, captivating, engrossing,
   enthralling, enchanting, enticing, gripping, intriguing, magnetic,
   mesmerizing, striking, stunning, impressive

artistry
   brilliance, drama, flourish, style, finesse, flair, virtuosity

atmosphere
   aura, mood, tone, ambiance, climate, color, scene

atrocious
   appalling, egregious, frightful, outrageous, ghastly, detestable,
   dreadful, hideous, wretched

august
   stately, courtly, dignified, gallant, glorious, kingly, lofty, majestic,
   noble, striking, distinguished

baffling
> puzzling, perplexing, bewildering, disconcerting, mystifying, cryptic, incomprehensible, unfathomable

barbaric
> ferocious, beastly, belligerent, fierce, monstrous, raging, inhumane, savage, cruel

beastly
> belligerent, fierce, ferocious, barbaric, monstrous, raging, savage, abominable

bedraggled
> disheveled, unkempt, scruffy, untidy, tousled, mangy, scraggly, shabby, messy, ragged

beguiling
> enchanting, charming, alluring, bewitching, arresting, disarming, hypnotic, captivating, engrossing, enticing, gripping, intriguing, magnetic, mesmerizing

bewilder, bewildering
> convoluted, confounding, inexplicable, mystifying, perplexing, puzzling, stunning, baffling

bewitch, bewitching
> enchanting, beguiling, mysterious, entrancing, captivating, magical, charming, fascinating, hypnotic, alluring, arresting, engrossing, gripping, intriguing, magnetic, mesmerizing, tantalizing, enticing, enrapturing, enthralling

bizarre
> unearthly, uncanny, freakish, mysterious, peculiar, outlandish, surreal

bleak
> desolate, stark, dreary, gloomy, barren, forlorn, godforsaken, grim, woeful, dismal, dreadful, deplorable, abysmal

blithe
> effervescent, breezy, exhilarating, carefree, sparkling, vivacious, joyous, buoyant, exuberant, lively, perky, bouncy, ebullient, airy, jaunty

bodacious
> bold, daring, remarkable, audacious, assured, unabashed, intrepid, gutsy

bold
> flamboyant, bright, colorful, showy, flashy, splashy, unabashed, brazen

bouncy
> ebullient, floating, jaunty, springy, effervescent, breezy, buoyant, exhilarating, sparkling, lively, perky, blithe, vivacious, exuberant, airy, light-hearted

brash
> energetic, assertive, bold, brazen, cocky, impulsive, rude, reckless

brassy
> saucy, flashy, brazen, brash, cheeky, daring, sassy, gaudy, jarring, cocky, pushy

brazen
> bold, unblinking, undaunted, saucy, flashy, brash, unabashed, showy, splashy, audacious

breathtaking
> captivating, spectacular, extraordinary, magnificent, stunning, wondrous, astounding

breezy
> effervescent, airy, exhilarating, frothy, sparkling, vivacious, lively, blithe, light-hearted

bucolic
> rustic, rural, pastoral, woodsy, serene, peaccful, tranquil

bumptious
pompous, overbearing, swaggering, pushy, obnoxious, haughty, cocky

bungling
clumsy, messy, careless, botched, inelegant, awkward, blundering, fumbling, graceless, bumbling, ungainly, sloppy

buoyant
energetic, joyful, lively, jaunty, exuberant, ebullient, effervescent, fluid, bouncy, blithe

canny
skillful, deft, shrewd, astute, crafty, wily

cantankerous
testy, bad-tempered, crotchety, fractious, ill-tempered, irritable, edgy, huffy, snappish, spiteful, feisty, crusty, cranky, grumpy, surly, ornery

captivate, captivating
charming, enchanting, fascinating, alluring, enticing, appealing, tempting, attractive, seductive, compelling, riveting, enthralling, tantalizing, enrapturing, bewitching, thrilling, arousing, enlivening, gripping, rousing

charismatic
magical, bewitching, enchanting, seductive, charming, magnetic

charming
disarming, arresting, delightful, alluring, enticing, appealing, tempting, captivating, enchanting, fascinating, hypnotic

cinematic
dramatic, theatrical, vivid, stellar, operatic, animated, colorful, picturesque

clumsy
awkward, bungling, bumbling, blundering, gauche, ham-handed

commanding
sweeping, powerful, expansive, decisive, superior, compelling, assertive, imposing, forceful, impressive

compelling
absorbing, engrossing, enriching, captivating, enthralling, gripping, inspiring, riveting, moving, powerful

composed
poised, refined, unruffled, unflappable, self-possessed, balanced, equanimous, calm, self-assured, placid

confounded
bewildered, baffled, puzzled, perplexed, befuddled, disconcerted, startled, mystified

contemptible
obnoxious, abhorrent, repugnant, offensive, deplorable, repellent, vile

courtly
kingly, lofty, stately, august, dignified, gallant, glorious, majestic, noble, striking

creepy
spooky, frightening, freaky, disturbing, eerie, ghoulish, hair-raising

crotchety
cranky, crusty, ill-tempered, feisty, fractious, testy, bad-tempered, cantankerous, edgy, huffy, irritable, snappish, spiteful, grouchy

crusty
ill-tempered, edgy, huffy, irritable, snappish, spiteful, testy, bad-tempered, cantankerous, cranky, crotchety, feisty, fractious

cultured
polished, refined, accomplished, graceful, impeccable, tasteful, sophisticated

curious
aberrant, odd, peculiar, strange, deviating, freakish, puzzling, exotic

dashing
sporty, dynamic, stylish, elegant, lively, flashy, showy, eye-catching, splashy, dapper, flamboyant, dazzling

daunting
formidable, intimidating, imposing, dismaying, ominous, forbidding, fearsome

decrepit
decaying, rickety, battered, ramshackle, worn, degraded, tottering, aged, dilapidated, crumbling

deft
masterful, accomplished, brilliant, consummate, superlative, skillful, proficient, superb

delirious
wild, fierce, deranged, frantic, howling, raving, savage, unhinged, ecstatic, rapturous, blissful, ecstatic

desolate
forlorn, abandoned, empty, dreary, godforsaken, bleak, deserted, grim, barren, remote, stark

despicable
abominable, atrocious, contemptible, despairing, dreadful, vile, miserable, worthless, repugnant, abhorrent, heinous, monstrous, vicious

devastated
ruined, wasted, wrecked, ravaged, blighted, demolished

diabolical
fiendish, demonic, villainous, devious, dastardly, vile, wicked

dignified
> gallant, glorious, stately, august, courtly, kingly, striking, majestic, noble, lofty

disarming
> beguiling, charming, arresting, stunning, striking, irresistible, bewitching

disheveled
> bedraggled, unkempt, disarrayed, messy, sloppy, untidy, scruffy, wrinkled, rumbled

dismal
> bleak, dreary, miserable, woeful, abominable, anguished, dreadful, sorrowful, tragic, deplorable, abysmal

distasteful
> unsavory, obnoxious, offensive, repulsive, repugnant, unpleasant, displeasing

dizzying
> woozy, befuddled, unsteady, dazed, witless, whirling, bewildering, giddy

dramatic
> climactic, cinematic, thrilling, stirring, stellar, sensational, striking, impressive, startling, vivid

dreadful
> atrocious, hideous, grim, ghastly, grisly, grotesque, gruesome, vile, heinous, horrendous, horrifying, loathsome, monstrous, odious

dreary
> desolate, forlorn, godforsaken, bleak, grim, colorless, dismal, lifeless, gloomy

droll
> quirky, wry, comical, dry, witty, amusing, eccentric, absurd, farcical, whimsical

ebullient
effervescent, lively, buoyant, exuberant, irrepressible, elated

edgy
explosive, bursting, volcanic, testy, feisty, restless, nervous, high-strung, uptight

eerie
mysterious, peculiar, strange, creepy, freakish, spooky, scary, spine-chilling, bone-chilling

effervescent
breezy, exhilarating, frothy, sparkling, vivacious, buoyant, ebullient, exuberant, lively, blithe, jaunty, bubbly

elegant
graceful, tasteful, refined, poised, polished, stylish

elevated
highfalutin, majestic, lofty, superlative, noble, grandiose, exalted, grand, dignified, eminent

eminent
outstanding, preeminent, illustrious, renowned, pre-eminent, distinguished, famed, esteemed

enamored
engrossed, riveted, beguiled, bewitched, enthralled, captivated, smitten, enchanted, charmed

enchanting, enchanted
captivating, bewitching, enlivening, riveting, mesmerizing, magical, beguiling, entrancing, charismatic, enamored

enduring
durable, sturdy, indestructible, impervious, persistent, resistant, unchanging, profound, unforgettable, inextinguishable, unfading, vital, indelible

engrossing, engrossed
enriching, gripping, inspiring, compelling, enthralling, absorbing, riveting, captivating

enraptured
enthralled, thrilled, enamored, captivated, bewitched, delighted

enriching
engrossing, inspiring, elevating, nourishing, stimulating

entrancing, entranced
bewitching, enchanting, beguiling, mysterious, captivating, mesmerized, hypnotized

evanescent
ephemeral, fading, vanishing, short-lived, fleeting, ethereal, transient, tenuous

evocative
powerful, vivid, stirring, moving, expressive, suggestive, graphic, haunting

exotic
mysterious, mystical, striking, curious, fascinating, alluring

exquisite
delicate, intricate, fine, dainty, elegant, polished, striking, charming, ornate, intense

extravagant
showy, ornate, fanciful, flamboyant, flashy, adorned, elaborate, ostentatious, indulgent

exultant
triumphant, elated, jubilant, euphoric, ecstatic, enraptured, joyous

fanciful
elaborate, whimsical, extravagant, imaginative, adorned, flowery, ornate, resplendent, frilly, embellished

fanfare
celebration, glitz, flourish, pageantry, splendor, spectacle

fastidious
exacting, finicky, meticulous, scrupulous, discriminating

fearsome
frightful, terrifying, imposing, intimidating, formidable, menacing, alarming, shocking

feisty
testy, touchy, edgy, spunky, gritty, gutsy, spirited, scrappy

ferocious
barbaric, beastly, belligerent, fierce, monstrous, raging, savage

festive
joyful, light-hearted, lively, gleeful, joyous, blithe, celebratory, jovial, jubilant

fiendish
diabolical, demonic, villainous, devious, dastardly, nefarious

finesse
artistry, mastery, flair, panache, craft, elegance, polish, wizardry, excellence, savvy

flair
artistry, brilliance, daring, drama, flourish, panache, style, savvy, polish, glitz, craft

flamboyant
bright, colorful, flowery, bold, elaborate, showy, flashy, garish, splashy, extravagant, dazzling, theatrical, glamorous

flashy
flamboyant, bright, colorful, bold, elaborate, eye-catching, splashy, garish, dashing, brazen, showy

flaunting
ostentatious, flamboyant, frilly, flashy, blatant, glaring, pretentious

flawless
impeccable, immaculate, exquisite, meticulous, pristine, spotless, unmarred, unblemished

flourish, flourishing
flair, brilliance, luxuriant, plentiful, abounding, lavish, teeming, thriving, swarming, bristling, bursting, exuberant, overflowing, copious

forbidding
gloomy, spooky, distant, menacing, remote, stern, unpleasant, uninviting, foreboding, sinister, ominous

forlorn
desolate, deserted, remote, dejected, dreary, bleak, barren, grim, hopeless, despondent, abandoned

formidable
imposing, intimidating, threatening, dismaying, daunting

freakish, freaky
strange, curious, peculiar, aberrant, creepy, eerie, surreal, uncanny, odd, bizarre

frightful
hideous, disturbing, appalling, alarming, shocking, calamitous, dreadful, ghastly

frothy
effervescent, bubbly, breezy, exhilarating, sparkling, vivacious, fizzy, foamy, soapy

gallant
fearless, dauntless, valorous, valiant, courageous, unflinching, bold, undaunted

galling
irksome, provoking, vexing, aggravating, wearisome, troubling, bothersome, disturbing, exasperating, tiresome

garish
gaudy, flashy, tacky, tawdry, lurid, vulgar, glaring, ostentatious, showy

gaudy
garish, tacky, showy, tawdry, ostentatious, flashy, harsh, tasteless, lurid

gawky
awkward, ungainly, unpolished, uncouth, ungraceful, clumsy

gauche
tasteless, awkward, gawky, inelegant, uncouth, unpolished, tactless, crude, unsophisticated

ghastly
appalling, dreadful, frightening, horrendous, hideous, horrifying, ghoulish, gruesome, grisly

glamorous
alluring, beguiling, dazzling, enchanting, lustrous, elegant, stylish, glittering, magnetic, stunning

glorious
luxurious, illustrious, majestic, striking, radiant, gallant, wondrous, noble

goon, goony
nincompoop, ninny, blockhead, imbecile, simpleton, nitwit, sap, dimwit, foolish, buffoon

gorgeous
exquisite, radiant, stunning, sparkling, dazzling, opulent, brilliant, luxurious, splendid, sumptuous

graceful

elegant, stylish, tasteful, refined, poised, polished, accomplished, cultured, sophisticated

graceless

inelegant, awkward, blundering, bungling, fumbling, indelicate, loutish, ungainly, bumbling, clumsy

grand

momentous, preeminent, ascendant, towering, stately, impressive, transcendent, magnificent, lavish, stellar

grandiose

elaborate, majestic, lofty, ostentatious, colossal, elevated, visionary, highfalutin, noble, grand, superlative

gripping

hypnotic, arresting, bewitching, engrossing, enthralling, magnetic, mesmerizing, thrilling, arousing, enlivening, rousing

grisly

ghastly, appalling, horrific, dreadful, frightening, horrendous, gruesome

gritty

feisty, spunky, gutsy, spirited, scrappy, tenacious, fierce, dogged, determined, plucky

grotesque

deformed, gruesome, monstrous, twisted, contorted, misshapen, gnarled, mangled, hideous

gruesome

dreadful, frightening, appalling, horrific, horrendous, hideous, ghastly, grisly

hapless

forlorn, doomed, hopeless, cursed, wretched, disastrous, woeful

haunted
tormented, cursed, tortured, possessed, frightful, creepy, obsessed, anguished, troubled

haunting
nagging, persistent, indelible, frightful, unforgettable, stirring, poignant, moving, eerie

hazardous
perilous, treacherous, uncertain, precarious, risky, unsound

hideous
heinous, horrendous, horrifying, grim, atrocious, dreadful, ghastly, grisly, grotesque, monstrous, odious, vile, appalling, detestable, wretched, gruesome, loathsome

histrionic
stagy, hysterical, cinematic, melodramatic, emotional, operatic, sensational, dramatic, showy

horrendous
hideous, grim, atrocious, heinous, horrifying, loathsome, dreadful, ghastly, grisly, grotesque, gruesome, monstrous, odious, vile

horrifying
gruesome, loathsome, vile, heinous, horrendous, dreadful, ghastly, monstrous, odious, hideous, grim, atrocious, grisly, grotesque

howling
raving, wild, fierce, delirious, deranged, frantic, savage, wailing, barking

hypnotic
beguiling, alluring, arresting, bewitching, captivating, engrossing, enthralling, enchanting, intriguing, magnetic, mesmerizing, riveting

idyllic
picturesque, ornate, charming, quaint, scenic, vivid, striking

impassioned
forceful, intense, fiery, passionate, resolute, rousing, stirring, fierce, vehement, fervent

impeccable
flawless, exquisite, meticulous, pristine, refined, precise, faultless, unblemished

indelible
enduring, keen, ingrained, poignant, profound, unforgettable, inextinguishable, pervading, piercing, unfading

indelicate
bungling, inelegant, awkward, blundering, fumbling, bumbling, graceless, ungainly, clumsy

inelegant
indelicate, loutish, ungainly, tasteless, awkward, graceless, clumsy, bungling, fumbling, blundering, uncouth

inscrutable
enigmatic, indecipherable, mystifying, puzzling, perplexing, incomprehensible

insolent
saucy, cocky, rude, ill-mannered, insulting, impertinent, brazen, arrogant

intriguing
enticing, magnetic, mesmerizing, hypnotic, beguiling, enthralling, arresting, bewitching, captivating, engrossing, alluring, enchanting

irksome
vexing, aggravating, bothersome, disturbing, exasperating, galling, provoking, tiresome, wearisome, troubling

ironfisted
adamant, unyielding, steadfast, headstrong, impervious, inflexible, unflinching, refractory, resistant

irreparable
> irrevocable, ruined, unsalvageable, impossible, hopeless, broken, irretrievable, impossible, irreversible, irreplaceable

irrepressible
> unrestrained, ebullient, exuberant, unbridled, boundless, buoyant, bubbling, vivacious

jaunty
> cheerful, lively, buoyant, ebullient, effervescent, breezy, sparkling, vivacious, exuberant, perky, bouncy, blithe, light-hearted

kingly
> stately, august, courtly, dignified, gallant, glorious, lofty, majestic, noble, striking

lackadaisical
> indifferent, careless, lazy, dreamy, halfhearted, apathetic, lethargic, idle, listless, spiritless, lax

languid
> listless, lumbering, sleepy, shuffling, leisurely, unhurried, poky, lazy, idle

languish, languishing
> deteriorating, listless, withering, drooping, wasting, dwindling

lavish
> luxuriant, adorned, embellished, extravagant, grand, lush, opulent, sumptuous, plush

lively
> buoyant, exuberant, cheerful, ebullient, spirited, sparkling, cheery, uplifting, bustling, animated, vigorous, bubbly

lofty
> elevated, grandiose, aerial, colossal, highfalutin, majestic, noble, soaring, superlative, visionary, stately, glorious

loony
> kooky, batty, cuckoo, daffy, flaky, crazy, unbalanced, unhinged, nutty

lurid
> gaudy, bright, blinding, intense, vivid, glaring, shocking, flaming, dazzling, loud, garish

luscious
> opulent, lavish, luxuriant, plush, sumptuous, showy, exquisite

magical
> bewitching, charismatic, enchanting, radiant, wondrous, wizardly, splendorous

magnetic
> hypnotic, alluring, arresting, engrossing, enthralling, beguiling, bewitching, captivating, enticing, gripping, intriguing, enchanting, mesmerizing

majestic
> gallant, glorious, elevated, grandiose, highfalutin, noble, visionary, superlative, stately, august, courtly, dignified, kingly, luxurious, lofty

masterful, masterly
> accomplished, brilliant, consummate, deft, superb, superlative

mercurial
> volatile, changeable, explosive, impulsive, wavering, erratic, flighty

mesmerize, mesmerizing
> enthralling, enchanting, hypnotic, riveting, beguiling, gripping, arresting, bewitching, captivating, engrossing, enticing, alluring, intriguing, magnetic

meticulous
> flawless, impeccable, scrupulous, precise, scrutinizing, exacting, conscientious

momentous
crucial, pivotal, earth-shattering, eventful, grand, preeminent, ascendant, stellar, towering, transcendent, seminal

monstrous
ferocious, vile, atrocious, heinous, vicious, barbaric, beastly, fierce, belligerent, raging

mysterious
cryptic, secret, enigmatic, perplexing, puzzling, obscure, baffling, inexplicable, inscrutable

mystifying
puzzling, baffling, cryptic, mysterious, secret, enigmatic, quizzical, perplexing, bewildering, inexplicable, confounding

noble
majestic, superlative, visionary, lofty, elevated, grandiose, kingly, highfalutin, stately, august, courtly, dignified, gallant, glorious

noxious
obnoxious, abhorrent, repugnant, toxic, odious, offensive, vile, repellent

obnoxious
abhorrent, repugnant, contemptible, odious, offensive, noxious, repellent, vile

odd, oddity
aberrant, curious, peculiar, freakish, irregular, bizarre, offbeat

odious
foul, obnoxious, abhorrent, repugnant, contemptible, offensive, noxious, repellent, vile

onerous
grueling, laborious, rigorous, vigorous, exhausting, formidable, arduous

operatic
cinematic, showy, histrionic, melodramatic, emotional, sensational, dramatic, stagy

opulent
rich, affluent, lavish, luscious, luxuriant, plush, sumptuous, showy, grand

ostentatious
flamboyant, frilly, flashy, flaunting, showy, pretentious

other-worldly
mystical, supernatural, unearthly, ethereal, dreamy, mysterious

outlandish
absurd, bizarre, wondrous, weird, preposterous, peculiar, fantastic, outrageous

outrageous
appalling, egregious, frightful, preposterous, exorbitant

passionate
explosive, bursting, volcanic, forceful, impassioned, vehement, fervent, spirited, ardent, intense

pastoral
rustic, bucolic, rural, woodsy, scenic, peaceful

peculiar
odd, aberrant, curious, strange, deviating, freakish, outlandish

perilous
hazardous, treacherous, uncertain, precarious, menacing, unsound, risky

perplexing
baffling, bewildering, confounding, cryptic, mysterious, secret, enigmatic, puzzling, obscure, inexplicable

pervading
indelible, enduring, ingrained, piercing, penetrating, permeating, keen, transfused

picturesque
idyllic, luxuriant, ornate, charming, quaint, scenic, vivid, striking, pastoral. bucolic

plagued
disintegrated, ravaged, blighted, corrosive, devastated, ruinous, wasted, wrecked

poignant
moving, touching, indelible, enduring, profound, unforgettable, pervading, unfading

ponderous
heavy, weighty, unwieldy, plodding, dreary, tedious, burdensome

precarious
hazardous, perilous, treacherous, uncertain, delicate, tenuous, unstable, tricky

preeminent
momentous, grand, ascendant, stellar, towering, transcendent, distinguished, illustrious

preposterous
outlandish, absurd, impossible, ludicrous, staggering, unthinkable, outrageous, shocking

provoking
galling, irksome, vexing, aggravating, exasperating, bothersome, disturbing, tiresome, wearisome, troubling

puzzling
baffling, mysterious, enigmatic, perplexing, bewildering, obscure, inexplicable, confounding, cryptic

quaint
> picturesque, idyllic, charming, scenic, whimsical, pleasing

racy
> bawdy, fiery, lusty, juicy, provocative, risqué, spicy, saucy, vivacious

ravening
> raging, ravenous, ferocious, voracious, predatory, greedy, savage

raving
> howling, savage, barking, wild, fierce, ranting, delirious, deranged, frantic, unhinged

reckless
> impulsive, headlong, dashing, plunging, rash, heedless, careless, thoughtless

refined
> poised, elegant, graceful, stylish, tasteful, self-possessed, calm, composed, assured, balanced

repellent
> repugnant, contemptible, odious, obnoxious, abhorrent, offensive, noxious, vile

repugnant
> offensive, noxious, obnoxious, abhorrent, contemptible, repellent, vile, odious

resplendent
> luxuriant, splendorous, radiant, dazzling, shining, lively, brilliant, sublime, spellbinding

rhapsodic
> blissful, euphoric, elated, ecstatic, exhilarated, joyous, rapturous

rich
> lavish, bountiful, abundant, profuse, opulent, intense, luscious, vibrant, vivid

risqué
racy, bawdy, fiery, lusty, juicy, provocative, salty, spicy, spirited, tart, saucy

riveting, riveted
enthralling, mesmerizing, hypnotic, thrilling, gripping, engrossing, spellbinding, enchanting, captivating, beguiling, magnetic, alluring, arresting, enticing

roaring
thriving, flourishing, uproarious, robust, swarming, teeming, vigorous, boisterous, rowdy

rotten
appalling, atrocious, decayed, detestable, dreadful, putrid, rancid, sordid, spoiled, wretched

rousing
thrilling, arousing, captivating, enchanting, enlivening, gripping, stirring, impassioned, animated

saucy
brash, brazen, cheeky, daring, sassy, rude, flippant

savage
howling, raving, wild, fierce, delirious, deranged, frantic, untamed, vicious, ferocious

scintillating
flashy, brilliant, sparkling, gleaming, glistening, effervescent, lively, dazzling, glimmering

scrupulous
impeccable, meticulous, flawless, precise, scrutinizing, unsparing, conscientious

seedy
chintzy, cheap, ragged, ratty, slipshod, squalid, tattered, tawdry, disreputable

shady
> unsavory, disreputable, slippery, unscrupulous, shoddy, suspicious, fishy, shifty

showy
> flashy, frilly, brash, ornate, garish, luxurious, plush, lavish, opulent, glittering

sophisticated
> cultured, graceful, impeccable, polished, refined, accomplished, tasteful

sorcery
> wizardry, witchcraft, magic, alchemy, incantation, mystique

sordid
> seedy, vile, sleazy, unsavory, squalid, grimy, foul, filthy, wretched, foul

spectacle
> array, display, splendor, extravagance, drama, curiosity, parade

spectacular
> breathtaking, phenomenal, extraordinary, magnificent, stunning, wondrous, astounding, sublime

spellbinding
> absorbing, alluring, beguiling, enchanting, engrossing, gripping, mesmerizing, enthralling

spirited
> animated, ebullient, lively, vivacious, passionate, dynamic, vibrant

splashy
> flashy, glittering, showy, glitzy, opulent, sensational, eye-catching

splendorous
> extravagant, magical, bewitching, charismatic, enchanting, radiant, brilliant, wondrous, glorious

sprightly
lively, spirited, vigorous, animated, ebullient, vivacious

staggering
astonishing, stunning, aghast, startling, astounding, unthinkable, alarming, shocking

stagy
cinematic, dramatic, histrionic, melodramatic, showy, operatic

stately
august, courtly, dignified, glorious, kingly, lofty, impressive, majestic, distinguished, noble, striking

stellar
preeminent, momentous, grand, ascendant, towering, sterling, transcendent, cinematic, dramatic, superlative

sterling
pure, refined, absolute, stellar, exceptional, superior, stunning

stormy
tumultuous, agitated, frenzied, raging, blustery, wild, passionate, turbulent, tempestuous

striking
disarming, beguiling, charming, arresting, stunning, extraordinary, compelling, dazzling, wondrous, vivid

stunning
striking, disarming, beguiling, charming, arresting, astonishing, phenomenal, tremendous, vivid

stylish
elegant, graceful, tasteful, poised, dapper, polished, refined

sublime
superb, glorious, transcendent, grand, heavenly, majestic, elevated

sumptuous
luxuriant, lavish, luscious, resplendent, stately, opulent, rich, plush, showy

superficial
petty, flat, hollow, shallow, tacky, frivolous, trivial

superior, superlative
majestic, noble, visionary, grandiose, masterful, brilliant, elevated, consummate, deft, superb

surreal
unearthly, bizarre, uncanny, freakish, mysterious, dreamlike, odd, fantastic, peculiar

tacky
garish, gaudy, tawdry, cheap, tasteless, shoddy, sleazy, crude, seedy, run-down

tantalizing
captivating, enrapturing, bewitching, alluring, enticing, appealing, tempting, fascinating, seductive, compelling, charming, riveting, enchanting, enthralling

tasteful
refined, polished, elegant, graceful, stylish, cultured, sophisticated, poised

tawdry
gaudy, tacky, shoddy, shabby, garish, sleazy, tasteless, cheap, vulgar, crude

thrilling
arousing, captivating, enchanting, enlivening, gripping, rousing, electrifying, riveting

thriving
radiant, flourishing, robust, swarming, teeming, vigorous

transcendent
preeminent, momentous, ascendant, stellar, towering, unparalleled, unmatched, grand, mystical

treacherous
precarious, hazardous, perilous, deceitful, deceptive, menacing, two-faced

treasure
gem, jewel, riches, masterpiece, fortune, prize

triumphant
elated, exultant, euphoric, delighted, jubilant

unabashed
bold, brazen, unblinking, undaunted, shameless, flagrant

uncanny
surreal, unearthly, bizarre, freakish, mysterious, unnatural, ghostly, magical

uncouth
gauche, boorish, crass, crude, tacky, clumsy

unearthly
dreamy, otherworldly, whimsical, mysterious, surreal, ethereal

unflappable
immovable, steely, unyielding, hardened, unbending, unruffled, flinty

unflinching
unyielding, headstrong, immutable, impervious, inflexible, ironfisted, refractory, resistant, steadfast, adamant

unglued
confused, unmoored, unhinged, unbalanced, unstable, unraveled, shaken, befuddled

unhinged

unmoored, unglued, deranged, unstable, demented, disturbed, crazed, batty

unholy

corrupt, depraved, base, unhallowed, profane, irreverent, dreadful, vile, immoral

unmoored

unstable, unhinged, unglued, deranged, crazed, adrift, unanchored

unruffled

calm, unflappable, composed, balanced, equanimous, cool-headed, poised, collected, placid

unsavory

distasteful, obnoxious, offensive, repugnant, disreputable, seedy, questionable, shady, repulsive

unseemly

indiscreet, tactless, crude, scandalous, tasteless, vulgar, distasteful, undignified

unsightly

ugly, dull, hideous, repulsive, grotesque, drab, deformed, appalling, hideous

unsound

perilous, hazardous, treacherous, uncertain, precarious

urbane

polished, refined, suave, sophisticated, affable, elegant, poised

valiant

gallant, fearless, unflinching, dauntless, heroic, intrepid, daring, undaunted

valorous

gallant, fearless, dauntless, valiant, courageous

vehement
forceful, intense, impassioned, fiery, passionate, resolute

vexing
aggravating, bothersome, provoking, tiresome, disturbing, galling, exasperating, troubling, irksome, wearisome

vibrant
robust, dynamic, hearty, spirited, vigorous, zestful

vigorous
forceful, fierce, robust, dynamic, full-bodied, spirited, staunch, rugged, sturdy, vibrant, zestful, thriving, roaring, swarming, teeming

vile
repugnant, abhorrent, atrocious, heinous, monstrous, vicious, wretched

virile
potent, robust, manly, forceful, vigorous, energetic

vivacious
sparkling, effervescent, airy, breezy, exhilarating, frothy

whimsy, whimsical
charmed, dreamy, fanciful, romantic, playful, mischievous

wild
fierce, feral, delirious, deranged, frantic, howling, raving, raging, savage, untamed, uncontrolled

witless
dim-witted, foolish, inane, kooky, moronic, wacky, zany

wizardly
magical, bewitching, charismatic, enchanting, spellbinding, wondrous, mystical

wondrous
   magical, enchanting, radiant, splendorous, glorious, brilliant

wretched
   abominable, atrocious, contemptible, despairing, despicable, vile,
   dreadful, miserable, worthless, forlorn, repugnant, abhorrent

GENERAL APPEARANCE

ancient
   age-old, primeval, antique, prehistoric, archaic, primordial, relic

antiquated
   archaic, ancient, heirloom, dated, aged, obsolete

archaic
   ancient, antiquated, prehistoric, obsolete, primitive

austere
   stern, unapproachable, uninviting, staid, bare, clinical, grave, bleak,
   unadorned

bare
   meager, gaunt, scant, spare, barren, empty, forsaken, void, blank,
   stripped

battered
   crumbling, ravaged, dilapidated, decaying, rickety, aged, damaged,
   deteriorated, shattered, demolished

bedraggled
   disheveled, unkempt, scruffy, untidy, mangy, shabby, scraggly,
   messy

besmirched
   marked, patchy, tarnished, splotchy, blemished, smudged, tainted,
   frayed, spotty

blemished
tarnished, besmirched, blotched, debased, smudged, tainted, gashed, deformed

blighted
ravaged, corrosive, devastated, disintegrating, haggard, hollowed, plagued, wasted

blotched, blotchy
marked, patchy, uneven, tarnished, besmirched, blemished, spotty, smudged, tainted, fragmented, frayed

craggy
weathered, weather-beaten, rugged, rocky, stony, jagged

cruddy
filthy, dirty, foul, grimy, grubby, grungy, polluted, soiled, squalid

crumbling
battered, dilapidated, rickety, decaying, aged, deteriorated, eroded, disintegrating

decaying, decayed
decrepit, rotting, deteriorated, rotten, spoiled, crumbling, eroding, deteriorating

decrepit
decaying, rickety, battered, ramshackle, worn, degraded, tottering, aged, dilapidated, crumbling

deteriorated
decayed, corroded, disintegrated, dilapidated, decrepit, decadent

dilapidated
decrepit, shabby, rickety, battered, decaying, aged, deteriorated, ruined, disheveled

disheveled
bedraggled, unkempt, disarray, messy, sloppy, untidy, scruffy

disintegrating, disintegrated

wasted, wrecked, ravaged, blighted, corrosive, devastated, haggard, plagued

disordered

disarray, chaotic, havoc, jumbled, unsettled, ruffled, untidy

dreary

desolate, forlorn, godforsaken, bleak, grim, colorless, ashen, pale, anemic, bland, faded, lifeless, pallid, sallow

drenched

awash, covered, flooded, overflowing, submerged, doused, soaked

dusty

sooty, grubby, grungy, gritty, crumbly, chalky, dirty

emaciated

sunken, frail, gaunt, haggard, withered, barren, scrawny, wasted, stark

filthy

dirty, cruddy, foul, grimy, grubby, grungy, odious, repugnant, vile, polluted, soiled, squalid

flooded

covered, overflowing, submerged, drenched, deluged, drowned, saturated, swamped, inundated, awash

grim

dreary, forlorn, bleak, forbidding, ghastly, grisly, gruesome

grimy

soiled, squalid, vile, filthy, dirty, repugnant, polluted, cruddy, foul, grubby, grungy, odious

grubby

foul, grimy, grungy, filthy, dirty, cruddy, polluted, soiled, squalid, sordid

grungy
soiled, squalid, filthy, dirty, grimy, grubby, cruddy, foul, polluted

hearty
robust, brawny, dynamic, full-bodied, rugged, sturdy, vibrant, vigorous, zestful

immaculate
unspoiled, untainted, spotless, flawless, unblemished, impeccable, untarnished, pristine

jowly
fleshy, mouthy, drooping

mangy
dingy, filthy, shabby, slovenly, unkempt, tattered, squalid, scruffy, shaggy

messy
bedraggled, bungling, careless, clumsy, dilapidated, disheveled, sloppy, unkempt, untidy

meticulous
flawless, impeccable, scrupulous, precise, fastidious, painstaking, detailed, exact

muddy
sludgy, oozy, murky, cloudy, hazy, foggy, opaque, obscure, fuzzy, turbid, milky

overgrown
weedy, teeming, leggy, flourishing, dense, spreading

polluted
filthy, odious, repugnant, foul, soiled, contaminated, poisoned, tainted

primordial
ancient, age-old, primeval, prehistoric, archaic, relic, primal

primeval
> pristine, ancient, age-old, primeval, prehistoric, archaic, primordial

pristine
> flawless, immaculate, exquisite, meticulous, refined, purified, pure, clarified, crystalline, primal, unblemished

pure
> refined, absolute, sterling, fresh, unblemished, unadorned, natural, spare

putrid
> rotten, decayed, hideous, rancid, stench, sordid, spoiled, stinking, wretched

ramshackle
> tottering, rickety, shifting, wobbly, flimsy, crumbling, decrepit, dilapidated, shabby

ratty
> seedy, ragged, slipshod, squalid, tattered, filthy, unkempt

ravaged
> blighted, corrosive, devastated, disintegrating, haggard, plagued, ruined, wasted, wrecked

rickety
> dilapidated, decrepit, shabby, flimsy, brittle, breakable, battered, decaying, fragile, deteriorated, ruined, shaky, wobbly, tottering, ramshackle

robust
> brawny, dynamic, full-bodied, hearty, muscular, sinewy, staunch, steely, rugged, sturdy, vibrant, vigorous, zestful, radiant

ruined, ruinous
> blighted, devastated, battered, decaying, ravaged, deteriorated, irreparable, unsalvageable, disintegrating, wasted, wrecked

rustic
  bucolic, rural, pastoral, woodsy, homespun, unrefined

scenic
  picturesque, idyllic, ornate, charming, quaint, vivid, striking

scraggly
  unkempt, scrawny, gawky, bedraggled, ragged, untidy, shoddy

scruffy
  shabby, untidy, bedraggled, mangy, ragged, scraggly, disheveled

seedy
  chintzy, cheap, ragged, ratty, slipshod, squalid, tattered, tawdry

severe
  grave, sharp, austere, biting, drastic, harrowing, harsh, forbidding, stark

shabby
  drab, dingy, dull, grungy, mangy, bedraggled, scraggly, ramshackle, scruffy

shoddy
  bedraggled, degraded, dilapidated, frazzled, tattered, scraggly

slipshod
  seedy, cheap, ragged, ratty, squalid, tattered, sloppy, dilapidated

sloppy
  unkempt, untidy, messy, bungling, careless, clumsy, slovenly

slovenly
  mangy, filthy, shabby, unkempt, tattered, squalid, ratty, dirty

sluggish
  heavy, listless, dragging, dull, groggy, laggard, languid, lethargic, lifeless

smudged, smudgy
  dusty, grubby, dingy, grimy, grungy, tarnished, blemished, sooty

sooty
  dusty, grubby, dingy, grimy, grungy, smudgy, blackened

spare
  scant, unadorned, stark, fine, precise, thin, confined, meager, bare, austere, gaunt

splattered
  splashed, splotched, smudged, doused, sprinkled, spattered

spotty
  scanty, sparse, diffuse, scarce, sporadic, patchy, uneven, erratic, thin

squalid, squalor
  ratty, slipshod, mangy, filthy, shabby, slovenly, unkempt, tattered, seedy, cheap, ragged, run-down, grimy, ramshackle

stark
  gaunt, barren, desolate, austere, bleak, severe, unadorned, spare, somber, distinct

straggly
  disheveled, unkempt, grimy, grungy, sloppy, filthy, stained, foul

submerged
  flooded, awash, overflowing, drenched, inundated, drowned

unadorned
  unembellished, unvarnished, natural, stark, spare, pure, austere, undecorated, modest

unblemished
  sterling, unspoiled, flawless, untarnished, unsullied, impeccable, pure

unkempt
> disheveled, bedraggled, mangy, dingy, filthy, slovenly, tattered, squalid, messy, untidy, scraggly

unsightly
> ugly, dull, hideous, repulsive, grotesque, unkempt, drab

untidy
> bedraggled, disheveled, sloppy, unkempt, cluttered, disheveled, messy

weedy
> reedy, scraggy, scrawny, puny, bony, gangly

withered
> decaying, haggard, emaciated, drooping, withered, shrunken, gaunt

wobbly
> faltering, bewildered, muddled, woozy, groggy, stunned, tottering, careening, toppling, bobbling, tumbling

wrecked
> disintegrating, ravaged, blighted, corroded, devastated, plagued, ruined, wasted, demolished

VISION *and* SIGHT

apparition
> illusion, ghost, delusion, phantom, hallucination, fallacy, figment

array
> display, splendor, spectacle, extravagance, display, throng, pattern

behold
> glimpse, discern, witness, glance, gaze, perceive, scan, spy, watch, observe

blatant
conspicuous, obvious, overt, unabashed, bald, flaunting, glaring, flagrant

blazon
blare, display, emblazon, broadcast, embellish, proclaim

bleary
blurry, foggy, drained, hazy, cloudy, unclear

blind
unseeing, sightless, oblivious, myopic, unaware

blindfold, blindfolded
curtain, blinder, cloak, mask, veil, blind

blind-side, blind-sided
blinded, hidden, unaware, unprepared, surprised, stampeded, blind spot

blink, blinking
flickering, glimmering, glinting, glittering, shimmering, twinkling, wink

blurry
bleary, foggy, hazy, nebulous, cloudy, fuzzy, murky, opaque

camouflage
disguise, hide, veil, conceal, screen, façade, mask, masquerade, smokescreen

charade
masquerade, farce, sham, pantomime, pretense

clandestine
hidden, surreptitious, secretive, stealthy, concealed, veiled, cloaked

clairvoyance
insight, perception, premonition, intuition, telepathy

SEE: VISION *and* SIGHT

clear-eyed
    unclouded, luminous, shining, perceptive, lucid

cloak, cloaked
    hidden, concealed, veiled, shrouded, masked, obscured

cloudy, clouded
    murky, foggy, hazy, opaque, muddy, obscure, fuzzy, turbid, shady, dreamy, distorted, shadowy, nebulous, blurry, milky, curtained

cogent
    perceptive, sharp, discerning, vigilant, alert, penetrating, piercing, shrewd, keen

conceal, concealed
    camouflage, disguise, hide, veil, screen, mask, masquerade, shroud, cloak, obscure

conspicuous
    noticeable, overt, blatant, striking, apparent, obvious, marked, pronounced

covert
    hidden, private, concealed, clandestine, camouflaged, disguised, furtive, incognito, shrouded, stealthy, surreptitious

cryptic
    mysterious, secret, enigmatic, perplexing, puzzling, obscure

curtained
    shady, clouded, shadowy, cloaked, lurking, undetected, occult, veiled, dark

decipher
    unravel, untangle, decode, unscramble, translate, deduce, solve, disentangle

decoy
    lure, snare, trap, entice, camouflage, deception, shill

delusion, delude
illusion, apparition, deception, phantom, mirage, fantasy, fallacy

detect
behold, glimpse, discern, perceive, scan, spy, view

discern
envision, insight, perceive, detect, behold, ascertain

discerning
sharp, perceptive, eagle-eyed, vigilant, astute, insightful, piercing, discriminating

disenchanted
disillusioned, indifferent, disappointed, embittered, jaundiced, soured, bitter, cynical

disguise, disguised
conceal, camouflage, hide, veil, screen, mask, masquerade

disillusioned
disenchanted, soured, embittered, world-weary, cynical, shattered, bitter

elusive
intangible, illusory, fleeting, mysterious, deceptive, evasive, ethereal, ghostly

enshrouded
enclosed, cloaked, concealed, masked, hidden, shrouded, veiled, swathed

espy
discern, view, detect, spot, discover, glimpse, observe

eye-catching
stunning, spectacular, breathtaking, striking, arresting, dazzling, flashy, dashing, brazen, showy, splashy

façade
> hide, masquerade, camouflage, disguise, veneer, conceal, screen, mask, veil

faint
> indistinct, pale, thin, hazy, faded, fuzzy, shadowy

fathom
> discern, grasp, decipher, understand, decode, unravel, interpret, pinpoint, probe

figment
> illusion, ghost, delusion, phantom, hallucination, fallacy, vision, apparition, fantasy

fixated
> engrossed, obsessed, enamored, focused, infatuated, riveted, gripped, fanatical

flagrant
> overt, conspicuous, obvious, noticeable, blatant, pronounced, glaring

focus
> concentrate, focal point, pinpoint, fixate, sharpen

foggy
> cloudy, murky, opaque, muddy, obscured, fuzzy, bleary, blurry, illusory, dreamy, awry, distorted, imaginary, shadowy, nebulous, amorphous, hazy

foresee, foresight
> anticipate, predict, envision, foretell, foreshadow, presage, vision, insight

furtive
> hidden, surreptitious, secretive, clandestine, stealthy, concealed, veiled, cloaked

gape
> gawk, gaze, ogle, stare, glare, peer, peek, search, pry, probe, seek, size up, scrutinize

gawk
> gape, gaze, goggle, stare, glare, peer, pry, probe

gaze
> gawk, gape, stare, glare, glimpse, plumb, peek, search, pry, probe, seek, size up, scrutinize, peer, glance, behold

ghost, ghostly
> apparition, illusion, delusion, phantom, hallucination, figment

glance
> glimpse, discern, witness, peer, gaze, peek, squint

glare
> glower, stare, gleam, peer, shine

glaring
> flagrant, overt, conspicuous, obvious, marked, noticeable, blatant, striking, apparent, pronounced

glimpse
> behold, discern, glance, peek, peer, gaze, squint, peep, flash, spot, view

groggy
> foggy, bewildered, fuzzy, muddled, numbed, dazed, stunned, woozy

hawk-eyed
> sharp, discerning, eagle-eyed, vigilant, clear-sighted, sharp-eyed, observant, perceptive

hazy
> cloudy, misty, murky, foggy, obscured, fuzzy, bleary, nebulous, opaque, shadowy, blurry

SEE: VISION *and* SIGHT

hide, hidden
>conceal, screen, masquerade, camouflage, clandestine, disguise, veil, façade, mask, secretive

hindsight
>retrospect, recollection, vision

illusory
>dreamy, foggy, cloudy, distorted, imaginary, shadowy, mystical, hallucinatory, unreal, deceptive

imaginary
>illusory, delusional, fantastic, mythic, shadowy, hallucinatory, dreamy, invented

imperceptible
>indiscernible, undetectable, unnoticed, inconspicuous, obscure, inconsequential, hidden, unseen

incognito
>camouflaged, disguised, masked, shrouded, stealthy, surreptitious, concealed, clandestine, secret

inconspicuous
>imperceptible, indiscernible, undetectable, unnoticed, concealed, inconsequential, obscure, unassuming

invisible
>imperceptible, intangible, hidden, veiled, concealed, unseen

keen
>perceptive, discerning, penetrating, piercing, shrewd, insightful, cogent, sharp

leer, leering
>ogle, glare, stare, peer, gawk, gaze, sneer, fixate, focus

mask, masked
>disguise, conceal, camouflage, hide, facade, guise, veneer, veil

masquerade
camouflage, veil, disguise, hide, screen, mask, conceal

mirage
illusion, delusion, hallucination, fallacy, figment, phantom

misty
wispy, gauzy, foggy, vapory, humid, cloudy, murky, bleary

muddled
jumbled, foggy, bewildered, fuzzy, confused, tottering, woozy, wobbly

murky
cloudy, hazy, foggy, opaque, muddy, obscure, fuzzy, nebulous, blurry, shadowy, turbid

myopic
short-sighted, narrow-minded, blind, unimaginative, biased, imperceptive

nebulous
amorphous, blurry, cloudy, fuzzy, hazy, murky, opaque, shadowy, ambiguous, vague

obscure, obscured
cloaked, hidden, concealed, veiled, shrouded, masked, cryptic, mysterious, vague, cloudy, shadowy

obstructed
jammed, blocked, impeded, barricaded, shrouded, occluded

ogle
leer, glare, stare, peer, fixate, focus, gawk, gape

opaque
nebulous, amorphous, blurry, cloudy, fuzzy, hazy, murky, shadowy, misty, muddied

overt
conspicuous, obvious, marked, noticeable, blatant, striking, glaring, apparent, pronounced

pantomime
charade, imitate, gesture, mime, mimic, signal, mirror

patrol
watch, lookout, scan, stare, spy, focus, gaze, safeguard

peek
peer, gaze, search, pry, probe, size up, scrutinize, stare

peep
glimpse, peer, glance, squint, scan, blink

peer
gape, glare, gaze, plumb, peek, probe, search, pry, stare, squint

perceive
discern, detect, grasp, distinguish, observe, identify

perceptive
vigilant, alert, cogent, sharp, discerning, eagle-eyed, keen, shrewd, penetrating, piercing

phantom
specter, illusion, apparition, ghost, mirage, hallucination, delusion

prism
crystal, facet, spectrum, glass, viewpoint

probe, probing
peer, gaze, gape, glare, plumb, search, pry, seek, scrutinize, stare, prod

pry, prying
probe, scrutinize, stare, peer, gaze, gape, glare, snoop, meddle

reverie
> daydream, musing, fantasy, trance

scan
> patrol, lookout, stare, spy, focus, gaze, peer, browse, skim

screen
> façade, hide, masquerade, camouflage, disguise, veil, conceal, mask, blind, smokescreen

semblance
> veneer, façade, guise, mask, pose, veil, aura

scrutinize, scrutinizing
> scrupulous, meticulous, probing, unsparing, peering, searching, prying, precise

shadowy
> illusory, dreamy, foggy, cloudy, distorted, imaginary, nebulous, amorphous, blurry, fuzzy, hazy, murky, opaque, concealed, vague

shady
> clouded, curtained, shadowy, dark, shrouded, screened

sharp
> perceptive, discerning, eagle-eyed, vigilant, piercing, penetrating, keen

short-sighted
> narrow-minded, blind, biased, unthinking, myopic, unimaginative

shrewd
> cogent, keen, penetrating, piercing, perceptive, sharp, discerning, vigilant, alert

shrouded
> shadowy, curtained, clouded, cloaked, hidden, concealed, veiled, masked, obscured

smokescreen
disguise, hide, veil, conceal, screen, façade, mask, masquerade, camouflage

spectacle
array, display, splendor, extravagance, drama, parade, scene

spectrum
scope, span, scale, purview, sphere, continuum

squint
peer, scrutinize, scan, glance, peek, gape, glimpse

spy
detect, behold, discern, perceive, snoop, uncover, spot, sleuth, eyeball, scan

stare
gawk, gape, gaze, glare, peer, pry, probe, scrutinize, ogle, fixate, focus

surreptitious
covert, veiled, hidden, concealed, clandestine, disguised, furtive, skulking, shrouded, stealthy, camouflaged

unblinking
unabashed, undaunted, fearless, focused, bold, unflinching, fixed, unswerving

undetectable
imperceptible, indiscernible, unnoticed, inconspicuous, invisible, obscured, shadowy, unseen

undivided
focused, unswerving, intense, engrossed, unbroken, unflagging, concerted, intent, fixed

unflagging
undivided, unswerving, unbending, fixed, focused, unremitting

unnoticed
   overlooked, unobtrusive, inconspicuous, obscure, disregarded, secret, unseen

unseen
   hidden, undetected, unnoticeable, obscure, concealed, invisible, imperceptible, shrouded, veiled

unswerving
   focused, determined, unfaltering, steady, undivided, unbroken, unflagging, intent, fixed

vantage
   viewpoint, slant, outlook, angle, standpoint, position

veil, veiled
   camouflage, disguise, screen, façade, masquerade, conceal, mask

vigilant
   perceptive, watchful, sharp, discerning, eagle-eyed, circumspect, guarded, mindful, observant, alert

visionary
   lofty, superlative, noble, grandiose, imaginative, starry-eyed

watch
   patrol, lookout, scan, stare, spy, focus, gaze, peer

watchful
   alert, cautious, circumspect, guarded, mindful, observant, vigilant

witness
   behold, glimpse, discern, perceive, glance, gaze, attest

HEAR

If you have the ears to hear, the whole existence is just music.
—*Sadhguru Jaggi Vasudev, yogi and mystic*

VIBRATIONS *and* PERCUSSIONS - DISCORD *and* NOISE
- MUSIC *and* HARMONY - ONOMATOPOEIA -
SPEECH *and* UTTERANCES - MOVEMENT -
LISTENING - VOLUME

Silence is the seat of all sound. From formlessness, the sounds of the Big Bang emerged, first as a low groan and then a deep roar. Colossal waves of sound, containing all future sounds, rippled out of the nascent universe as an expanding hiss, their acoustic patterns unwinding and unfolding across the emerging cosmos. We carry the echoes of these primordial sounds within us, reverberations from the distant past.

The universe is mostly empty space—dark matter and vibrations to which we are largely deaf. Yet, in our narrow band of hearing, about 10 octaves, the world is a cacophony of sounds. It is a complex mixture of rhythms, tones, melodies, and percussions, from the barely perceptible ring to deafening booms—music, laughter, machines, wind, birds and animals, traffic, planes, sirens, conversations, crowds. Even in silence, we hear the hum of ambient noise.

Speech is our splendid sound currency. We speak in a myriad of languages and dialects. Our collective vocabulary tops billions of words that we richly arrange into innumerable patterns. In dialogue, we mimic each other, rearrange sounds, and invent new ways of communicating. Not even birds can match our vocal range of expression.

We are acutely receptive to a sound's quality, pitch, and timbre. From rhythmic cues, we hear the intention and cadence behind spoken words. Over our lifetimes, we build a vast aural library to identify and recognize sounds. We try to filter out distortions. Unfamiliar sounds surprise and sometimes deeply unsettle us.

From just a handful of core notes, we create music and harmonies of sublime quality. We sing, strike chords, and beat drums to express our deepest joys and sorrows. In song, we resonate with the transcendent emotion of music. We strive to be in tune with others and at the same time find our own voice. We play it by ear. At times, we find perfect pitch with the world.

Discordant sounds—screaming, scraping, grating, dripping—set our nerves on edge. We respond viscerally to shrillness, clamor, and ear-splitting volumes. We sense when something has a hollow ring or when others are tone deaf or strike a false note. Sometimes, we crave stillness and soundproofing.

Sound orients us. With both ears, we hear in stereo. Faraway rumbles. Murmurs. Oncoming collisions. Whistling trajectories. Every sound we hear tells us something about itself—its form, its essence. And every form suggests its latent, hidden sound.

Finally, in our own private world, we are in continual dialogue with an inner voice, a constant guide who knows our hopes, doubts, and dreams. Turning inward, we can tap into the deep well of silence within us—a sanctuary of eternality that connects us to our origins.

In this section, lend your ears to the dynamic range of hearing words: vibrations and percussions, discord and noise, music and harmony, movement, speech and utterances, volume, and the delightful music that is onomatopoeia.

VIBRATIONS *and* PERCUSSIONS

backfire
> explode, bang, blast, burst, erupt, flare, boom, thunder, ricochet, backlash

bang
> batter, bat, beat, belt, deck, crash, detonate, hammer, rap, knock, smash, strike, slam, whack, explode, blast, thunder, thud, clash, rumble

bash
> bang, belt, clobber, deck, drub, knock, slam, smack, smash, thump, wallop, whack, bat

bell
> ring, clang, chime, toll, peal, resound, gong, ting, knell, alarm, buzz, siren

bellow
> roar, bawl, grunt, screech, sob, howl, gasp, growl, rave, rant, bark, shriek, squawk, trumpet, thunder, wail, holler, bark, bluster, bray, boom

blare

reverberate, ring, roar, bellow, boom, clamor, echo, wail, thunder, trumpet, resound, rumble, blast

blaring

ringing, booming, wailing, thunderous, resounding, shrill, raucous, dissonant

blast

boom, thunder, explode, backfire, bang, burst, erupt, flare

bluster

blast, thunder, bellow, bombast, cacophony, commotion, uproar, clamor, melee, rumble, tumult, rant, roar

boom

reverberate, resound, resonate, thunder, echo, pound, bellow, roar, explode, bang

booming

deafening, ear-piercing, ringing, blaring, resounding, bellowing, roaring, crashing

brassy

resounding, noisy, brash, blaring, boisterous, jarring, thunderous, tinny, clanging

clack

clatter, rattle, clank, clang, clamor, clap, din, commotion, clink, rattle

clang

ring, clink, chime, clank, jingle, peal, knell, ting, resound, jangle, gong, crash, clatter, clash, tinkling, ping, toll

clank

chime, ding, jangle, peal, ring, ting, clink, clang, toll, jingle, knell, resound, rattle, din, clatter, ping

clap
> bang, clash, clatter, commotion, knock, rumble, swat, thunderclap, thwack, wallop, whack, whomp, applaud, cheer

clash
> commotion, brawl, collide, crash, discord, flap, quarrel, rumble, snarl, tussle, wrangle, bat, bang, batter, beat, belt, clobber, smash, hammer, knock, pummel, whack, jangle, clang

clatter
> rattle, clank, clang, clack, clamor, clap, din, commotion, ruckus, spout, clink, jangle, clash, jingle, peal, ping

click
> clink, clack, clop, clunk, flick, plunk, snap, tick, pop

clink
> clatter, clank, ping, ring, peal, tinkling, clang, jangle, clash, jingle, ding

clomp
> stomp, clop, trudge, smash, bang, knock, rap, thump, plod, thud

clop
> clunk, stomp, plunk, thud, clatter, rattle, clank, clang, clack, clap

crack
> crackle, sizzle, snap, blast, clap, pop, bang, smash

crackle
> crack, hiss, crash, buzz, fizz, snap

crash, crashing
> bang, boom, burst, jolt, knock, whack, batter, hammer, punch, smash, strike, beat

detonate
> bang, crash, hammer, knock, smash, strike, blast, explode

drone

burble, gurgle, murmur, purr, whir, hum, rumble, whine, whistle, buzz, whir

drum

beat, call, hammer, drone, hum, resound, thunder, thrum, boom, strum, throb, tap

echo

resound, reverberate, thunder, explode, repercussion, ringing, chant

gong

toll, bell, chime, clang, ting, knell, crash, alarm, cymbal

hammer

thrash, wallop, whack, bang, pummel, batter, clobber, crash, knock, rap, smash, strike, beat

high-pitched

reedy, shrill, shrieking, acute, piercing, sharp, cutting, falsetto

jangle, jangly

clang, clink, clatter, clash, jingle, peal, tinkling, ping, clank, rattle

jingle

clang, ring, clink, chime, toll, clank, ding, peal, knell, ting, resound, jangle

knell

clang, clink, chime, clank, jingle, peal, toll, ting, resound, summon, warning, ring

low-pitched

bass, drum, buzz, drone, rumble, muffled, echo, boom, thunder, hum

nuance

overtone, shade, hint, tinge, trace, distinction

peal
> jangle, clang, clink, clatter, clash, jingle, tinkling, ping, bell, ring, chime, toll, resound

quiver, quivering
> tremulous, shaky, trembling, vibrato, shuddering, jittery, tremulous, quavering

reedy
> thin, fragile, high-pitched, shrill, harsh, nasal, cutting

repercussion
> echo, resound, reverberate, thunder, explode, ringing, booming

resonate
> chime, chant, sing, ring, clang, peal, toll, echo, resound

resonant
> booming, consonant, harmonic, resounding, pulsating, pulsing, sonorous, ringing, throbbing, thunderous, vibrating, echo

resound, resounding
> bell, ring, clang, chime, toll, peal, resonate, boom, echo, thunder, ringing

reverberate, reverberating
> boom, echo, rebound, rumble, sound, thunder, resound

ring
> peal, toll, clang, jingle, tinkling, jingling, jangle, chime, ding, bell, knell, resound

roar
> thunder, wail, whoop, bark, bellow, shout, burst, clamor, growl, rave, rant, bawl, boom, explode, holler, grunt, howl

roaring
> resounding, thunderous, ringing, crashing, deafening, uproarious, boisterous, rowdy, pealing, piercing

rumble, rumbling

thunder, resonant, hum, bellow, roar, resound, reverberate, echo, blast, boom, clap, drone, whir, clash, throb, jolt, shudder

shudder

tremor, rumble, jolt, vibrato, shimmy, tremble, shiver, gyrate

sonic

acoustic, sound, tune, chord, aural, vibration, reverberation, music, echo

thud

clobber, bang, crash, hammer, knock, rap, smash, thrash, wallop, thump

thunder, thunderous, thundering

rumble, wail, trumpet, echo, uproar, commotion, tumult, resound, blast, bellow, boom, clamor, crash, explode, rail, roar

thunderbolt, thunderclap

rumble, blast, slap, boom, bang, roar

tinny

thin, brassy, metallic, jingly, jangly, twangy

toll

bell, chime, clang, gong, ting, knell, ring, signal, strike, summon, peal

tremble, trembling

tremulous, quivering, shaky, vibrato, quiver, throb, shudder, quake

tremor

rumble, jolt, shudder, vibrato, quake, quiver, ripple, shiver

tremulous

quavering, quivering, trembling, vibrato, shaky, wobbly, warbling, wavering

undercurrent
murmur, overtone, hint, tenor, vibe, riptide, undertow, tinge

undertone
undercurrent, whisper, hint, murmur, buzz, nuance, tenor

vibrate
whine, whistle, whir, hum, drone, chant, trill, purr, murmur, buzz, rumble, throb

vibrato
tremor, rumble, vibration, quiver, warble, quaver, trill

DISCORD *and* NOISE

acrimonious, acrimony
discordant, cacophonous, harsh, abrupt, biting, jarring, grating, gruff, raucous, screeching, shrill, clashing, cutting

atonal
dissonant, cacophony, discordant, off-key, sour, unmelodious, jangling, jarring

biting
harsh, abrupt, acrimonious, jarring, grating, raucous, discordant, piercing, screeching, shrill, cacophonous, clashing, cutting

bluster
blast, thunder, bellow, bombast, cacophony, commotion, uproar, clamor, melee, rumble, tumult, rant, roar

booming
deafening, ear-piercing, ringing, blaring, resounding, bellowing, roaring, crashing

cacophony
racket, clamor, discord, dissonance, discordance, uproar, raucous, screeching, din

caterwaul
> scream, screech, howl, bawl, bay, bellow, squawk, wail, shriek, cry, yowl

clamor, clamorous
> commotion, uproar, tumult, roar, ranting, raucous, raving, blaring, boisterous, brassy, cacophonous, jarring, deafening, clanging, racket, resounding, shrill, thunderous

commotion
> clamor, uproar, tumult, roar, rant, racket, upheaval, turbulence

cutting
> harsh, abrupt, acerbic, acrimonious, biting, jarring, grating, shrill, raucous, discordant, piercing, screeching, clashing

deafening
> booming, ear-piercing, earthshaking, piercing, resounding, ringing, thundering, rattling

diatribe
> tirade, denunciation, attack, screed, harangue, outburst, rant

din
> racket, tumult, ruckus, commotion, clamor, roar, clang, clash, clatter, rattle, rumble

discord, discordant
> cacophony, racket, clamor, uproar, acrimonious, biting, jarring, grating, raucous, screeching, shrill, clashing, din, cutting

dissonant
> atonal, cacophony, discordant, off-key, sour, jangling, jarring, clashing

ear-piercing
> deafening, booming, resounding, thundering, rattling, ear-splitting, ringing

ear-splitting
> deafening, booming, ear-piercing, piercing, resounding, ringing, thundering, rattling

fracas
> flap, tumult, strife, turmoil, uproar, racket, rumble, melee, scuffle, clash, tussle, brawl, riot, disturbance

frenzy, frenzied
> ranting, clamorous, hysterical, raging, raucous, raving

furor
> racket, agitation, cacophony, clamor, commotion, discord, uproar, turmoil, shrill, thunder

grating
> piercing, jarring, biting, raucous, discordant, screeching, clashing, cacophonous, cutting, shrill

jarring
> grating, shrill, raucous, raspy, dissonant, atonal, cacophony, sour, discordant, off-key, unmelodious, piercing, biting, screeching, clashing, cutting

melee
> uproar, bluster, roar, brawl, clamor, commotion, embroil, rumble, thunder, tumult, furor

noisy
> blaring, boisterous, brassy, cacophonous, clamorous, jarring, shrill, deafening, clanging, resounding, riotous, rip-roaring, thunderous

off-key
> dissonant, atonal, cacophonous, discordant, sour, jangling, jarring, flat, tuneless, off-pitch, clashing

piercing
> deafening, booming, earthshaking, resounding, ringing, rattling, thundering, thunderous, shrill

racket

agitation, cacophony, clamor, commotion, discord, furor, uproar, turmoil, thunder

raging

clamorous, hysterical, ranting, raucous, raving, stormy, seething, tempestuous, turbulent

raucous

agitated, clamorous, frenzied, hysterical, raging, ranting, raving, acrimonious, biting, jarring, grating, discordant, screeching, shrill, cacophonous, clashing, cutting

riot

turmoil, uproar, commotion, racket, rumble, storm, anarchy, strife, rampage, revolt, melee, furor, brawl, clamor, fracas, clash, tussle, tumult

riotous, rioting

unruly, uproarious, boisterous, tumultuous, brawling, chaotic, wild, turbulent

rip-roaring

noisy, blaring, boisterous, brassy, cacophonous, clamorous, jarring, deafening, clanging, racket, resounding, riotous, rowdy, screaming, shrill, thunderous

ruckus

clatter, rattle, clank, clang, clack, clamor, clap, din, commotion, upheaval, racket

screech, screeching

cackle, squawk, whoop, yelp, scream, holler, yell, bellow, howl, bay, bawl, squeal, wail, bark, bleat

shriek

blare, caterwaul, cry, holler, roar, screech, scream, squawk, wail, thunder, whoop, bawl, hail, moan, whine

shrill
dissonant, ear-piercing, ear-splitting, grating, harsh, high-pitched, piercing, reedy, sharp, wailing, jarring, screeching

siren
alarm, alert, buzzer, warning, bell, horn

stormy
raging, clamorous, hysterical, ranting, raucous, raving, turbulent, tempestuous

tempestuous
raging, clamorous, hysterical, ranting, raucous, raving, turbulent, stormy

tirade
bawl, rant, attack, onslaught, blast, tongue-lash, scream, harangue, wail, cry, lament, shriek, diatribe, rail

tumult, tumultuous
clamor, commotion, uproar, roar, hysteria, raging, ranting, raving, raucous

turbulent
raging, clamorous, hysterical, ranting, raucous, raving, stormy, tempestuous

turmoil
racket, agitation, cacophony, clamor, commotion, discord, furor, uproar, thunder

uproar, uproarious
roaring, raucous, deafening, clamorous, booming, boisterous, rowdy, rambunctious

vehement
forceful, intense, impassioned, fiery, passionate, resolute, violent, powerful

vitriol, vitriolic
  biting, scathing, spiteful, venomous, vicious, cutting, withering, sharp

vociferous
  vehement, clamorous, blaring, clanging, boisterous, shrill, ranting, loud-mouthed, strident, shouting

MUSIC *and* HARMONY

acoustic, acoustical
  music, echo, reverberation, sound, tune, chord, aural, sonic

attuned
  receptive, tuned, harmonized, unified, integrated, matched

bugle
  trumpet, horn, pipe, whistle, clarion, cornet

cadence
  tone, rhythm, music, lilt, intone, accent, tempo, accent, inflection, intonation, meter, swing, measure

catchy
  memorable, musical, melodic, harmonious, tuneful, lyrical

chime, chiming
  chant, sing, resonate, clang, peal, toll, clink, jingle, gong, harmonic, mellifluous, harmonious, ring, melodious, ting

chord
  chorus, blend, harmony, tune, overtone, melody, chime, string, note

dulcet
  mellifluous, melodious, lyrical, musical, poetic, sonorous, tuneful, harmonious, harmonic, chiming, flowing

harmonious, harmonic, harmonized
    blended, tuneful, harmonic, melodious, mellifluous, sonorous,
    chiming, attuned, lyrical

honeyed
    lyrical, musical, expressive, golden-tongued, melodic, sonorous,
    poetic, songful, mellifluous, tuneful, harmonious, harmonic

hum, humming
    drone, whine, whistle, whir, purr, murmur, buzz, vibrate, rumble,
    throb, chant, trill, thrum, strum

lyrical
    musical, expressive, golden-tongued, melodic, poetic, sonorous,
    songful, honeyed, mellifluous, tuneful, harmonious, harmonic,
    melodious, chiming, flowing

mellifluous
    tuneful, harmonic, mellow, melodic, sweet sounding, sonorous,
    chiming, flowing, harmonious, melodious, musical, catchy, lyrical,
    dulcet

melodious, melodic, melody
    mellifluous, lyrical, musical, poetic, sonorous, tuneful, harmonious,
    harmonic, chiming, flowing

mingled
    medley, chorus, blended, melded, mixed, harmonized

musical
    lullaby, melody, tuneful, lyrical, expressive, poetic, sonorous,
    songful, harmonious, harmonic, melodious, mellifluous, chiming

nuance
    overtone, undercurrent, mood, tenor, murmur, tone

octave
    note, frequency, vibration, scale, tone, range, interval

overtone
    undercurrent, mood, nuance, chord, tone

pitch
    cadence, tone, frequency, harmonic, music, timbre

poetic
    lyrical, musical, expressive, golden-tongued, melodic, sonorous,
    songful, honeyed, tuneful, harmonious, harmonic, melodious,
    mellifluous, chiming, flowing

resonating, resonant
    booming, consonant, harmonic, resounding, pulsating, pulsing,
    sonorous, ringing, throbbing, thunderous, vibrating, full-throated,
    echoing

rhythm, rhythmic
    cadence, intermittent, pulsating, oscillating, pulsing, throbbing,
    staccato, undulating, tone, beat, tempo

scale
    octave, note, frequency, vibration, tone

songful
    mellifluous, tuneful, harmonious, harmonic, melodious, lyrical,
    musical, expressive, golden-tongued, melodic, poetic, sonorous,
    honeyed, chiming

sonorous
    reverberating, resonant, resounding, silver-tongued, melodious,
    round, vibrant, harmonious, tuneful, harmonic, lyrical, chiming,
    mellifluous, flowing, fluent, expressive, golden-tongued, honeyed,
    songful, rich

tempo
    lilt, cadence, accent, inflection, meter, intone, rhythm, beat

tenor
    tone, mood, trend, drift, essence

timbre
tone, resonance, voice, pitch, accent, inflection, intonation

tone, tonal
timbre, resonance, pitch, accent, sound

tuneful
harmonious, blending, harmonic, lyrical, melodious, mellifluous, chiming, flowing, fluent, sonorous

ONOMATOPOEIA

babble, babbling
chatter, blather, ramble, blabber, murmur, gurgle, drivel, gibberish

blabber
blather, chatter, ramble, yammer, murmur, gurgle, jabber, babble, gab, prattle, ramble

bubble, bubbling
effervesce, foam, froth, fizz, gurgle, boil, percolate, gush, fizz

burble
gurgle, bubble, rumble, blather, babble, murmur, purr, whir, drone, hum

buzz
hum, drone, whine, whistle, whir, purr, murmur, vibrate, rumble, throb, trill

cackle
snicker, snort, chuckle, bark, screech, squawk, whoop, chortle, smirk

caterwaul
scream, screech, howl, bawl, bay, bellow, squawk, wail, shriek, yell, yowl

chatter
> jabber, gab, blather, chit-chat, babble, ramble, blabber, murmur, drivel, gibberish

cheep
> trill, burble, cluck, croon, gaggle, tweet, peep, chirp, chirrup

chirp, chirpy
> cluck, squawk, sing, trill, cheep, peep, chirrup, bellow, lilt, warble, quack, trumpet, creak, whistle

chirrup
> call, chitter, cluck, quack, chirp, cackle, hoot, tweet, clack, warble, crow, gobble, honk, whistle, trill, twitter

chitter
> quack, chirp, cackle, call, chirrup, cluck, clack, crow, gobble, honk, hoot, tweet, warble, whistle

chortle
> hee-haw, roar, hoot, snicker, cackle, smirk, giggle, snort, chuckle, snort, guffaw, crow

clack
> clatter, rattle, clank, clang, clamor, clap, clunk, click, clink, crash, tap

clang
> ring, clink, chime, toll, clank, ding, jingle, peal, knell, ting, resound, gong, crash, jangle, clatter, clash, tinkling, ping

clank
> chime, ding, jangle, peal, ring, ting, clink, clang, toll, jingle, knell, resound, rattle, din, clatter, ping

clap
> bang, clash, clatter, commotion, knock, rumble, swat, thunderclap, thwack, wallop, whack, whomp, applaud, cheer, celebrate

clash
> commotion, brawl, collide, crash, discord, flap, quarrel, rumble, snarl, tussle, wrangle, hammer, knock, jangle, clang

clatter
> rattle, clank, clang, clamor, clap, din, commotion, ruckus, jangle, clink, clack, clash, jingle, peal, ping

click
> clink, clack, clop, clunk, flick, plunk, snap, tick, snap, pop

clink
> clatter, clank, ping, peal, tinkle, clang, jangle, clash, jingle, chime, ting, ring

clomp
> stomp, clop, trudge, smash, bang, knock, rap, thump

clop
> clunk, stomp, plunk, thud, clatter, rattle, clank, clang, clack, clap

cluck
> chirp, clack, squawk, burble, cheep, croon, gaggle, tweet, peep, chirrup, trill

clunk
> clatter, rattle, clank, clang, clack, clap, clink, clomp, plod, thump, tromp, clonk, thud

crackle
> burn, clack, spark, sizzle, snap, crinkle, crack, fizz, hiss

creak
> screech, squeak, squeal, wail, whine, whistle, groan, scrape, chirp, rasp, grind

crinkle
> scrunch, rumple, crease, crimp, ripple, rustle, twist, wring, pucker, crumple

ding
clang, ring, clink, chime, toll, clank, jingle, peal, knell, ting, resound

dribble
drool, froth, gurgle, percolate, spit, sprinkle, drizzle, drip

drizzle
percolate, seep, trickle, drip, dribble, leak, pour, spray, sprinkle

fizz, fizzle
buzz, bubble, simmer, sparkle, sputter, effervesce, foam, froth, hiss

flick, flicker
flip, flitter, pulse, tweak, click, snap, tick, tap

flutter
flap, fly, jangle, whirl, wag, twirl, hover, beat, bat, wiggle, wave

gabble
babble, chatter, drivel, gibberish, spout, sputter, jabber, rattle

gargle
guzzle, swig, swill, gurgle, swish, gulp

gasp
choke, pant, wheeze, shriek, squawk, grunt, screech, gulp, huff, puff

giggle
chortle, hee-haw, roar, hoot, snicker, cackle, smirk, snort, chuckle

growl
bark, hiss, howl, snarl, snort, gnarl, grunt, moan, bellow

gruff
gravelly, husky, hoarse, guttural, testy, blunt, truculent, jarring, harsh, abrupt, biting, grating, raspy

gurgle, gurgling
dribble, ripple, babble, bubble, splash, trickle, murmur, percolate, burble, rumble

guzzle
gargle, swig, swill, gurgle, slosh, imbibe

hiss, hissing
fizz, whistle, jeer, heckle, wheeze, sizzle, whine, bark, gnarl, snort, sneer

lisp
drawl, nasal, snort, sniff, twang, sputter, spit, stutter

mumble
murmur, whisper, mutter, babble, blather, chatter, ramble, blabber, gurgle, sigh

murmur
whisper, mumble, mutter, sigh, babble, chatter, blather, ramble, blabber, gurgle, bellow, purr, vibrate, whir, rustle

mutter
mumble, murmur, whisper, sigh, snort, splutter, stammer, babble, chatter, blather, blabber

peep
chirp, chirpy, sing, trill, cheep, warble, chirrup, coo, tweet, squeal, squeak

ping
clink, clatter, clank, ring, peal, jangle, tinkling, clang, ting

plunk
bang, crash, hammer, knock, strike, wallop, plop

prattle
chatter, chat, jabber, blather, yammer, babble, blabber, rattle

purr
> burble, gurgle, murmur, whir, drone, hum, rumble, trill

raspy, rasping
> abrasive, throaty, scratchy, chafing, gravely, husky, gruff, hoarse, croaky

rattle
> clank, clatter, jingle, jangle, clink, joggle, ramble, bang, jolt, shatter, jounce, shake

rustle, rustling
> crinkle, crackle, swish, ripple, whistle, whisper, whish, whoosh, hum, murmur, whir

screech, screeching
> cackle, squawk, whoop, yelp, scream, holler, bellow, howl, squeal, bawl, wail, yell

seethe, seething
> bellow, boil, erupt, explode, fume, rant, rage, fume, flare

sizzle, sizzling
> boil, effervesce, fizzle, sear, seethe, burn, crackle, hiss, whistle

snap
> click, clink, clack, clop, flick, plunk, tick, crack, crackle, snarl, bark, pop

snarl
> growl, bark, hiss, howl, snort, gnarl, grumble, snap

sneer
> jeer, decry, hiss, heckle, snort, mock, scorn, deride, scoff, taunt, ridicule, revile

snicker
> chortle, hee-haw, roar, hoot, cackle, smirk, giggle, snort, chuckle

snort
    growl, bark, gnarl, hiss, howl, snarl, chortle, cackle, hoot, smirk, giggle, snicker, chuckle, lisp, drawl, sniff, twang, splutter, spit

spew
    billow, spit, gush, belch, burp, spittle, expel, heave

splash
    gurgle, gurgling, babble, bubble, dribble, ripple, trickle, percolate, sprinkle, spray

splat
    clash, crash, smash, plop, splatter, splash

splutter, spluttering
    spit, stammer, lisp, drawl, nasal, snort, sniff, cough, choke, spout, stammer

spout
    gush, spew, squirt, sputter, billow, spit, exude, surge, shoot, spray, belch

sputter
    fizzle, bubble, spit, spout, burst

squawk
    groan, moan, grouse, gripe, grumble, lament, shriek, snipe, whoop, wail, bark, bawl, screech, sob, bay, bellow, bleat, blare, caterwaul, groan, howl, yell, yelp, cry

squeak
    creak, chirp, screech, squeal, wail, whine, whistle, grate

stomp
    clomp, clop, trudge, smash, bang, knock, rap, thump, trample

swoosh
    rush, ripple, undulate, flutter, flap, twirl, whirl, whorl, pivot, swirl

thrash
smash, strike, bang, batter, chop, clobber, crash, hammer, knock, pummel, punch, wallop, beat

thump
bang, biff, belt, clobber, deck, drub, crack, hammer, flog, knock, pelt, pound, pummel, slug, smack, slam, smash, rap, wallop, whack

ting
clang, ring, clink, chime, clank, ding, jingle, peal, knell, resound, bell, gong, toll

tinkle, tinkling
clink, clatter, clank, ping, ring, peal, jangle, clang, click, clack, clunk

trill
burble, cheep, cluck, croon, gaggle, tweet, peep, warble, bellow, chant, chirp, drawl, lilt, murmur, trumpet, whistle, twitter

twang, twangy
accent, nasal, tonal, lisp, drawl, snort, sniff

wail, wailing
groan, howl, squeal, whimper, bellow, roar, bark, holler, rave, rant, shriek, squawk, thunder, whoop, yelp, yell, bawl, screech, whine, snivel, sob, weep, lament, blubber, moan

warble
bray, croon, chirrup, trill, bellow, chant, chirp, drawl, lilt, murmur, trumpet, twitter, whistle

whack
bash, bang, beat, belt, clobber, deck, drub, knock, slam, smack, smash, thump, wallop, bonk, crack, hammer, flog, pelt, pound, pummel, slug, bat, biff, rap

wheeze
breathy, hoarse, choke, quaver, tremulous, gasp, blow, pant, snort, whistle, breathe, huff, puff

whimper
blubber, cry, moan, snivel, sob, weep, wail, whine

whir, whirring
hum, fly, buzz, revolve, flutter, swish, vibrate, whistle

whirl, whirling
flap, fly, flutter, jangle, wag, flurry, surge, twirl, whir

whish
whistle, rustle, howl, whoosh, hum, warble, trill, whirl, murmur,
buzz, vibrate

whisper, whispering
murmur, sigh, babble, blather, gurgle, purr, vibrate, whir, breathe,
coo, rustle, sigh, hush, subdued, muffled, muted

whistle, whistling
rustle, howl, whish, whoosh, hum, warble, trill, whirl, murmur,
buzz, vibrate, creak

whoop
screech, sob, squawk, yelp, bark, bawl, bay, bellow, bleat, cackle,
grunt

whoosh
whistle, rustle, howl, whish, hum, warble, trill, whirl, murmur,
vibrate, hum, buzz

yodel
croon, ballad, chant, chirp, chorus, hum, lilt, serenade, sing, trill,
warble, whistle

Speech *and* Utterances

accent
inflection, meter, intonation, beat, tempo, modulate, twang, lisp,
tone, drawl, articulation, cadence, inflection, timbre

applaud
> clap, cheer, celebrate, laud, salute, hail, roar, shout

articulate
> eloquent, expressive, diction, enunciate, utter, fluent

babble
> chatter, blather, ramble, blabber, murmur, gurgle, drivel, gibberish, jargon, clamor

ballad
> croon, chant, chirp, chorus, hum, intone, lilt, serenade, sing, trill, warble, whistle, yodel, serenade

banter
> quip, retort, wit, wise-cracking, repartee, chitchat, jest, mock

bark, barking
> bawl, bay, bellow, bang, bleat, cackle, chant, grunt, screech, yell, squawk, whoop, yelp, howl, growl, wail, snarl, snort

bawl
> whine, lament, shriek, wail, weep, bark, bay, bellow, bang, bleat, cackle, yell, holler, rant, squawk, chant, grunt, screech, sob, whoop, yelp, tirade, bemoan, snivel, whimper

bay
> screech, sob, squawk, bark, bawl, wail, howl, bellow, bleat, whoop, yelp, yell

beg
> beseech, implore, plead, cajole, cry, insist, urge, appeal, pray

belch
> burp, spew, spittle, spit, gush, emit, expel, erupt, hiccup

bellow
> roar, bawl, grunt, screech, sob, howl, gasp, growl, rave, rant, wail, shriek, squawk, trumpet, thunder, bark

bemoan
weep, bawl, lament, wail, cry, mourn, grieve, whimper

benediction
blessing, eulogy, invocation, prayer, praise, gratitude

berate
scold, rebuke, chide, tongue-lash, vilify, besmirch, decry, denounce

beseech
implore, plead, beg, cry, pray, urge

besmirch
vilify, berate, decry, denounce, tongue-lash, defile, slander, slam

blab, blabber
blather, chatter, ramble, murmur, gurgle, jabber, babble, gab

blather
babble, blabber, chatter, ramble, murmur, gurgle, jabber, drivel, gab

bleat
screech, sob, squawk, bark, bawl, bay, grunt, hail, keen, bellow, cackle, chant, murmur, whoop, yelp, yell, wail, howl

blow
breathe, huff, expel, puff, gasp, wheeze, whistle, bluster, pant

blubber
whimper, cry, moan, snivel, sob, weep, wail, whine

blurt
blab, babble, diverge, leak, spout, ramble

boisterous
noisy, blaring, brassy, cacophonous, clamorous, jarring, deafening, clanging, racket, resounding, riotous, rip-roaring, screaming, shrill, thunderous, rowdy

bombast, bombastic
blabber, blather, boast, brag, drivel, prattle, rant, swagger, strut, bully, verbose, overblown

brawl
uproar, bluster, roar, clamor, commotion, quarrel, melee, rumble, tumult

bray
warble, bellow, chant, chirp, drawl, murmur, trill, trumpet, whistle, neigh, whinny, lilt

breathe
huff, inhale, exhale, puff, pant, blow, gasp, wheeze, whisper, sigh, murmur, gulp, sniff, snore, snort

breathless
panting, gasping, wheezing, winded, gulping, choking

breathy
hoarse, gravelly, gruff, tremulous, guttural, husky, throaty

broadcast
announce, circulate, telegraph, blazon, blare, disseminate, relay, transmit

brusque
blunt, gruff, sharp, husky, raspy, gravelly, guttural, snippy, curt

burp
belch, spew, spittle, billow, spit, gush, hiccup

cackle
hee-haw, roar, hoot, snicker, cackle, smirk, giggle, snort, chuckle, chortle, guffaw, cluck

cajole
plead, beg, cry, insist, rally, implore, beseech, coax, wheedle, entice

Hear: Speech *and* Utterances

call
> signal, yell, shout, holler, crow, honk, hoot, tweet, whistle, plea, command

catchphrase
> slogan, jingle, motto, watchword, saying

caterwaul
> scream, screech, howl, bawl, bellow, squawk, wail, shriek, yowl, bay

catty
> spiteful, snippy, biting, rancorous, backbiting

celebrate
> applaud, clap, cheer, honor, laud, praise, revere

chant
> call, sing, bay, bellow, chime, clang, hum, warble, chirp

chastise
> criticize, rebuke, reprimand, berate, lambaste, scold, castigate, lash

chatter
> jabber, blather, chit-chat, babble, ramble, blabber, murmur, gurgle, drivel, gibberish, gab

chatty
> effusive, flip, gabby, gassy, gossipy, gushy, gregarious, long-winded, loquacious, verbose, windy, talkative, wordy

cheer
> applaud, clap, celebrate, shout, roar, salute

chide
> berate, scold, rebuke. lambaste, chastise, criticize

chortle
> hee-haw, roar, hoot, snicker, cackle, smirk, giggle, snort, chuckle

chorus
croon, ballad, chant, chirp, hum, intone, lilt, serenade, sing, trill, warble, whistle, yodel, medley, blend

chuckle
chortle, cackle, hoot, smirk, giggle, snicker, snort, guffaw

close-lipped
tight-lipped, reticent, silent, taciturn, mute, terse, hushed, subdued, muffled, private, reserved, discreet

conniption
outburst, explosion, eruption, burst, tantrum, blowup, upheaval

coo
whisper, breathe, murmur, rustle, sigh, hush, cry

croaky
throaty, guttural, raspy, husky, gravelly, growling, scratchy

croon
ballad, chant, chirp, chorus, hum, lilt, serenade, sing, trill, warble, whistle, yodel

crow
chirrup, chitter, cluck, quack, chirp, warble, whistle, cackle, call, clack, gobble, honk, hoot, tweet

cry
groan, moan, grouse, gripe, grumble, lament, outcry, shriek, sob, squawk, tirade, wail, howl, blubber, whimper, snivel, weep

decry
ridicule, revile, vilify, jeer, hiss, sneer, scoff, heckle, bark, gnarl, snort, mock, scorn, deride, berate, besmirch, denounce

denounce
vilify, berate, besmirch, decry, tongue-lash, assail, revile, attack, rail, lambaste, condemn, rebuke

deride
mock, jeer, sneer, scorn, decry, scoff, taunt, mimic, ridicule, revile, insult

diatribe
tirade, denunciation, attack, screed, onslaught, harangue

drawl
lisp, crack, nasal, snort, sniff, twang, spit, splutter, warble, bellow, chirp, lilt, murmur, trill, trumpet, whistle

drivel
flummery, jabber, blather, dither, gibberish, dribble, ramble, rant, rubbish, spittle

dumbstruck
tongue-tied, speechless, stupefied, startled, dumbfounded, dazed, wordless, stammering

ebullient
exuberant, gushing, lavish, teeming, voluble, gossipy, gabby, windy, loquacious, verbose

effusive
abundant, ebullient, exuberant, gushing, lavish, teeming, voluble, gossipy, gabby, loquacious, verbose, windy, wordy, garrulous

elaborate (v)
embellish, amplify, magnify, clarify, energize, intensify, refine

elegy
lament, chant, hymn, march, dirge, requiem

eloquent
articulate, expressive, impassioned, passionate, ardent, outspoken, poignant, fluent

embellish
elaborate, amplify, magnify, exaggerate, intensify

enunciate
 fluent, articulate, utter, express, vocalize, vent, affirm, proclaim

eulogy
 accolade, homage, laudation, valediction, tribute, praise

exaggerate
 embellish, hyperbole, puffery, hype, fabricate, distort, overstate, inflate

exhale
 breathe, huff, inhale, puff, pant, blow, gasp, wheeze, emit, eject, expel

exhort
 urge, implore, beg, plead, warn, admonish, caution

express
 utter, articulate, vocalize, vent, enunciate, fluent, assert, convey

expressive
 eloquent, articulate, impassioned, passionate, melodic, sonorous, melodious, fluent

extol
 praise, acclaim, exalt, tout, applaud, commend, laud, glorify

exuberant
 gushing, animated, lavish, vivacious, buoyant, energetic, profuse, ebullient

flout
 taunt, disdain, deride, jeer, jest, quip, scoff, decry, ridicule, revile, scorn, spurn

fluent
 articulate, enunciate, utter, lyrical, melodious, flowing, sonorous, eloquent

flummery
    drivel, blather, dither, dribble, jabber, ramble, rant, rubbish, spittle,
    malarkey, poppycock, puffery

full-throated
    bellowing, resonant, deep, resounding, loud-mouthed, vociferous

gab
    blab, blabber, blather, chatter, cackle, flummery, jabber, rattle

gabby
    loquacious, chatty, garrulous, gassy, long-winded, talkative, windy,
    verbose, wordy, effusive, gushy

garrulous
    effusive, loquacious, verbose, windy, wordy, long-winded, babbling

gasp
    choke, pant, wheeze, shriek, squawk, grunt, screech, huff, puff,
    gulp, sob

gassy
    verbose, chatty, gabby, gossipy, gushy, gregarious, long-winded,
    loquacious, effusive, windy, flip, garrulous

gibberish
    babble, drivel, jabber, blather, chatter, gobbledygook, malarkey,
    rant

gobbledygook
    babble, blather, gibberish, malarkey, drivel, rubbish

golden-tongued
    lyrical, musical, expressive, melodic, sonorous, eloquent, moving,
    mellifluous, tuneful, harmonious, melodious, stirring

gossipy
    chatty, effusive, flip, gabby, gassy, gushy, long-winded, loquacious,
    verbose, windy, blabber, garrulous

gravelly
> throaty, rasping, husky, gruff, hoarse, abrasive, scratchy, croaky, growling, raspy, guttural

gripe
> groan, moan, cry, grouse, grumble, lament, outcry, shriek, squawk, tirade, snipe, wail, mutter, grouch

groan
> wail, bawl, bellow, cry, squeal, howl, moan, grouse, gripe, grumble, lament, outcry, shriek, squawk, tirade

grouse
> quibble, nit-pick, grumble, groan, moan, gripe, lament, squawk, growl

growl
> bark, hiss, howl, snarl, snort, grunt, moan, gnarl

growling
> croaky, throaty, guttural, raspy, husky, grunting, snarling

grumble
> groan, moan, quibble, nit-pick, grouse, gripe, lament, squawk

grunt
> bellow, bleat, screech, bawl, bark, bay, squawk, whoop, yelp, growl

gushy, gushing
> chatty, effusive, flip, gabby, gassy, gossipy, gregarious, long-winded, loquacious, verbose, windy, spewing

guttural
> throaty, croaky, husky, gravelly, growling, breathy, hoarse, gasping, choked, quavering, tremulous, wheezing, raspy

hack
> gasp, choke, pant, wheeze, wail, whoop, yelp, bark, huff, puff

hail
applaud, call, shout, salute, holler, signal

harangue
tirade, bawl, shriek, berate, onslaught, blast, tongue-lash, scream, wail, rant

hoarse
gruff, growling, husky, raspy, gravelly, guttural, raucous

holler
bawl, clamor, growl, roar, shout, yell, bellow, bark, gasp, rave, rant, shriek, squawk, trumpet, thunder, wail, whoop, warble, yelp, bleat, screech, sob

homage
eulogy, accolade, laudation, valediction, tribute, homage, esteem, salutation

honk
quack, chirp, chirrup, chitter, cluck, clack, gobble, hoot, whistle, tweet, warble, crow

hoot
chortle, hee-haw, roar, snicker, cackle, smirk, giggle, snort, chuckle

howl, howling
hiss, snarl, snort, groan, squeal, wail, scream, screech, bellow, roar, bay, bleat, caterwaul, moan, holler, growl

huff
breathe, inhale, exhale, puff, pant, blow, gasp, wheeze

husky
croaky, throaty, guttural, raspy, gravelly, growling, gruff, hoarse

implore
beseech, plead, beg, cajole, cry, insist, rally, exhort, urge, appeal

incantation
chant, spell, invocation, enchantment, wizardry, sorcery

incoherent
inarticulate, unintelligible, stuttering, muffled, mumbling, garbled

ineffable
unutterable, unspoken, indescribable, inexpressible, unimaginable

inexpressible
indescribable, ineffable, unspoken, unutterable, unthinkable

inflection
lilt, cadence, accent, meter, intonation, rhythm, beat, tempo

inhale
breathe, huff, exhale, puff, pant, blow, gasp, wheeze, sniff

innuendo
tone, overtone, insinuation, implication, intimation, hint

insist
rally, implore, plead, beg, cajole, cry, beseech, urge

intimate (v)
allude, imply, hint, infer, insinuate, vent, signal, divulge

intone
lilt, cadence, chant, croon, sing, accent, inflection, rhythm

invocation
prayer, chant, devotion, appeal, command

jabber
drivel, blather, dither, dribble, flummery, ramble, rant, rubbish, spittle

jawbone
persuade, pressure, cajole, wheedle, pester, entice, tempt

jeer
decry, boo, hiss, sneer, heckle, bark, gnarl, snort, mock, scorn, deride, scoff, taunt, ridicule, revile

jest
jeer, mock, scoff, scorn, wit, wisecrack, banter, quip, crack, retort, tease, taunt, sneer, decry, ridicule, revile

jubilation
applaud, clap, cheer, celebrate, triumph, elation

laconic
terse, pithy, reticent, silent, taciturn, close-lipped, mute

lambaste
criticize, rebuke, reprimand, berate, chastise, scold

lament
groan, moan, grouse, gripe, grumble, outcry, shriek, squawk, wail, tirade, snipe, whine, weep

laudation
eulogy, accolade, homage, valediction, praise, acclaim

lilt
cadence, accent, inflection, meter, intone, rhythm, beat, tempo, sing, warble, trill, serenade, bellow, chant, chirp, drawl, murmur, trumpet, whistle

lisp
drawl, nasal, snort, sniff, twang, splutter, spit

long-winded
chatty, gregarious, verbose, windy, wordy, effusive, flip, gabby, gassy, gossipy, gushy, loquacious

loquacious
gassy, long-winded, talkative, chatty, garrulous, verbose, effusive, windy, wordy, gushy, gabby

loud-mouthed

full-throated, obnoxious, bellowing, vociferous, clamorous, crude, boisterous

lullaby

melody, song, tune, lull, croon, hum

malarkey

gobbledygook, babble, blather, gibberish, drivel

maunder

blather, mumble, ramble, babble, prattle, mutter, drivel

medley

chorus, blend, mingled, mash-up, mix

mimic

mock, parrot, parody, spoof, mirror

moan

groan, cry, grouse, gripe, grumble, lament, outcry, shriek, squawk, tirade, wail, howl

mock, mocking

jeer, sneer, scorn, decry, deride, scoff, taunt, mimic, ridicule, revile, lampoon

monotonous

banal, colorless, dreary, tiresome, tedious, wearying, repetitive, toneless, flat, dull

mouthy

wordy, chatty, effusive, gabby, gossipy, loquacious, gushy, windy, gregarious, long-winded, loud-mouthed

mumble

murmur, whisper, mutter, sigh, babble, blather, chatter, ramble, blabber, gurgle

mutter
    mumble, murmur, whisper, sigh, snort, splutter, stammer, babble, chatter, blather, blabber

nasal, nasally
    lisp, crack, drawl, snort, sniff, twang, splutter, spit

onslaught
    tirade, bawl, rant, attack, blast, tongue-lashing, scream, harangue, wail, cry, lament, shriek

outburst
    explosion, eruption, burst, tantrum, conniption, upheaval, outcry, outpouring, flare-up

outcry
    groan, moan, cry, grouse, gripe, grumble, lament, shriek, squawk, tirade, wail, protest, outburst, outpouring

pant
    breathless, gasp, wheeze, winded, blow, gulp, heave, huff, snort, puff, whiff, hiss

parrot
    mimic, mock, parody, spoof, mirror, lampoon

pitch, pitched
    tone, timbre, lingo, blather, prattle, drivel, chatter, parlance, saga, blurb

plead
    beg, cajole, cry, insist, rally, implore, beseech

prattle
    chatter, chat, jabber, blather, yammer, babble, blabber

puffery
    exaggeration, hype, praise, ballyhoo

quack
> chirp, cackle, call, chirrup, chitter, cluck, clack, crow, gobble, honk, hoot, tweet, warble, whistle

quaver, quavering
> breathy, tremulous, gasp, wheeze, tremble, shake, falter, warble, quiver, shudder, vibrate, oscillate, crack

quibble
> grouse, nit-pick, grumble, protest, niggle, moan, gripe

quip
> retort, chitchat, tease, crack, wit, jest, wisecrack, banter, repartee

rail
> protest, condemn, rage, denounce, blast, berate, attack, rant, scold, revile

rally
> plead, cajole, cry, insist, cheer, implore

ramble, rambling
> jabber, rattle, gurgle, babble, blabber, blather, chatter

rant, ranting
> shriek, wail, whoop, screech, tirade, clamorous, frenzied, hysterical, raging, raucous, raving

rasping, raspy
> abrasive, throaty, scratchy, chafing, gravely, husky, gruff, hoarse, croaky

rave, raving
> holler, rant, rail, raucous, shriek, wail, clamorous, frenzied, hysterical, raging, extol

rebuff
> reject, snub, spurn, repel, dismiss, rebuke, slight

rebuke
> berate, scold, chide, tongue-lash, reprimand, rebuff, snub

repartee
> wit, quip, jest, banter, wisecrack, gag

reticent
> restrained, silent, taciturn, close-lipped, close-mouthed, terse, curt, mute

retort
> quip, crack, wit, jest, wisecrack, chitchat, tease, banter

revile
> condemn, denounce, berate, attack, lambaste, vilify, scold, blast, slander

revelry
> celebration, festivity, spree

ridicule
> mock, jeer, sneer, scorn, decry, deride, scoff, taunt, revile

roister
> carouse, celebrate, rollick, revel, romp, carouse, rejoice

scoff
> taunt, annoy, deride, flout, jest, quip, mock, sneer, scorn, decry, ridicule, revile, jeer

scold
> chide, denounce, rant, rebuke, berate, revile, admonish

scorn
> decry, deride, scoff, mock, jeer, sneer, taunt, ridicule, revile

scream
> holler, yell, bellow, screech, howl, tirade, bawl, squeal, rant, blast, wail, blare, shriek, racket

screech, screeching
cackle, squawk, whoop, shriek, scream, holler, bellow, howl, squeal

seethe
bellow, boil, erupt, explode, fume, rant, bristle, simmer, smolder

serenade
ballad, hymn, chorus, chant, melody, croon, dirge, lilt, trill, warble

sharp-tongued
harsh, biting, scathing, cutting, caustic, acid, shrill

shout
squawk, shriek, outcry, tirade, applaud, bark, bawl, wail, caterwaul, cackle, chortle, clamor, holler, howl, roar, scream, screech, squeal

shriek
blare, bugle, caterwaul, cry, holler, roar, screech, scream, squawk, wail, thunder, whoop, bawl, moan, whine

shrill
dissonant, ear-piercing, ear-splitting, grating, harsh, high-pitched, piercing, reedy, sharp, wailing, jarring, screeching

shush
quell, muffle, squelch, subdue, quash, stifle, hush, lull

sigh
murmur, whisper, mumble, babble, gurgle, mutter

signal
announce, echo, beacon, message, proclaim, beckon, call, holler

sing, song
lilt, cadence, accent, inflection, intone, rhythm, tempo, warble, trill, serenade, tune

smirk
laugh, chortle, cackle, hoot, giggle, snicker, snort, simper, chuckle

HEAR: SPEECH *and* UTTERANCES

snarl
growl, bark, hiss, howl, snort, mutter

sneer
jeer, decry, hiss, heckle, snort, mock, scorn, deride, scoff, taunt, ridicule, revile

snicker
chortle, hee-haw, roar, hoot, cackle, smirk, giggle, snort, chuckle, guffaw

sniff, sniffle
lisp, crack, drawl, nasal, snort, twang, splutter, spit, snuff

snipe
jeer, attack, sneer, scoff, mock, deride

snivel
whimper, blubber, cry, moan, sob, weep, wail, bawl, gripe, groan, whine, sniffle

snore
snort, grunt, sniff, growl, hiss, lisp, huff, puff, wheeze

snort
growl, bark, gnarl, hiss, howl, snarl, chortle, cackle, hoot, smirk, giggle, snicker, chuckle, lisp, drawl, sniff, twang, splutter, stammer, spit

snuff
snort, sniff, snore, pant, puff, wheeze, sniffle

sob
whimper, snivel, weep, wail, bawl, blubber, groan, moan, snort, whine, yelp, screech, squawk, cry

speechless
breathless, dazed, dumbfounded, shocked, tongue-tied, wordless, hushed, silent, subdued, tight-lipped, dumbstruck, mute

spit
   lisp, drawl, snort, sniff, splutter, spittle, sputter

splutter
   spit, stammer, lisp, drawl, nasal, snort, sniff, burst, explode, choke

squawk
   caterwaul, groan, howl, yell, grouse, gripe, outcry, shriek, tirade,
   snipe, wail, whoop, bark, bawl, screech, bellow, bleat, blare

squeak
   creak, chirp, screech, squeal, wail, whine, whistle, grate, peep

squeal
   wail, bawl, bellow, cry, lament, groan, whine, screech, blare, blurt,
   gasp, hail, howl, shout, shrill, trumpet, yelp

squelch
   stifle, quell, muffle, subdue, quash, stifle, hush, lull, crush, squash

stammer
   mutter, mumble, murmur, sigh, snort, splutter, babble, chatter,
   blather, blabber

stifle
   squash, shush, quell, muffle, quash, hush, lull, squelch, subdue

strident
   grating, harsh, shrill, jarring, raucous, blaring, clashing

stutter
   mutter, stammer, mumble, snort, splutter, babble, blather, blabber

summon
   arouse, beckon, command, conjure, invoke, hail, rally

swagger
   brag, boast, rant, strut, parade, bluster, crow

taciturn
> laconic, reticent, close-lipped, mute, tight-lipped, unexpressive, silent, withdrawn

talkative
> articulate, chatty, fluent, gabby, garrulous, gassy, gossipy, gushy, mouthy, outspoken, gregarious, talky, verbose, vocal, wordy

tantrum
> tirade, conniption, outburst, explosion, eruption, burst, blowup, upheaval

taunt
> annoy, deride, flout, mock, jest, quip, scoff, sneer, scorn, ridicule, decry, revile, jeer

telegraph
> relay, broadcast, blazon, announce, circulate, blare, disseminate, transmit

testy
> gruff, blunt, truculent, edgy, uptight, ill-tempered

throaty
> raspy, gravelly, brassy, brazen, husky, hoarse, squawking, rasping, tremulous, croaky, abrasive, scratchy, gruff, growling

tight-lipped
> reticent, restrained, close-mouthed, mute, taciturn

tirade
> bawl, rant, attack, onslaught, blast, tongue-lash, scream, harangue, wail, cry, lament, shriek

tongue-tied
> speechless, wordless, dumbstruck, lulled, hushed, garbled

tout
> acclaim, praise, extol, trumpet, proclaim, herald, laud

trill

burble, cheep, cluck, croon, gaggle, tweet, peep, warble, bellow, chant, chirp, drawl, lilt, murmur, trumpet, whistle

truculent

gruff, testy, blunt, combative, quarrelsome, belligerent, bullying

trumpet

boom, explode, rant, thunder, wail, whoop, bugle, whistle, warble, bellow, chant, chirp, trill

twang, twangy

accent, nasal, lisp, tonal, drawl, snort, sniff

tweet

quack, chirp, cackle, call, chirrup, chitter, cluck, clack, crow, hoot, gobble, honk, warble, whistle

unexpressed

indescribable, inexpressible, ineffable, unutterable, unspoken

unexpressive

taciturn, close-lipped, mute, tight-lipped, reticent, emotionless

unintelligible

incoherent, unintelligible, stuttering, muffled, mumbling, garbled

unspeakable

unutterable, indescribable, inexpressible, inconceivable, ineffable

unspoken

ineffable, indescribable, inexpressible, unutterable, unexpressed

unutterable

inexpressible, ineffable, unthinkable, indescribable, unspeakable

uproar

bluster, roar, brawl, clamor, commotion, embroil, melee, rumble, thunder, tumult

utter
express, articulate, vocalize, vent, enunciate, blurt

vent
utter, express, articulate, vocalize, enunciate, voice

verbose
gushy, gregarious, long-winded, chatty, effusive, flowery, fluent, gabby, gossipy, loquacious, wordy, windy

vilify
berate, slander, slam, besmirch, decry, denounce, tongue-lash, condemn

vitriol, vitriolic
biting, scathing, spiteful, venomous, vicious, cutting, withering, sharp

vocalize
utter, express, articulate, vent, enunciate, fluent, chant, croon

voice
timbre, tone, resonance, lilt, express, utter, vent

voluble
ebullient, exuberant, gushing, teeming, gossipy, gabby, verbose, loquacious, windy, lavish

wail
groan, howl, squeal, whimper, shriek, squawk, yelp, bawl, bay, screech, sob, weep, lament, blubber, moan

weep
bawl, bemoan, lament, wail, whimper, blubber, moan, snivel, cry, sob

whine
bawl, bellow, gasp, lament, wail, howl, whistle, creak, gripe, grouse

whinny
> cry, wail, shriek, whistle, neigh, bray, squawk, squeal

whisper
> mutter, murmur, rustle, hiss, mumble, sigh, buzz, hum

winded
> breathless, panting, gasping, wheezing, puffing

windy
> garrulous, rambling, loquacious, verbose, wordy, long-winded

wordless
> unspoken, quiet, hushed, silent, muted, whisper, tight-lipped, speechless, unsaid, subdued

wordy
> chatty, effusive, flowery, fluent, gabby, gossipy, loquacious, gushy, gregarious, long-winded, windy

yell
> bellow, scream, wail, growl, roar, thunder, cry, bawl, bark, bay, bleat, cackle, chant, grunt, hail, keen, screech, squawk, whoop

yelp
> yowl, bark, bawl, bay, whimper, neigh, squeal, bellow, bleat, cackle, grunt, screech, sob, squawk, whoop, yell

yodel
> croon, ballad, chant, chirp, chorus, hum, lilt, serenade, sing, trill, warble, whistle

MOVEMENT

bash
> knock, slam, smack, bang, belt, clobber, deck, drub, smash, thump, wallop, whack, bat

bat
>   bang, batter, beat, belt, deck, drub, clobber, crash, knock, hammer, pummel, smash, strike, thrash, wallop, smack, whack, rap

batter
>   bang, beat, clobber, hammer, knock, pummel, rap, smash, strike, thrash, wallop, whack

billow
>   spew, spittle, spit, gush, burp, surge, pitch, ripple

blast
>   boom, thunder, explode, backfire, bang, burst, erupt, flare

burst
>   downpour, cascade, drench, monsoon, torrent, explode, blast, erupt, flare, boom, thunder, surge

cascade
>   downpour, burst, drench, monsoon, surge, torrent, avalanche, deluge, flood

chop
>   smash, strike, thrash, wallop, bang, batter, beat, clobber, crash, hammer, knock, pummel

collide
>   bang, smash, strike, crash, slam, shatter, clash, sideswipe, bump, shatter

downpour
>   burst, cascade, drench, monsoon, surge, torrent, deluge

drip
>   dribble, drizzle, leak, pour, percolate, trickle, drool, leach, sprinkle, gurgle, seep

drum
>   beat, hammer, drone, hum, resound, thunder, thrum, strum, strike

effervesce
bubble, boil, fizzle, sizzle, foam, froth, fizz, lather

erupt
explode, backfire, bang, blast, burst, flare, smolder, thunder, boom

explode
backfire, bang, blast, burst, erupt, flare, boom, thunder

flap
fly, flutter, jangle, whirl, wag, flail, flop

flare
explode, backfire, blast, burst, erupt, smolder, boom, thunder

flick, flicker
flip, flitter, pulse, tweak, click, plunk, snap, tick, quiver, oscillate, wave

flutter
flap, fly, jangle, whirl, wag, hover, quiver, flit, flitter, dance, ripple

fracture
crack, snap, chisel, chip, fissure, rupture

hammer
thrash, wallop, whack, bang, pummel, batter, beat, clobber, knock, crash, rap, smash, strike

jolt
tremor, rumble, shudder, shock, blow, clash, collision, jar

knock
rap, bang, thump, slam, tap, hammer, strike, batter, beat, clobber, crash, pummel, smash, thrash, wallop

leach
trickle, drip, drizzle, percolate, seep, sprinkle, gurgle, dribble

pelt
slug, smack, slam, smash, wallop, whack, thump, bang, biff, belt, clobber, deck, drub, crack, hammer, flog, knock, pound, pummel

percolate
drip, dribble, drizzle, leak, pour, seep, trickle, sprinkle, leach

pound
boom, thunder, bellow, explode, bang, strike, hammer, thrash

pummel
strike, thrash, wallop, bang, batter, beat, clobber, crash, detonate, hammer, knock, punch, rap, smash

rail
thunder, blast, bellow, clamor, crash, explode, resound, rumble, wail, trumpet, echo, boom

rap
crash, detonate, hammer, whack, tap, pound, bang, batter, beat, clobber, knock, pummel, plunk, punch, smash, strike, thrash, wallop

rattle
clank, clatter, jingle, jangle, clink, joggle, ramble, jolt, clatter

ripple
crinkle, bristle, rustle, twist, wring, undulate, wave, flow, flutter, pulsate

seep
trickle, drip, drizzle, percolate, leach, sprinkle, gurgle, dribble, leak

shake, shaky
tremulous, quivering, trembling, quaking, jittery

slam
punch, smash, thump, hammer, strike, bang, batter, crash, deck, clobber, pummel, thrash, wallop, bash, bat, drub, smack, whack

smash
plunk, bang, beat, chop, clobber, crash, hammer, knock, pummel, punch, rap, strike, thrash, wallop, batter

spew
billow, spit, gush, belch, burp, spittle, heave, expel

splat
clash, crash, smash, splash, thud

spout
gush, spew, squirt, sputter, billow, spurt, expel

sprinkle
trickle, drip, drizzle, percolate, leach, seep, gurgle, dribble

stomp
clomp, clop, trudge, smash, bang, knock, rap, thump, trample

strike
bang, batter, beat, crash, hammer, knock, pummel, punch, smash, thrash, wallop, rap

strum
thrum, hum, rhythm, drum, beat, pluck

surge
burst, cascade, downpour, drench, monsoon, torrent, upsurge, gush, rush

tap
knock, drum, rap, strike, bump, flap, flick, pat, whack, thump

teem, teeming
gushing, abundant, ebullient, lavish, exuberant, swarming

thrash
smash, strike, bang, batter, chop, clobber, crash, hammer, knock, pummel, punch, rap, wallop, beat

throb, throbbing
pulsate, pound, purr, rumble, hum, drum, thud, thump

thump
bang, clobber, deck, drub, crack, hammer, flog, knock, pound, pelt, belt, pummel, slug, smack, slam, smash, rap, wallop, whack

thrum
strum, hum, rhythm, drum, purr, buzz, drawl, murmur, throb, trill

torrent
downpour, cascade, drench, surge, burst, monsoon, deluge

trickle
drip, drizzle, percolate, leach, seep, sprinkle, gurgle, dribble

wallop
smash, strike, thrash, bang, batter, beat, clobber, crash, hammer, knock, pummel, punch, rap, bash, thump, stomp

wrangle
clash, brawl, collide, quarrel, rumble, snarl, tussle, fracas, ruckus, flap

Listening

attuned
receptive, tuned, harmonized, aligned, integrated, connected

aural
acoustic, audio, phonic, audible, sonic

discern
perceive, detect, recognize, distinguish

eavesdrop
listen, snoop, hearken, heed, overhear, spy, tune in, monitor

heed
> hearken, listen, eavesdrop, tune in, overhear

listen
> eavesdrop, overhear, attend, snoop, heed, tune in

overhear
> eavesdrop, hearken, heed, spy, tune in, monitor

VOLUME

amplify
> magnify, crescendo, energize, elaborate, embellish, intensify, swell, boost

blare, blaring
> ringing, booming, wailing, thunderous, resounding, shrill

booming
> deafening, ear-piercing, ringing, blaring, resounding, bellowing, roaring

choke, choked
> muffle, deaden, dampen, breathy, hoarse, quavering, tremulous, guttural, gasp, pant, stifle, squelch, wheeze, hack, mask, smother, deafen, hushed, muted

clipped
> pithy, concise, compact, terse, succinct, blunt, curtailed, pointed, laconic, curt

close-lipped
> tight-lipped, reticent, silent, taciturn, mute, terse, hushed, subdued, muffled, private, reserved

crescendo
> amplify, magnify, energize, embellish, intensify, escalate, upsurge

dampen
>   muffle, deaden, muted, squelch, mask, choke, hushed, stifle

deaden
>   muffle, muted, dampen, squelch, mask, hush, subdue, stifle, quiet, blunt

deafening
>   booming, ear-piercing, earthshaking, piercing, resounding, ringing, thundering, rattling

decibel
>   loudness, volume, intensity, amplification

ear-piercing
>   deafening, booming, resounding, thundering, rattling, ear-splitting, ringing

ear-splitting
>   deafening, booming, ear-piercing, piercing, resounding, ringing, thundering, rattling

high-pitched
>   screaming, shrill, shrieking, acute, piercing, sharp

hush, hushed
>   subdued, muffled, murmur, muted, whisper, lull, tranquil, silent

inaudible
>   undetectable, imperceptible, muffled, hushed, muted, mumbled, soundless, silent, faint

incoherent
>   inarticulate, unintelligible, stuttering, muffled, mumbled, garbled

lull
>   soothe, calm, assuage, hush, quiet, silence, stillness, respite, quell, temper

magnify
> intensify, amplify, crescendo, energize, embellish, elaborate, boost, surge, swell

mask
> dampen, squelch, muffle, deaden, smother, choke, hush, subdue, shield, stifle, mute

modulate
> accent, inflection, rhythm, harmonize, attune, balance, temper, tweak, tune, adjust

muffle, muffled
> deaden, mute, dampen, stifle, squelch, smother, choke, smother, hushed, subdued, whisper, drown, silence, mask

mute
> laconic, reticent, silent, taciturn, close-lipped, terse, stifle, deaden, dampen, squelch, smother, hushed, subdued, muffled, whisper, choke, mask

piercing
> deafening, booming, earthshaking, resounding, ringing, rattling, thundering, thunderous, shrill

pithy
> clipped, concise, compact, terse, succinct, crisp, curt

quell
> stifle, squash, shush, muffle, quash, hush, lull, squelch, subdue

quiet
> hush, silent, muted, whisper, still, subdued, faint, tight-lipped, speechless, wordless, muffled

rip-roaring
> noisy, blaring, boisterous, brassy, clamorous, jarring, deafening, clanging, resounding, riotous, rowdy, screaming, shrill, thunderous

roaring
resounding, thunderous, ringing, crashing, deafening, uproarious, boisterous, rowdy, clanging, piercing, rumbling

secret
clandestine, censored, close-mouthed, encrypted, unspoken, hushed, furtive

shrill
dissonant, ear-piercing, ear-splitting, grating, harsh, high-pitched, piercing, reedy, sharp, wailing, jarring, screeching

silent, silence
hushed, mute, reserved, restrained, still, tight-lipped, unspoken, wordless, mum, reticent, speechless, stillness

smother
muffle, deaden, muted, dampen, stifle, squelch, mask, choke, deafen, hushed, subdued, quash, snuff

squelch
muffle, deaden, dampen, stifle, mask, smother, choke, hush, mute, subdue, shush, suppress

stifle, stifled
assuage, censor, dampen, extinguish, hush, mute, suppress, muffle, deaden, squelch, smother, deafen, subdue

still, stillness
hush, silence, soundless, tranquil, calm, placid

subdue, subdued
hushed, muffled, murmur, muted, whisper, quell, overwhelm, suppress

terse
clipped, blunt, pointed, restrained, truncated, reticent, concise, brusque, pithy, curt

thready
feeble, thin, weak, reedy

tight-lipped
reticent, restrained, close-mouthed, muted

truncated
terse, clipped, blunt, pointed, restrained, reticent, abbreviated, curt, truncated

unsung
unexpressed, overlooked, unheralded, unacknowledged, nameless

uproarious
roaring, raucous, deafening, clamorous, booming, boisterous, rowdy, rambunctious

whisper
murmur, sigh, babble, blather, gurgle, purr, vibrate, whir, breathe, coo, rustle, hush, subdued, muffled, muted

TOUCH

The body says what words cannot.
—Martha Graham, dancer and choreographer

SKIN & BODY SENSATIONS *and* VISCERAL RESPONSES
TEXTURES *and* STRUCTURES
MOVEMENT, PRESSURE, *and* SPEED

Touch is our second set of eyes and ears through which we sense the world. In the absence of light, we can feel our way through darkness. Without hearing, we can intimately sense vibrations in our fingertips, bones, and skin. Touch even extends beyond our physical boundaries. We can kinesthetically get a "feel" for a place or situation. Or physically sense another person's gaze. Or our feelings can "go out" to someone in need.

The body remembers touch. Healing touch, revulsion, pain, pleasure all leave an indelible mark. Touch and our reactions to it communicate without words. *You are cherished. That gives me the creeps.* Deep-seated, blissful, gut-wrenching, profound.

We talk in the language of touch. When we are deeply moved, we say we are *touched*. When we are insulted, our *feelings* are hurt.

Some people are *touchy*, *abrasive*, *out of touch*, or *tactless*. Others are *tactful*, *tactical*, or have a *light touch*.

We cannot completely shut off touch, though we can feel numb to it. We constantly float in a sea of sensations. We luxuriate in clothes and fabrics, breezes, water, movement and dance, the cuddle or caress of another. We feel the electric charge of arousal and the throbbing dagger of pain. We itch for something. Emotions burn and bubble within us. Essential for survival, touch is our blessing and curse. Our reminder that we are alive, feeling every sensation.

In this section, we get a feel for tactile words describing various body and skin sensations and visceral responses, textures and forms, and words that convey movement, pressure, and speed.

SKIN & BODY SENSATIONS *and* VISCERAL RESPONSES

abhor, abhorrent
> repellent, atrocious, heinous, obnoxious, repugnant, contemptible, odious, offensive, noxious, loathsome, vile

absorbing
> immersing, engrossing, gripping, riveting, enthralling, arresting, spellbinding, consuming

aching
> throbbing, bruised, paining, panging, twinging, stabbing, shooting, stinging, tender, raw, nagging

acidic
> bracing, stinging, cutting, biting, sharp, acrid, caustic, astringent, bitter, sour

aflame
> fiery, blistering, burning, blazing, ablaze, flaring, searing, singeing, ignited

aggravating
> disturbing, exasperating, provoking, vexing, bothersome, galling, irksome

agitated
> roiled, flustered, ruffled, rattled, unsettled, aggravated, provoked, disquieted, shivering, shuddering, vexed

agitating
> aggravating, disturbing, galling, irksome, exasperating, provoking, vexing, bothersome

airless
> windless, stifling, choking, constrictive, oppressive, squelching, stuffy, strangling, suffocating, stuffy

airy
> light, subtle, flowing, dreamy, languid, tranquil, breezy, buoyant, windy, feathery, fluffy, willowy, wispy, soft

anoint
> smooth, lubricate, daub, oil, smear, rub

antsy
> edgy, fretful, panicky, jittery, squirmy, touchy, uneasy, fidgety

apprehensive, apprehension
> trembling, disquieted, frightened, quivering, trepidation, shivering, uneasy, fearful, frozen

arduous
> grueling, backbreaking, irksome, tiresome, toilsome, strained, wearying, laborious, crushing, back-breaking, rigorous, taxing, strenuous, wearisome, onerous

arid

bone-dry, barren, dusty, parched, dry, scorched, waterless, wilted, dehydrated, desiccated, shriveled, withered, baked

arousing, aroused

stimulating, agitating, stirring, enlivening, provoking, thrilling, vexing, invigorating, startling, electrifying, alarming

assailed

besieged, beleaguered, blockaded, stressed, surrounded, encircled, beset, racked, harassed

assuage, assuaged

soothe, allay, soften, appease, balm, comfort, hush, lull, smooth, quell, subdue, pacify, mollify, calm

astringent

caustic, stinging, biting, constricting, cutting, sharp, bitter, harsh, acrid

averse, aversion

animosity, revulsion, hostility, abhorrence, antipathy, repulsion, disgust, reluctance, loath, distaste

awash

drenched, covered, flooded, overflowing, submerged, inundated, flushed

balm

emollient, soothe, moisten, soften, lubricate, salve, solace, relief, comfort, restorative

balmy

soothing, gentle, tranquil, temperate, pleasant, refreshing, mild

bare

stark, plain, unadorned, unclothed, stripped, barren, harsh, naked, bald, denuded, disrobed, primal

bathe
deluge, drown, dunk, imbue, infuse, inundate, saturate, submerge, permeate, pervade, drench, steep, instill, refresh, rinse, cleanse, douse

beset
assailed, beleaguered, besieged, surrounded, encircled, plagued, entangled, harassed

besieged
assailed, surrounded, encircled, beleaguered, harassed, stressed, beset, trapped

biting
acid, acerbic, brisk, bracing, bitter, cutting, edgy, stinging, sharp, acrid, caustic, astringent, intense, piercing, searing, scathing

bitter
astringent, cutting, caustic, stinging, biting, scathing, sharp

blanch, blanched
wince, pale, recoil, twitch, grimace, flinch, crouch, cringe, shrink, reel, retract, shudder, retreat, quiver, tremble, squirm

blazing
fiery, blistering, burning, flaring, searing, seething, aflame

blistering, blistered
bleeding, boiling, parched, heated, searing, seething, sizzling, sweltering, burning, torrid, feverish, flushed, inflamed, intense, fierce, fiery

blood-curdling
spine-chilling, creepy, spooky, bone-chilling, hair-raising, chilling, shocking, scary, terrifying, frightening, horrifying, spine-tingling

bloody, bloodied
bruised, wounded, blood-stained, gory, brutal, savage, ferocious

blush, blushed
 warm, flushed, fiery, heated, radiant, reddened

blustery
 windy, gusty, tumultuous, stormy, windswept, breezy, brisk, drafty, howling, turbulent

boiling
 burning, torrid, searing, steamy, stifling, blistering, flushed, heated, feverish, seething, simmering, sultry, sizzling, sweltering, inflamed, fiery

bone-chilling
 eerie, strange, creepy, freakish, spooky, spine-chilling, shocking, disturbing, scary

bothersome
 irksome, provoking, tiresome, aggravating, disturbing, troubling, exasperating, galling, wearisome, vexing

bracing
 chilly, crisp, exhilarating, invigorating, reviving, biting, nippy, brisk, bitter, cutting, stinging, caustic, astringent

breezy
 airy, bubbly, buoyant, lively, spirited, windy, stormy, gusty, brisk, drafty

brisk
 sharp, windy, biting, bracing, cutting, stinging, blustery, stormy, gusty, breezy, drafty

bristle, bristling
 flare, ruffle, seethe, fume, rage, boil

bruised
 aching, throbbing, welted, swollen, blackened, battered, marred, bloodied, wounded

buoyant
   breezy, airy, bubbly, lively, spirited, windy, resilient

burn
   ignite, fan, inflame, kindle, stoke, torch, scald, scorch

burning
   blazing, blistering, simmering, fiery, boiling, seething, smoldering, impassioned, sweltering, torrid, ablaze, aflame, flaring, searing, stinging, parched

caress
   embrace, nuzzle, stroke, touch, nudge, squeeze, cuddle

cathartic, catharsis
   releasing, purifying, purging, cleansing, venting

caustic
   acidic, acerbic, bitter, biting, cutting, piercing, stinging, astringent

chafe
   rub, scrape, abrade, erode, graze, grate, chisel, scour, file, scratch, scuff, grind, corrode

charged
   electric, electrify, thrilling, rousing, stirring, pervading, intense, fraught, saturated, tense

chilling
   horrifying, blood-curling, spine-chilling, disturbing, shocking, hair-raising

chilly
   shivering, frozen, brisk, bracing, frigid, exhilarating, invigorating, biting, nippy, reviving, icy, frosty, crisp

choking
   stifling, constrictive, oppressive, squelching, stuffy, strangling, suffocating, windless, airless

choppy
jolting, agitating, bumpy, jarring, rough, turbulent, violent

clammy
sweaty, damp, misty, moist, sticky, slithery, slimy, tacky, humid, muggy, steamy

cleanse
freshen, purge, spruce, wash, bathe, refresh, lather, scrub, douse, swab, rinse, wipe

clench, clenching
clasp, cling, clutch, grasp, grip, clamp, vise, grapple, constrict

congested
stuffy, cramped, stifling, constricted, choked, clogged, grid-locked, jammed, blocked

constricted
stifling, choking, oppressive, strangling, suffocating, squelching

contort, contorted
wince, writhe, convulse, twitch, blanch, grimace, flinch, shudder, crouch, cringe, shrink, reel, retract, recoil, retreat, quiver, tremble, squirm, twist, mangle, warp, wring, wrench, flail

convulse, convulsing
quake, bobble, fidget, flutter, heave, joggle, quiver, shake, tremble, twitch, waver, wobble

cower, cowering
recoil, quake, cringe, tremble, shake, flinch, crouch, wince, shrink

cramped
constricted, confined, congested, crowded, jammed

creepy
bone-chilling, eerie, strange, freakish, spooky, scary, spine-chilling

cringe
recoil, retract, shudder, retreat, quiver, swerve, tremble, squirm, flinch, wince, reel

crisp
bracing, brisk, chilly, exhilarating, invigorating, reviving, nippy

cuddle
nuzzle, touch, embrace, cling, clutch, cradle, grip, caress

cutting
stinging, biting, sharp, acerbic, brisk, bracing, bitter, edgy, pointed, scathing, caustic, acid

damp
moist, humid, muggy, clammy, misty, steamy, watery, drizzly, dank, dewy, rainy, sticky, swampy, tacky

dank
damp, dewy, humid, moist, muggy, rainy, sticky, swampy, clammy, chilly

daub
smooth, lubricate, anoint, crown, oil, rub, massage

deadened
lifeless, numb, muffled, hardened, stifled

deluged
drenched, drowned, inundated, saturated, submerged, flooded, doused, soaked, swamped, overwhelmed

devastating, devastated
shattering, shocking, crushing, tormenting, stunning, mortifying, distressing, traumatic

dewy
muggy, rainy, damp, humid, moist, sticky, swampy, misty

discombobulated
> flummoxed, bewildered, perplexed, confused, confounded, rattled, baffled, disconcerted, unsettled

disconcerting
> unsettling, upsetting, disturbing, rattling, troubling, disquieting, perturbing, unnerving, shaken

disgust, disgusting
> sickening, unsettling, repulsive, shocking, revolting, detestable, repugnant, appalling

disquiet, disquieted, disquieting
> flustered, agitated, ruffled, rattled, unsettled, befuddled, roiled, bewildered, shaken

disrobe, disrobed
> bare, naked, primal, unclothed, stripped, stark, plain, undressed, unclad

distorted
> scarred, blistered, defaced, disfigured, gashed, welted, gnarled, warped, twisted

distressing, distressed
> alarming, shattering, disturbing, shocking, crushing, devastating, tormenting, stunning, mortifying, traumatic

douse
> submerge, drench, bathe, deluge, drown, dunk, inundate, quench, saturate, soak

drafty
> windy, blustery, windswept, gusty, breezy, brisk, airy, nippy, chilly

drenched
> saturated, covered, flooded, overflowing, submerged, bathed, doused, drowned, imbued, infused, inundated, sopping, awash

drizzly
    damp, moist, humid, muggy, clammy, misty, steamy, watery

edgy
    antsy, fretful, panicky, prickly, squirmy, touchy, uneasy, skittish,
    uptight, tense

eerie
    bone-chilling, strange, freakish, spooky, spine-chilling, creepy,
    scary

effervescent
    swishing, fizzling, bubbly, burbling, rustling, frothy, bouncy, airy,
    sparkling, foaming

electric, electrifying
    charged, thrilling, rousing, stirring, tingling, surging, arousing

embroiled
    entangled, ensnared, intertwined, entrenched, mired, enmeshed

emollient
    soothing, moistening, softening, balm, lubricating, pacifying, salve

encircled
    beleaguered, besieged, blockaded, stressed, assailed, surrounded,
    beset

engrossed, engrossing
    enticing, beguiling, magnetic, alluring, riveting, hypnotic, thrilling,
    gripping, enthralling, spellbinding, captivating, mesmerizing,
    arresting, enchanting

enliven, enlivening
    arouse, stimulate, stir, excite, thrill, invigorate, brighten, rejuvenate

enrapture, enraptured
    tantalize, attract, beckon, enthrall, stimulate, tempt, enamored,
    enchanted, mesmerized, charmed, fixated

enraged
livid, seething, incensed, furious, infuriated, irate, outraged

entangled
twisted, intertwined, tangled, snarled, embroiled, ensnared

enthrall, enthralling
absorbing, immersing, engaged, riveting, hypnotic, thrilling, gripping, mesmerizing, engrossing, spellbinding, captivating, beguiling, magnetic, alluring, arresting, enchanting, enticing

entice, enticing
engrossing, spellbinding, arresting, enchanting, captivating, hypnotic, gripping, enthralling, mesmerizing, alluring, beguiling, magnetic, tempting

entrenched
ingrained, embedded, deep-seated, barricaded, blockaded, lodged, deep-rooted, deep-seated

exasperate, exasperated
aggravated, inflamed, provoked, enraged, infuriated, incensed, maddened

excite
arouse, stimulate, stir, enliven, kindle, thrill, invigorate, energize, rouse, electrify

excruciating
agonizing, consuming, intense, piercing, shooting, tearing, acute, unbearable, racking, tormenting, stabbing

exhilarating
invigorating, electrifying, thrilling, breathtaking, bracing, rousing, stirring, intoxicating

fervent
impassioned, intense, passionate, vehement, ardent

feverish
flushed, burning, boiling, fervent, flaming, fiery, heated, seething, frenzied, frantic, overwrought

fidget, fidgety
quake, quiver, shake, tremble, twitch, waver, wobble, restless

fiery
burning, searing, boiling, flaming, heated, impassioned, seething, fierce, flushed, fervent, hot-headed, hot-tempered, vehement

fitful
restless, unsettled, erratic, jumpy, flighty, sporadic

flail, flailing
wave, flap, twist, writhe, thrash, writhe, flounder, lash

flaming
flushed, raging, feverish, boiling, fervent, heated, fiery, seething, sweltering, burning, searing, scathing, livid

flare, flaring
bursting, erupting, burning, blazing, seething, boiling, fuming

flighty
careening, dispersed, erratic, jumpy, sporadic, restless, twitchy, volatile, impulsive, scattered, capricious, fickle, fitful

flinch, flinching
crouch, recoil, shrink, wince, cringe, reel, retract, shudder, retreat, quiver, tremble, squirm, writhe, contort, twitch, grimace

flummoxed
bewildered, baffled, confused, confounded, discombobulated, perplexed, rattled

flushed
fiery, seething, blushing, boiling, heated, feverish, burning, searing, flaming

flustered

agitated, ruffled, rattled, unsettled, befuddled, bewildered, roiled, disquieted, shaken

frantic

frenetic, feverish, fraught, agitated, frenzied, agitated, distraught, hectic

frenetic

feverish, frantic, hectic, frenzied, raving, obsessive, maniacal, wild

frenzied

frenetic, hectic, feverish, frantic, raving, manic, crazed, hysterical, fraught, furious

freshen

cleanse, purge, scrub, spruce, wash, invigorate, refresh, revitalize, restore, clean

fretful

uneasy, fitful, panicky, squirmy, agitated, jittery, unsettled, anxious, antsy, fidgety, edgy

frightened

apprehensive, shivering, trembling, disquieted, fearful, startled, uneasy

frigid

chilly, bracing, freezing, shivering, frozen, brisk, numbing, frosty, biting, nippy

frosty, frosted

cold, chilly, brisk, biting, bracing, frozen, icy, shivering, freezing, numb, frigid

frozen

chilly, bracing, frigid, shivering, brisk, biting, nippy, frosted, numb, icy, impassive

gashed
scarred, blistered, defaced, disfigured, welted, gouged, slashed

gnawing
biting, consuming, gripping, piercing, shooting, tearing, alarming, harrowing, heart-rending, nerve-racking

grating
jarring, abrasive, biting, screeching, clashing, rasping, irksome

grimace, grimacing
flinch, cringe, reel, retract, tremble, twinge, pang, wince, writhe, contort, recoil, twitch, blanch, shudder, retreat, quiver, squirm

gripping
spellbinding, captivating, magnetic, riveting, hypnotic, thrilling, enthralling, mesmerizing, engrossing, arresting, enticing

grueling
arduous, backbreaking, irksome, tiresome, toilsome, strained, wearying, taxing, tortuous

gusty
blustery, windy, tumultuous, stormy, windswept, breezy, brisk, drafty

gutsy
unshrinking, bold, unflinching, undaunted, valiant, fearless

gut-wrenching
stunning, distressing, alarming, startling, shocking, disquieting

hair-raising
spine-chilling, electrifying, creepy, spooky, bone-chilling, chilling, bloodcurdling, spine-tingling, shocking

harrowing
alarming, heartrending, gripping, terrifying, traumatic, nerve-racking, disturbing

harsh
   biting, coarse, caustic, jarring, rugged, scraping, scratchy, grating

headstrong
   unflinching, unyielding, adamant, ironfisted, steadfast, bullheaded

heart-rending
   harrowing, alarming, gnawing, piercing, nerve-racking, gripping,
   terrifying, tragic, heartbreaking

heartsick
   despairing, grieving, melancholy, despondent, disheartened

heated
   fiery, passionate, intense, fierce, stormy, spirited, bitter, violent,
   acrimonious, vehement

high-strung
   edgy, tense, temperamental, excitable, unstable, restless, neurotic

hot-headed
   reckless, passionate, volatile, fiery, explosive, quick-tempered

humid
   clammy, sweaty, damp, misty, moist, sticky, muggy, dank, stifling,
   steamy, sweltering

icy
   frozen, biting, bitter, detached, cutting, dispassionate, freezing,
   distant, frosted, impassive, numb, reticent, shivery, cold, stony

ignite
   spark, kindle, energize, arouse, trigger, provoke

immersed
   absorbed, enthralled, soaked, permeated, engrossed, spellbound

incendiary
   provocative, inflammatory, combustible, inflaming, inciting

indignant

irate, aggravated, aggrieved, furious, livid, incensed

inflamed

feverish, boiling, fervent, heated, seething, aggravated, provoked, irked, flushed, burning, searing, fiery

ingrained

entrenched, embedded, deep-seated, lodged, unshakable, deep-rooted, enduring

infuriated

seething, livid, incensed, enraged, furious, outraged, indignant, irate

instilled

imbued, permeated, pervaded, bathed, steeped, drenched, doused, deluged, infused, inundated, saturated

instinctive

visceral, gut, deep-rooted, deep-seated, impulsive, reflexive, spontaneous

insufferable

unbearable, intolerable, unendurable, shattering, excruciating, gnawing, tormenting

intolerable

insufferable, unbearable, unendurable, shattering, excruciating, gnawing, tormenting

intrusive

meddling, invasive, prying, interfering, pushy, meddlesome, nosy, forward

invigorating

bracing, brisk, crisp, exhilarating, reviving, enlivening, revitalizing, refreshing, energizing

irate
>incensed, enraged, furious, infuriated, outraged, livid, seething, raging, indignant

irksome
>grueling, arduous, backbreaking, tiresome, toilsome, straining, wearying, bothersome, troubling

ironfisted
>unflinching, unyielding, headstrong, stubborn, impervious, resistant, unbending, relentless, adamant

itchy, itching
>ticklish, prickly, touchy, scratchy, tingling, crawling

jarring
>harsh, biting, coarse, caustic, rugged, scraping, grating, jolting, bumpy, unsettling, cutting

jaundiced
>disenchanted, disillusioned, indifferent, cynical, embittered, bitter, soured

jittery
>trembling, uneasy, agitated, edgy, quivering, quaking, fidgety, shaky, twitchy, uptight, jumpy

jumpy
>erratic, flighty, sporadic, restless, twitchy, fidgety, high-strung, skittish, spooked, edgy, fitful

labored
>stilted, strained, forced, leaden, laborious, burdensome

laborious
>arduous, grueling, taxing, strenuous, wearisome, cumbersome

languid
>relaxed, lethargic, unhurried, sluggish, fatigued

lethargic
drowsy, languid, leaden, sluggish, stagnant, listless

lifeless
deadened, drab, torpid, listless, passive, lethargic, dull, lackluster, emotionless

listless
feeble, languid, moribund, sluggish, stagnant, lifeless, leaden, spiritless

livid
seething, incensed, enraged, furious, infuriated, irate, outraged, indignant

loathsome
deplorable, obnoxious, revolting, repugnant, abhorrent, detestable, execrable, vile

lubricate, lubricated
smooth, daub, emollient, soothe, anoint, oil, moisten, soften, balm

lull
soothe, calm, assuage, hush, quiet, silence, quell, temper

malaise
unease, distress, angst, disquiet, despair, affliction, discomfort

magnetic
arresting, enchanting, enticing, riveting, hypnotic, engrossing, thrilling, gripping, enthralling, alluring, spellbinding, beguiling, captivating, mesmerizing

misty
damp, moist, sticky, humid, muggy, foggy, bleary, steamy

moist
clammy, sweaty, damp, misty, humid, muggy, steamy

moisten
emollient, soothe, soften, balm, lubricate, dampen, saturate, soak

muggy
damp, humid, clammy, misty, moist, soggy, sticky, stuffy

naked
bare, bald, denuded, disrobed, primal, unclothed, stripped, stark, unadorned, exposed

needle, needling
goad, provoke, pester, irk, infuriate, taunt, badger, ruffle, prod, harass

nestle
burrow, cuddle, nuzzle, snuggle

nippy
chilly, bracing, brisk, exhilarating, invigorating, reviving, biting, frosty, crisp

numb, numbing
blunt, deadened, subdued, icy, frozen, detached, cold, impassive, stony, bewildered, stunned

nuzzle
caress, embrace, stroke, burrow, touch, cuddle, snuggle

off-putting
revolting, creepy, offensive, disagreeable, distasteful, repellent, vile, odious, unappealing

oil (v)
anoint, smooth, lubricate, daub, grease, smear, slather

oily
greasy, unctuous, slimy, slithery, lubricated, slippery, pomaded, smeary, slick

oppressive
stifling, choking, constrictive, airless, squelching, stuffy, strangling, suffocating, windless

pacify
placate, appease, console, soothe, calm, assuage, quell, comfort

pained
wounded, aggrieved, anguished, distressed, troubled, tormented, aggravated

painstaking
meticulous, scrupulous, exacting, tedious, diligent, rigorous, fussy careful

palpable
tangible, apparent, conspicuous, detectable, evident, perceptible, distinct

palpitate, palpitation
trepidation, apprehension, shiver, tremble, disquiet, fright, quiver, unrest, unease

pang
throb, tremble, twinge, grimace, pulse, vibrate, thump, ache, stab, spasm, wrench

panicky
fretful, squirmy, antsy, touchy, uneasy, frenzied, startled, aghast, apprehensive, edgy

paralyzed
startled, alarmed, crippled, frightened, perturbed, stunned, incapacitated, unnerved

parched
shriveled, withered, dry, arid, dusty, waterless, dehydrated, wilted, desiccated, dried, scorched, thirsty

penetrating
> sharp, piercing, pointed, stinging, cutting, biting, puncturing, intense

perturbed
> startled, alarmed, stunned, unnerved, flustered, uneasy, troubled

piercing
> excruciating, gripping, pinching, scathing, scorching, puncturing, intense, sharp, skewering, stabbing, biting

pinched
> strained, tense, edgy, uneasy, winced, taut, drained, worn, fraught, distressed

placate
> soothe, mollify, pacify, appease, calm

pleasing
> delightful, pleasurable, gratifying, agreeable, engaging, satisfying, enchanting

pleasurable
> salubrious, pleasing, delightful, satisfying, sensuous, gratifying, sumptuous

pomaded
> oily, unctuous, lubricated, greasy, slick

provoking
> arousing, agitating, aggravating, stirring, vexing, rankling, irksome, needling, baiting, taunting, goading

punishing
> grueling, backbreaking, excruciating, strenuous, exhausting, crushing, tortuous, onerous, taxing, relentless, arduous

queasy
> squeamish, nauseated, faint, sickly, dizzy, woozy

quell
soothe, soften, appease, assuage, calm, comfort, hush, lull, subdue

quiver
flinch, wince, jitter, teeter, totter, shiver, shudder, quaver, tremor, quake, bobble, convulse, fidget, flutter, joggle, shake, tremble, twitch

rankled
vexed, irked, annoyed, provoked, galled, tormented

rattled
unnerved, flustered, agitated, ruffled, unsettled, befuddled, shaken, bewildered, disquieted

recoil
retreat, tremble, waver, squirm, repulse, cringe, retract, shudder, quiver, flinch, swerve, wince, reel, balk, dodge

reel
recoil, shudder, quiver, flinch, wince, squirm, tremble, cringe

refresh, refreshing
invigorate, freshen, rejuvenate, revitalize, cleanse, revive, enliven

relish
revel, savor, bask, indulge, enjoy, delight in, cherish, luxuriate in

repose
rest, calm, stillness, ease, peace, serenity, poise

repulse, repulsive
recoil, balk, dodge, qualm, retreat, tremble, waver, wince, cringe, retract, shudder, quiver, flinch, swerve, squirm, reel

restless
fitful, erratic, edgy, uneasy, flighty, jumpy, twitchy, fidgety, agitated, unsettled

revel
 savor, relish, bask, indulge, enjoy, delight in, cherish, wallow

riveting
 enchanting, hypnotic, thrilling, gripping, enthralling, mesmerizing, engrossing, spellbinding, captivating, beguiling, magnetic, alluring

rousing
 electric, charged, thrilling, stirring, spirited, arresting

salacious
 vulgar, suggestive, lewd, crude, obscene, lascivious, risque

salubrious
 pleasing, delightful, healthful, pleasurable, agreeable, salutary, invigorating, revitalizing

salutary
 healing, salubrious, nourishing, beneficial, restorative

scald, scalding
 seared, burning, scorched, parched, smoldering, singed, charred, stinging

scar, scarred, scarring
 blistered, defaced, disfigured, distorted, welted, pockmarked, pitted, gashed

scathing
 caustic, searing, stinging, scalding, withering, cutting, blistering, fierce, devastating, biting

scintillating
 dazzling, effervescent, flickering, gleaming, glimmering, radiant, sparkling

scorching, scorched
 searing, scalded, singed, seething, blackened, burned, parched, smoldering, steaming

searing
> blistering, scorching, scalding, singeing, seething, burning, fiery, parched, sweltering, sizzling, stinging, withering

seethe, seething
> flaring, roiled, stewing, fuming, smoldering, simmering, boiling, bristling, infuriated, livid

sensation
> tingling, tremor, undercurrent, rush, charge

sensuous, sensual
> luscious, voluptuous, luxurious, pleasurable, arousing, stimulating, pleasing, sumptuous, lush

serene
> tranquil, soothing, peaceful, calm, placid, restful, still, undisturbed

shaky
> jittery, wobbly, twitchy, unsteady, quivering, giddy, dizzy, woozy, insecure

shattering
> shocking, crushing, devastating, tormenting, stunning

shiver, shivering
> tremble, quiver, shudder, quake, quaver, tremor, twitch, twinge, shake

shocking
> stunning, distressing, alarming, startling, gut-wrenching, disgusting, horrifying

shooting
> excruciating, biting, gripping, piercing, cutting, stabbing, agonizing

shrill
> sharp, piercing, penetrating, stinging, cutting, biting, earsplitting

shrink
flinch, crouch, cringe, recoil, wince, reel, retract, shudder, retreat, quiver, tremble, squirm, wilt

shudder, shuddering
shiver, tremble, quiver, quake, quaver, tremor, twitch, cringe, reel, recoil, retract, flinch, wince, swerve, squirm

sickening
disgusting, shocking, revolting, detestable, unsettling, repulsive, repugnant, appalling

simmer, simmering
sizzling, burning, sweltering, parched, flushed, searing, singeing

singed, singeing
blistering, burning, flaring, blazing, ablaze, aflame, fiery, searing, smoldering

sizzling
blistering, boiling, flushed, heated, feverish, seething, sweltering, burning, searing, singeing

skittish
antsy, fretful, panicky, jumpy uneasy, uptight, tense, edgy, fearful, jittery, anxious, excitable

sluggish
fatigued, languid, lethargic, listless, sluggardly, leaden, stagnant

slumberous
languid, tranquil, lethargic, listless, sedated

smolder, smoldering
simmering, sizzling, sweltering, blazing, sultry, blistering, burning, searing, singeing, fiery

snuggle
nestle, burrow, cuddle, nuzzle, caress

soft, soften
fuzzy, furry, squishy, doughy, pliable, emollient, soothe, moisten, balm, lubricate

soggy
drenched, saturated, sopping, soaked, waterlogged, damp, sodden

solace
comfort, soothe, calm, relief

soothe
soften, appease, assuage, balm, calm, comfort, hush, lull, quell, smooth, subdue

soothing
tranquil, comforting, calming, consoling, pacifying, warming, peaceful

sopping
drenched, saturated, soggy, soaked, sodden, waterlogged, dripping, drowned

spasm
shudder, twitch, tremor, outburst, frenzy, convulsion, eruption, shiver, shake

spine-chilling
eerie, creepy, freakish, spooky, scary, bone-chilling, hair-raising, chilling, blood-curdling, spine-tingling, shocking

spruce
cleanse, clean, freshen, purge, scrub, wash, tidy

spurn
rebuff, reject, scorn, snub, repulse, slight, jilt

squeamish
nauseated, queasy, faint, uneasy, sickly, shaky, disgusted

squirm, squirmy

cringe, reel, recoil, retract, shudder, retreat, quiver, flinch, wince, swerve, tremble, uneasy

startled

stunned, astonished, astounded, stupefied, dazed, flabbergasted, shocked, aghast, dumbfounded, dumbstruck, thunderstruck

steamy

feverish, boiling, flaming, heated, seething, sweltering, parched, flushed, sizzling, burning, searing, singeing, sultry, fiery

steely

steadfast, unflinching, unswerving, unwavering, stony, inflexible, unyielding, gritty

stifling

windless, choking, constrictive, oppressive, squelching, sweltering, suffocating, airless

stilted

awkward, clumsy, stodgy, leaden, unwieldy, wooden

stinging

acrid, caustic, biting, bitter, acid, cutting, sharp, scathing

stirring

thrilling, rousing, electrifying, lightning, charged, energizing, exhilarating, gripping, provocative, electric

stony

detached, cold, cutting, dispassionate, distant, frosted, impassive, numb, reticent

stormy

windswept, breezy, blustery, windy, gusty, tumultuous, passionate

strained

uneasy, pinched, winced, tense, edgy, distressed, forced, awkward

strenuous
laborious, arduous, crushing, grueling, hefty, jaw-breaking, taxing, rigorous, wearisome

stuffy
musty, stale, congested, stifling, suffocating, oppressive, stagnant

stunned
astonished, astounded, staggered, stupefied, dazed, flabbergasted, shocked, aghast, dumbfounded, dumbstruck, thunderstruck

stunning
startling, alarming, arousing, frightening, unnerving, devastating, bewildering, amazing, shocking

stunted
hampered, hindered, restricted, impeded, stymied

suffocated, suffocating
stifling, choking, constrictive, oppressive, squelching, strangling, stuffy

sultry
fiery, sizzling, burning, searing, scorching, humid, sensual, sticky, smoldering, steamy

swab
refresh, lather, scrub, douse, cleanse, wipe, scrub, daub

swampy
dank, damp, dewy, humid, moist, muggy, rainy, sticky

sweaty
clammy, damp, moist, sticky, slithery, slimy, humid, muggy

sweltering
stifling, sultry, blistering, burning, fiery, melting, roasting, scalding, scorching, sizzling, boiling, parched, flushed, feverish, seething, searing, singeing

swoon, swooning
faint, tremble, quiver, shaky, dizzy, ecstatic, collapse, weak, giddy, unsteady, wobbly

tactful
gracious, polished, sensitive, perceptive, poised, deft, delicate, discreet

tactile
tangible, palpable, discernible, perceptible

tactless
crude, blunt, gauche, thoughtless, boorish, blundering, bungling, clumsy, gruff, crass

tangible
palpable, distinct, tactile, concrete, perceptible, conspicuous

tantalizing
alluring, attractive, beckoning, charming, enrapturing, enthralling, provoking, seducing, stimulating, tempting

taxing
laborious, crushing, grueling, rigorous, strenuous, wearisome, arduous

tedious
dreary, dull, lifeless, repetitive, tiresome, wearisome, monotonous, irksome

temperate
balmy, soothing, gentle, tranquil, pleasant, steady

tense
charged, rigid, stern, stiff, taut, strained, clutched, pinched

tepid
lukewarm, cool, feeble, muted, weak, dull, lifeless, languid

thrill, thrilling
   arouse, enthrall, excite, rush, surge, electrify, stimulate, enliven, kindle, charged, rousing, stirring, riveting, gripping, arresting, mesmerizing, engrossing, spellbinding, enticing, excite

throb, throbbing
   tremble, twinge, pang, grimace, pulse, vibrate, thump, aching, stabbing, piercing

thunderstruck
   startled, stunned, astonished, astounded, stupefied, flabbergasted, shocked, aghast, dumbfounded, dumbstruck, dazed

tickle, ticklish
   tingle, itchy, arouse, excite, touch, tease, prickly, scratchy

tinge
   touch, smattering, sprinkling, dash, pinch, sprinkling

tingle, tingling
   burn, shiver, tremor, twinge, itch, sting, throb, prickly, quiver, rush

tiresome
   grueling, arduous, toilsome, strained, wearying, wearisome, exasperating, irksome

toilsome
   grueling, arduous, backbreaking, irksome, tiresome, strained, wearying

tormenting
   excruciating, biting, gnawing, intense, piercing, unbearable

torpid
   lethargic, dull, numb, sluggish, languid, lackadaisical

torrid
   blistering, boiling, feverish, fiery, flushed, heated, searing, stifling, simmering, sultry, steamy, hot, sweltering

touchy
> prickly, squirmy, uneasy, antsy, fretful, uptight, volatile, sensitive, testy, edgy

toxic
> venomous, bitter, caustic, poisonous, deadly, noxious, lethal

tranquil
> soothing, temperate, composed, calm, placid, serene, undisturbed, balmy

tremble, trembling
> quiver, quake, fidget, shake, twitch, waver, wobble, cringe, flinch, wince, jitter, shiver, reel, recoil, shudder, squirm

tremor
> shiver, tremble, quiver, shudder, quake, quaver, twitch, rattle, jerk, bobble, jolt, jostle, quake, shake, throb, tic, tingle, vibrate

tremulous
> quivering, jittery, wobbly, tottering, teetering, twitchy, shivering, trembling, shaky

trepidation
> apprehension, shiver, tremble, disquiet, fright, palpitation, quiver, unrest, unease

twinge
> twitch, grimace, tweak, gnaw, throb, tremble, pang, pulse, spasm, prick, stab, jab

twitch, twitchy
> fitful, flighty, jumpy, sporadic, restless, quake, fidgety, quiver, shake, tremble, tremor

unbearable
> intolerable, unendurable, insufferable, shattering, excruciating, gnawing, tormenting

undercurrent
hint, tenor, vibe, riptide, undertow, tinge, murmur, overtone

uneasy, unease
edgy, antsy, fretful, panicky, prickly, squirmy, touchy, fitful, jittery, unsettled, unstable

unendurable
unbearable, intolerable, insufferable, shattering, excruciating, gnawing, tormenting

unflappable
immovable, flinty, unyielding, hardened, unbending, unflinching, unruffled, cool-headed, steely

unflinching
unyielding, adamant, headstrong, inflexible, refractory, resistant, steadfast, steely

unnerved
flustered, rattled, perturbed, stunned, agitated, ruffled, dismayed, disquieted

unnerving
rattling, agitating, perturbing, stunning, disquieting, disconcerting, unsettling

unruffled
calm, unflappable, composed, balanced, equanimous, placid, poised, cool-headed, collected, serene

unswerving
steadfast, unflinching, unwavering, undaunted, gutsy, determined, focused, gritty

unwavering
steadfast, unflinching, unswerving, intense, resolute, undaunted, unyielding

venomous
> bitter, caustic, cutting, toxic, poisonous, noxious, vile, hostile

vexing
> agitating, aggravating, rankling, irksome, provoking

vigor
> brute, robustness, exuberance, hardiness, vitality, zeal, intensity

visceral
> gut, instinctive, deep-rooted, deep-seated, ingrained

vitality
> vigor, brute, robustness, exuberance, hardiness, zeal

vivacious
> lively, breezy, ebullient, buoyant, sparkling, playful, effervescent, bubbly

volatile
> capricious, fickle, volatile, mercurial, explosive, erratic, unstable, turbulent, unpredictable

wallow, wallowing
> revel, luxuriate, roll, wade, tumble, splash, delight, indulge, lurch, toss, plunge

wearisome, wearying
> tiresome, exasperating, galling, pestering, toilsome, aggravating, bothersome, disturbing, provoking, troubling, laborious, arduous, grueling, taxing, strenuous, vexing, irksome

welt
> scar, blister, wound, gash, bruise, swelling, pockmark

wince
> writhe, contort, twitch, blanch, grimace, flinch, crouch, cringe, recoil, shrink, retract, shudder, retreat, quiver, tremble, squirm, reel

windless
 stifling, choking, constricting, airless, stuffy, suffocating, still

windswept
 windy, breezy, brisk, drafty, blustery, stormy, gusty

windy
 gusty, breezy, blustery, stormy, windswept, brisk, drafty

wrenching
 gut-wrenching, distressing, alarming, startling, shocking, jarring, agonizing

writhe
 contort, recoil, twitch, wince, quiver, tremble, squirm, blanch, grimace, flinch, cringe, reel, retract, shudder, convulse

yearn
 hunger, itch, pine, crave, ache, lust, thirst

Textures *and* Structures

airy
 light, subtle, flowing, languid, breezy, buoyant, windy, feathery, fluffy, willowy, wispy, soft

arid
 bone-dry, barren, dusty, parched, dry, scorched, baked, waterless, dehydrated, desiccated, shriveled, wilted, withered

armored
 unbreakable, impervious, resistant, unyielding, indestructible, shatterproof, durable

baked
 desiccated, shriveled, wilted, crisp, withered, parched, scorched, arid, dusty, waterless, dry, dehydrated

barbed
  spiny, bony, thorny, pronged, spiky, bristly, prickly, sharp, pointed

bare
  stark, unadorned, barren, naked, bald, denuded, primal, unclothed, stripped, plain

barren
  stripped, stark, plain, unadorned, sapless, bare, naked, bald, harsh, denuded

bearded
  furry, hairy, fuzzy, shaggy, feathery, downy, fluffy, woolly

bendable
  supple, flexible, lithe, willowy, rubbery, springy, limber, resilient, agile

blubbery
  thick, chunky, meaty, plump, stout, burly, heavy, doughy, fatty, heavy

blunt
  dull, rounded, abrupt, stark, worn, stubby

bone-dry
  barren, dried, dusty, parched, seared, scorched, desiccated, arid, baked

bony
  spiny, barbed, thorny, pronged, bristly, prickly, sharp, pointed, spiky

bouncy
  springy, buoyant, elastic, flexible, lithe, stretchy, willowy

braided
  textured, lattice, meshed, lacy, weaved, interlaced, twisted

brambly
> thorny, prickly, spiky, pointed, stinging, tangled, bristly, barbed, knotty

brawny
> sinewy, fleshy, muscular, rugged, buffed, ropy

bristly
> coarse, rough, bumpy, scratchy, prickly, ragged, spiny, brambly, thorny, spiky, harsh

brittle
> delicate, crumbly, fragile, breakable, crisp

buffed
> polished, silken, satiny, sleek, smooth, shiny, glossy

bulletproof
> impenetrable, impervious, indestructible, resistant, unyielding, dense

bumpy
> coarse, bristly, rough, scratchy, prickly, ragged, choppy, lumpy

burly
> plump, stout, thick, chunky, meaty, blubbery, heavy, doughy

bushy
> woody, scrubby, shaggy, bristly, furry, prickly, woolly, fuzzy

busty
> voluptuous, buxom, plump, ample, curvy

buxom
> busty, voluptuous, curvy, plump

caked
> lumpy, chunky, clotted, congealed, curdled, jelled, encrusted, bumpy

calloused
> leathery, rugged, wrinkled, weather-beaten, sinewy, ropy, tough, hardened

chalky
> dusty, crumbling, gritty, flaky, scaly, sooty, powdery

chunky
> lumpy, bumpy, caked, clotted, congealed, curdled, jelled, meaty, plump, burly, blubbery, doughy

clayey
> earthy, coarse, muddy, sandy, sticky

clingy
> gluey, sticky, gooey, gummy, tacky

clotted
> caked, chunky, lumpy, bumpy, congealed, curdled, jelled

coarse
> rough, bumpy, harsh, scratchy, bristly, prickly, ragged, textured, rugged

congealed
> lumpy, bumpy, caked, chunky, clotted, jelled, curdled

corroded
> rusted, tarnished, disintegrating, abraded, scratched, scraped

cottony
> fuzzy, soft, gauzy, silky, satiny, velvety, gossamer, plush, smooth

cozy
> plush, snug, luxurious, frilly, posh, cushy, comforting

craggy
> rugged, harsh, rough, coarse, jagged, pitted, weather-beaten

creased
 wrinkled, withered, shriveled, furrowed, grooved, aged, crinkled, ruffled, worn, leathery

crinkled
 ruffled, crumpled, tousled, tangled, disheveled, rumpled, wrinkled, scrunched

crisp
 smooth, starched, clean, brittle

crumbly
 flaky, sooty, dried, dusty, shriveled, wilted, withered, brittle

curdled
 lumpy, bumpy, caked, congealed, jelled, chunky, clotted

dainty
 airy, wispy, lacy, delicate, fragile, fine

denuded
 stripped, exposed, barren, bare

desiccated
 dry, parched, scorched, arid, dusty, waterless, dehydrated, wilted, shriveled, withered

disfigured
 mangled, crippled, lacerated, shredded, torn, scarred, defaced, distorted, gashed

disheveled
 ruffled, crinkled, crumpled, tousled, tangled, rumpled, bedraggled, slipshod, wrinkled, unkempt

distorted
 blistered, defaced, disfigured, gashed, welted, gnarled, crooked, askew, scarred

doughy
    soft, squishy, mushy, spongy, thick, chunky, meaty, plump, stout, burly, blubbery, heavy

downy
    feathery, fluffy, fuzzy, furry, velvety, woolly, fleece, shaggy, silky

dried
    bone-dry, dusty, parched, desiccated, shriveled, arid

droopy
    dangling, flapping, draped, slumped, sagging, crumpled, wilted, limp, flaccid, flimsy, wobbly, floppy, bent, flabby, slouching

dry
    parched, baked, dusty, waterless, dehydrated, desiccated, shriveled, wilted, crisp, withered, arid

dull
    blunt, worn, flat

durable
    rigid, immobile, steely, strong, stiff, solid, resistant, shatterproof, indestructible

dusty
    arid, chalky, crumbly, sooty, dried, parched, waterless, dehydrated, desiccated, powdery

earthy
    clayey, coarse, muddy, sandy, gritty, grainy

elastic
    flexible, malleable, supple, springy, bouncy, buoyant, stretchy, pliant

embedded
    entrenched, ingrained, deep-seated, lodged, rooted

feathery
> downy, flossy, fluffy, fuzzy, furry, velvety, woolly, fleecy, shaggy, airy

feeble
> flaccid, limp, weak, frail, flimsy, fragile, debilitated

fibrous
> stringy, thready, pulpy, sinewy, woody, ropy

filthy
> dirty, grimy, sticky, muddy, sooty, smudgy, grungy, soiled, cruddy, mucky

firm
> taut, stretched, tense, tight, rigid, stiff, sturdy

flabby
> droopy, flaccid, languid, flimsy, floppy, lax, baggy, limp, sagging

flaccid
> limp, droopy, flimsy, fragile, wobbly, shaky, floppy, slack

flaky
> dusty, chalky, crumbly, scaly, peeling

fleecy
> feathery, woolly, downy, fluffy, furry, shaggy

fleshy
> meaty, blubbery, rotund, plump, pudgy, stout, chunky, portly, heavyset

flexible
> pliant, elastic, malleable, supple, springy, lithe, spongy, stretchy, bendable

flimsy
> fragile, brittle, wobbly, rickety, wispy, shaky, floppy, willowy

floppy
   flimsy, wobbly, shaky, limp, willowy, slack, loose, sagging

flossy
   feathery, downy, fluffy, fuzzy, furry, velvety, woolly

fluffy
   fleecy, woolly, fuzzy, furry, downy, shaggy, hairy, feathery, velvety

fluid
   liquid, juicy, watery, flowing, runny, molten

foamy
   bubbly, frothy, velvety, soapy, fizzy, lathery

fossilized
   rigid, stiff, ossified, bony, calcified, hardened, petrified, solidified

fragile
   rickety, delicate, shaky, flimsy, brittle, wobbly, frail

frail
   withered, wilted, feeble, flimsy, delicate, brittle, tenuous, weak

frilly
   luxurious, posh, plush, trimmed, lacy, ornate, gauzy, filigree

frothy
   bubbly, fizzy, foamy, soapy, lathery, sudsy

furrowed
   wrinkled, grooved, crinkled, ruffled, creased, crumpled, fluted

furry
   fuzzy, bearded, shaggy, feathery, downy, fluffy, woolly, cottony, hairy, whiskered

fuzzy
   furry, woolly, shaggy, feathery, downy, fluffy, hairy, woolly

Touch: Textures *and* Structures

gauzy
   flimsy, thin, sheer, wispy, lacy, gossamer, papery, slinky, silken, silky

glossy
   satiny, smooth, sleek, slick, shiny, shining, gleaming, lustrous, silky, glassy

gluey
   sticky, gooey, gummy, tacky, clingy, viscous

gooey
   sticky, gummy, jellied, gluey, clingy, tacky, syrupy, viscous

gossamer
   lacy, airy, gauzy, wispy, flimsy, fine, silky, fibrous

greasy
   slippery, slimy, gunky, oily, slithery, lubricated, slick, smeared

grimy
   muddy, filthy, sooty, dingy, dirty, smudgy, grungy, soiled, mucky

gritty
   sandy, earthy, clayey, coarse, gravelly, muddy, powdery, granular

grungy
   grimy, dingy, dirty, muddy, filthy, sooty, smudgy, unkempt, greasy, gunky

gummy
   gluey, clingy, sticky, gooey, gelled, tacky, syrupy, viscous, gunky

gunky
   slimy, clammy, grungy, gluey, gooey, sticky, slithery, tacky, grimy

hairy
   furry, feathery, downy, fluffy, fuzzy, bearded, shaggy, woolly

hardy
vigorous, muscular, vital, robust, firm, hearty, rugged

heavy
thick, chunky, plump, stout, burly, blubbery, bulky, hefty, unwieldy, weighty

immobile
rigid, stern, stiff, stationary, motionless, frozen, stagnant

impervious
impermeable, airtight, impenetrable, unyielding, immutable, inflexible, refractory, resistant

indestructible
shatterproof, unbreakable, impervious, resistant, unyielding, armored, durable

inflexible
taut, rigid, dense, unyielding, immutable, impervious, refractory, resistant

infused
drenched, permeated, instilled, doused, drowned, inundated, saturated, bathed

itchy
prickly, scratchy, tingling, rough, grating

jagged
rough, coarse, cutting, scratchy, sharp, notched, irregular, pointed, spiked, serrated, ragged

jelled, jellied
gummy, gooey, gluey, clingy, sticky, tacky, syrupy, viscous

juicy
liquid, fluid, watery, flowing, moist, oozy, oily, slippery

jumbled
tangled, disordered, twisted, knotted, matted, coiled, muddled, knotty, garbled

knotted
tangled, gnarled, twisted, matted, coiled, muddled, jumbled

knotty
tangled, convoluted, jumbled, intricate, knotted, gnarled, thorny, twisted

lacy
airy, gauzy, gossamer, papery, slinky, wispy, frilly, meshed

leaden
wooden, heavy, plodding, weighty, dense

leathery
rugged, wrinkled, weather-beaten, sinewy, ropy, fibrous, tough

limber
supple, flexible, lithe, willowy, rubbery, springy, resilient, bendable, agile

limp
flimsy, floppy, droopy, flimsy, flaccid, feeble

liquid
fluid, juicy, watery, flowing, smooth, molten, moist, melted

lithe
springy, bouncy, buoyant, elastic, flexible, stretchy, willowy

loose
slack, limp, flabby, saggy, droopy, flaccid, flimsy, floppy

lubricated
smooth, oily, wet, greasy, moistened, slippery, smooth

lumpy
bumpy, caked, chunky, clotted, congealed, curdled, jelled

luscious
lush, voluptuous, luxurious, sumptuous, luxurious, smooth

lustrous
silky, satiny, smooth, sleek, slick, velvety, glossy

luxurious
cozy, frilly, posh, plush, sensual, voluptuous, lush

malleable
flexible, pliant, elastic, supple, willowy, rubbery, springy, bendable

marshy
boggy, swampy, dank, damp, dewy, humid, moist, muggy, rainy

matted
tangled, snarled, twisted, knotted, coiled, muddled, jumbled

meaty
stout, burly, blubbery, thick, chunky, heavy, plump

moistened
wet, lubricated, dampened, humid, misted

moldy
mildew, sooty, fusty, rotting, decaying

mucky
sticky, tacky, gooey, gummy, gunky, clammy, oozy

mucous
viscous, sticky, tacky, thick, gummy, gooey, oozy, slimy, mucky

muddy
earthy, clayey, sandy, grimy, dirty, filthy, sooty, smudgy, grungy, gritty

muscular
sinewy, brawny, rugged, strapping, burly

mushy
squishy, doughy, spongy, sloshy, sludgy, slushy, oozy

netted
woven, braided, lattice, laced, weaved, webbed, interwoven, lacy, meshed

oily
slimy, greasy, gooey, sticky, slithery, pomaded

ooze, oozing
drain, effuse, leach, seep, trickle, exude, emit, secrete, drip

oozy
slimy, sludgy, oily, slithery, slushy, muddy

ossified
rigid, stiff, fossilized, bony, calcified, hardened, solidified

papery
lacy, airy, gauzy, gossamer, slinky, wispy, paper-thin, flimsy

parched
seared, shriveled, singed, withered, dry, dusty, waterless, crispy, dehydrated, baked, desiccated, dried, arid

pliant, pliable
flexible, elastic, malleable, supple, springy

plump
thick, chunky, meaty, stout, burly, blubbery, heavy, doughy

plush
luxurious, frilly, posh, sensual, voluptuous, silken, silky, cottony, satiny, velvety, cozy

pockmarked
scarred, blistered, defaced, disfigured, distorted, welted, gashed

pointed, pointy
barbed, cutting, edged, stinging, sharp, piercing, thorny, spiked, pronged

porous
spongy, absorbent, permeable, squishy

posh
luxurious, cozy, frilly, plush, sensual, voluptuous

prickly
thorny, spiky, pointed, stinging, tangled, brambly, barbed, knotty, bristly, spiny

pronged
spiny, bony, barbed, thorny, spiky, bristly, prickly, sharp, pointed

protrude, protruding
bulge, jut, overhang, extend, project, poke

ragged
coarse, bristly, rough, bumpy, harsh, scratchy, tattered

razor-edged
sharp, piercing, cutting, biting, razor-sharp

refractory
inflexible, resistant, unyielding, immutable, impervious

resilient
supple, flexible, pliable, agile, durable, sturdy, buoyant, bendable

resistant
protected, immutable, unyielding, impervious, inflexible, repellent, refractory

rickety
> flimsy, fragile, wobbly, shaky, floppy, brittle, tottering, teetering, ramshackle, dilapidated, unsound

rigid
> steely, stern, stiff, tense, wooden, taut, sturdy, durable, immobile

robust
> hardy, rugged, brawny, tough, exuberant, hearty, muscular, strong, sturdy

ropy
> thready, stringy, leathery, fibrous, sinewy, pulpy, coarse

rough
> coarse, cutting, scratchy, jagged, rugged, textured, bumpy, ridged, ruffled, irregular

rubbery
> flexible, lithe, willowy, springy, bendable, elastic, pliable

ruffled
> crinkled, crumpled, tousled, disheveled, rumpled, frilly, disordered

rugged
> harsh, rough, coarse, jagged, pitted, muscular, craggy, weathered, rocky, leathery

rumpled
> ruffled, crinkled, crumpled, tousled, tangled, disheveled, crimped, creased

sagging, saggy
> floppy, slumping, droopy, crumpled, dangling, shrinking, wilted, flabby, flaccid, flimsy

sandy
> earthy, clayey, coarse, gravelly, muddy, gritty, powdery

sapless
arid, bone-dry, dried, dusty, parched, baked, sapped, shriveled, withered

sappy
sticky, tacky, gooey, syrupy, oozy, runny

satiny
smooth, sleek, slick, velvety, shiny, glossy, gleaming, lustrous, silky

saturated
doused, drenched, bathed, deluged, imbued, infused, inundated, submerged

scaly
dry, flaky, flaking, peeling, flaking, rough

scarred
scratched, blistered, ripped, torn, pockmarked, disfigured, pitted, blemished, defaced

scratchy
raspy, abrasive, scraping, chafing, gravelly, ragged, coarse, jagged, itchy

scruffy
tattered, ragged, disheveled, raggedy, ratty, unkempt, mangy, shaggy, worn

shaggy
fleecy, feathery, woolly, downy, fluffy, furry, hairy

sharp
piercing, razor-edged, pointy, penetrating, pointed, stinging, cutting, razor-sharp

shatterproof
unbreakable, impervious, indestructible, durable, unyielding, armored

sheer
thin, wispy, gauzy, translucent, gossamer, papery, lacy, flimsy

shriveled
desiccated, wilted, withered, shrunken, deflated, sunken

silken, silky
buffed, cottony, satiny, velvety, gossamer, plush, sleek, smooth

sinew, sinewy
fleshy, muscular, brawny, leathery, rugged, ropy

slack
loose, limp, flabby, sagging, flaccid, floppy, baggy, flimsy

sleek
slick, shiny, satiny, smooth, lustrous, silky, glassy, polished

slick
velvety, shiny, satiny, smooth, glossy, shining, gleaming, lustrous, silky, slippery, sleek

slimy
slippery, clammy, gummy, gunky, slithery, slobbery, sloshy, slushy, squishy, greasy, slick, gooey, oozy, oily

slinky
gauzy, gossamer, papery, wispy, lacy, airy, willowy

slippery
silky, glassy, oily, slithery, lubricated, slick, greasy, soapy

slithery
clammy, viscous, gooey, ropy, stringy, slippery, glossy, oily, sleek, soapy

slobbery
slimy, slippery, gunky, oily, slithery, sloshy, slushy, squishy, sticky, greasy, slick, sludgy, drooling, spitting, frothy

sloppy
> careless, fumbling, gawky, clumsy, blundering, muddy, messy

sloshy
> slimy, slippery, slithery, slushy, squishy, sludgy, slick, splashing, splattering, sticky

sludgy
> squishy, mushy, sloshy, spongy, slimy, slippery, slithery, slobbery, slushy, oozy

slushy
> slimy, slippery, slobbery, sloshy, squishy, clammy, mucky, oozy, sludgy

smooth
> polished, lubricated, satiny, sleek, slick, velvety, silken, buffed, creamy, glossy, silky

smudgy, smudged
> grimy, dingy, dirty, muddy, filthy, sooty, grungy, smeary, streaky

soggy
> drenched, saturated, sopping, soaked, water-logged, sodden

sooty
> chalky, muddy, dusty, grimy, dingy, filthy, smudgy, grungy

sopping
> drenched, saturated, water-logged, sodden, soggy, soaked, flooded, drowned

spiky
> prickly, bristly, thorny, ticklish, pointed, spiny, bony, barbed, sharp, pronged, sharp, pointy

spiny
> barbed, thorny, pronged, spiky, bristly, prickly, sharp, edgy, pointed

spongy
   absorbing, porous, permeable, springy, elastic, resilient

springy
   bouncy, buoyant, elastic, flexible, lithe, stretchy, willowy, rubbery

squishy
   mushy, spongy, cushiony, squelchy, soft

stark
   bare, bald, stripped, plain, barren, harsh, blunt

static
   stagnant, inert, fixed, frozen, immobile, motionless, rigid

steely
   rigid, durable, immobile, stern, stiff, taut, firm

sticky
   gluey, gooey, tacky, gummy, mucky, sappy, syrupy, viscous, mucous

stiff
   wooden, leaden, stodgy, stilted, awkward, clumsy, rigid, immobile,
   stern, tense, constrictive, turgid

stout
   blubbery, heavy, thick, chunky, meaty, plump, burly, doughy, portly,
   stocky

stretchy
   elastic, elongated, springy, bouncy, buoyant, flexible, extended,
   lithe, willowy

stringy
   ropy, straggly, wiry, lanky, gangly, bony, fibrous, sinewy, spindly

sturdy
   tough, solid, hefty, robust, durable, resilient, stiff, robust

supple
flexible, lithe, willowy, springy, agile, limber, resilient, bendable, nimble, pliant

syrupy
gooey, viscous, jellied, sticky, tacky, sappy, sugary, clingy, gummy

tacky
sticky, gooey, gummy, gluey, viscous

tangled
twisted, knotted, matted, coiled, muddled, jumbled

tattered
ripped, shredded, threadbare, torn, frayed, worn, ragged

taut
firm, stretched, tense, tight, rigid, stiff, flexed, strained

tender
soft, delicate, fragile, frail, gentle

texture, textured
braided, fabric, lattice, meshed, lacy, netting, weaved, rough

thick, thickened
chunky, meaty, plump, stout, burly, blubbery, heavy, doughy, stocky, gooey

thin
flimsy, fragile, brittle, sheer, wispy, willowy, delicate, narrow, sparse, thinning

thorny
prickly, spiky, pointy, stinging, tangled, bristly, brambly, barbed, knotty

thready
ropy, stringy, leathery, fibrous, sinewy, stranded

turgid
swollen, bloated, distended, puffy, bulging

uncoiled
unraveled, unearthed, untangled, unfurled, disentangled, flattened, unfolded, unwound

unwieldy
stilted, awkward, clumsy, leaden, wooden, cumbersome, ungainly, hefty, bulky

unyielding
immutable, impervious, inflexible, unflinching, adamant, resistant, headstrong, ironfisted, refractory, shatterproof

velvety
feathery, downy, fluffy, silken, silky, cottony, satiny, plush, sleek, creamy

viscous
sticky, tacky, thick, mucous, gummy, gooey, gluey, syrupy

voluptuous
curvy, curvaceous, shapely, buxom, alluring

waterless
parched, scorched, arid, dusty, dehydrated, desiccated, shriveled, bone-dry, wilted, withered, dry

watery
damp, moist, humid, muggy, misty, steamy, drizzly, liquid, fluid, juicy, flowing

weighty
wooden, plodding, leaden, cumbersome, heavy

well-trodden
worn, threadbare, tattered, frayed, ragged

whiskered
   woolly, furry, fuzzy, feathery, fluffy, hairy, shaggy, downy, bristly, velvety, fleecy

willowy
   wispy, lanky, lithe, supple, graceful, agile, elastic, springy

wilted
   withered, shriveled, wrinkled, shrunken, droopy, sagging

wiry
   sinewy, burly, lean, stringy, skinny, supple, ropy

wispy
   airy, dainty, flimsy, gauzy, lacy, papery, sheer, willowy

withered
   shriveled, faded, emaciated, wilted, wrinkled, shrunken, droopy, dehydrated, desiccated, sunken

wobbly
   flimsy, rickety, floppy, teetering, tottering, unsteady, unstable, shaky, ramshackle

wooden
   plodding, leaden, stiff, stilted, awkward, rigid, weighty

woody
   bushy, scrubby, stiff, fibrous, sinewy, stringy, stalky, pulpy

woolly
   furry, fuzzy, feathery, fluffy, hairy, shaggy, whiskered, downy, velvety, fleecy

worn
   threadbare, tattered, ragged, shabby, dull, frayed

wrinkled
   withered, shriveled, furrowed, ridged, crinkled, worn, creased

Movement, Pressure, *and* Speed

abrade
erode, scratch, scrape, grind, corrode, chafe, scuff, graze, grate, disintegrate, rub

adept
deft, skillful, agile, savvy, nimble, dexterous, masterful

agile
deft, adept, nimble, dexterous, light-footed, flexible, lithe

amble
totter, trudge, idle, saunter, meander, loiter, mosey, lurch, sidle, toddle, shimmy, gyrate, sashay

anchor
clamp, brace, clasp, clench, clutch, shackle, tether, strap, yoke, fasten

annihilate
obliterate, destroy, decimate, shatter, crush, demolish

backfire
backlash, repercussion, ricochet, explosion, boomerang

backlash
blowback, repercussion, backfire, boomerang, retaliation

bait
ensnare, trap, entangle, enmesh, embroil, snare, entrap, snag, lure, hook

balk
recoil, resist, flinch, shirk, reject

barricade, barricaded
obstruct, impede, blockade, defend, fortify

bash
punch, smash, strike, clobber, bang, blast, trounce, whack, wallop

bat, batter
smack, slap, swat, thump, whack, wallop, drub, bang, crack, bash, beat, pelt, pummel, jab

batten
clamp, fasten, fix, secure, tighten

beckon
gesture, flag, mime, wave, charm, tempt, entice, signal, lure, coax, summon

befall
ensue, transpire, materialize, emanate, arise, emerge

belabor
thrash, pound, thump, hammer, overwork, dwell on, overdo

bind
fetter, bridle, encumber, entangle, impede, hobble, restrain, saddle, tether, tie, yoke

blast
clobber, bang, bash, bonk, punch, smash, strike, trounce, whack

blend
churn, emulsify, stew, whisk, fuse, merge, meld, mingle, unite

blockade, blockaded
barricade, surround, besiege, isolate, seal, close off

blowback
backlash, repercussion, backfire, boomerang, retaliation

blunder, blundering
bungle, grabble, stumble, grope, flounder, botch, bobble, misstep, clumsy, cloddish, sloppy, uncouth, fumbling

bobble
> blunder, fumble, bungle, botch, stumble

bolt
> scurry, hasten, burst, scuttle, gallop, hustle, scramble, dash, rush, scamper, scoot, sprint, trot

boomerang
> ricochet, backfire, backlash, recoil, rebound, deflect

botch
> fumble, blunder, bungle, grabble, stagger, stumble, flounder

brace
> clamp, anchor, clasp, clench, clutch, grasp, grip, vise

bridle
> fetter, bind, encumber, impede, hobble, restrain, saddle, tether, tie, yoke

browbeat
> bully, harass, coerce, hound, bulldoze, pressure

brunt
> impact, force, shock, clash, onslaught, repercussion

bubble
> foam, froth, fizzle, burble, swish, effervesce, simmer, gurgle, overflow

bungle
> fumble, blunder, grabble, stagger, stumble, grope, flounder, botch

burden
> strain, load, weight, drag, encumbrance, impose, hinder, impede

burrow
> nestle, cuddle, nuzzle, snuggle

burst, bursting
spew, cascade, erupt, flare-up, outbreak, heave, pour, spit, surge, squirt, spurt

bustle, bustling
swarm, stream, spill, flit, scurry, flutter, scamper, rush

calibrate
fine-tune, adjust, align, connect, sharpen, balance, correct, fiddle with

capture
grab, grasp, grip, seize, snatch, snag, snare, entrap, lasso, rope, trap, hook, harpoon

careen, careening
hurtle, bolt, dash, crash, lurch, sway, pitch, tilt

caress
embrace, nuzzle, stroke, touch, nudge, cuddle, fondle, snuggle, squeeze

carve
chisel, engrave, mold, sculpt, shave, hew, trim

cast
fling, heave, lob, sling, hurl, pitch, toss

catapult
fling, propel, launch, blast, spur, cast, pitch, sling

chafe
rub, scrape, abrade, erode, graze, grate, chisel, scour, file, scratch, scuff, grind, rub

chain
shackle, yoke, saddle, fetter, tether, anchor, bridle, batten, hamper, harness, leash, muzzle, restrain, bind, encumber, impede, entangle

chisel

carve, engrave, mold, sculpt, shave, scrape, scuff, knead, weld, hew, shape

churn

agitate, blend, emulsify, ferment, stew, whisk, ripple, flutter, swirl, roll, ruffle

clamp

anchor, brace, clasp, clench, clutch, grasp, grip, vise, fasten, batten

clasp

clamp, clutch, envelop, grasp, grip, pin, clench

claw

chip, grasp, puncture, rip, scuff, stab, tear, scratch, dig, scrape

clench

clasp, cling, clutch, grasp, grip, clamp

cling

clutch, grasp, grip, clench, clasp, cradle, adhere, cuddle, linger, embrace

clobber

bang, blast, bonk, punch, smash, strike, trounce, whack, wallop

cloister

seclude, protect, seal, shelter, confine, enclose

clop

stomp, clump, stamp, shuffle, trot, tramp, trudge, plod

cluster

bundle, huddle, flock, gather, crowd, bunch

clutch

clench, clasp, cling, grasp, grip, clamp, anchor, brace

coalesce
> fuse, unite, merge, blend, integrate, join

coast
> glide, drift, hover, sail, skate, skim, float, waft, buoy, soar, flit, dart, flutter, dance, flicker, flurry, fly, wave

collapse
> crumble, fail, shatter, topple, disintegrate, cave in, buckle, slump, faint, fold, sag

constrain
> strap, yoke, cloister, impede, shackle, fetter, anchor, tether, hem in, hinder, leash, muzzle, hobble, hamper, cripple

contort
> wince, writhe, convulse, recoil, twitch, blanch, grimace, flinch, crouch, cringe, shrink, reel, retract, shudder, retreat, quiver, flail, tremble, squirm, twist, mangle, warp, wring, wrench

convulse
> quake, bobble, fidget, flutter, heave, joggle, quiver, shake, tremble, twitch, waver, wobble

cower
> recoil, quake, cringe, tremble, grovel, flinch, wince, shrink, hide, crouch

cradle
> rock, support, shelter, steady, embrace, cling, clutch, cuddle, grip, caress, nuzzle, encircle

crawl
> limp, amble, stagger, totter, trudge, inch, squirm, creep, drag, plod

creep, creeping
> crouching, prowling, lurching, inching, worming, slithering, groveling, skulking, wriggling, crawling, sneaking

cringe
recoil, retract, shudder, retreat, quiver, tremble, squirm, flinch, wince, reel

cripple
debilitate, sabotage, shackle, rattle, unnerve, mangle, hinder, impede, hobble, hamper

crouch
flinch, cringe, shrink, wince, reel, recoil, retract, shudder, retreat, quiver, tremble, squirm

crown
adorn, festoon, enthrone, coronate, endow, honor, anoint

crumble
churn, crush, erode, grind, pulverize, pound, grate, smash, mash

crumple
crinkle, rumple, crush, squash, smash, scrunch, crease

crush
crumble, erode, squish, grind, pulverize, squash, trample, mash, crunch

cuddle
nuzzle, touch, embrace, cling, clutch, cradle, grip, caress

dance
twirl, whirl, flap, frolic, shimmy, gyrate, twist, trot, sashay, saunter, flit, prance, waltz, strut, swing

dangle
bobble, flap, flaunt, drape, droop, flutter, unfold, toss, wag

dapple
splatter, splash, shower, speckle, slosh, sprinkle, flick, streak, fleck, speck

dart
> flit, flutter, dance, flicker, float, flurry, skate, waft, skim, soar, glide, bolt, fly

dash
> scurry, hasten, bolt, burst, scuttle, gallop, hustle, scramble, rush, scamper, scoot, sprint, trot, dart, pell-mell

debilitate
> cripple, sabotage, shackle, rattle, unnerve, paralyze, immobilize

decimate
> destroy, obliterate, shatter, explode, ruin

deface
> scar, blister, disfigure, distort, gash, welt, mar, mangle, sully

deft, deftness
> adept, nimble, dexterous, proficient, skillful

delve
> pry, dig, poke, wedge, root, ferret, wrench, wring, squeeze, extract, wrest, rummage, fish

dexterous
> skilled, proficient, agile, deft, artful, masterful, adept, nimble, smooth, facile

diffuse (v)
> spread, pour, scatter, disperse, strew, dissipate

disengage
> unravel, extract, extricate, uncoil, untangle, detach, unfasten, untie, loosen

disentangle
> extricate, extract, unravel, disengage, release, untangle, detach, unwind

disfigure, disfigured
mangled, misshaped, scarred, defaced, distorted, gashed, marred, deformed

dispel
quell, ease, allay, banish, dismiss

disperse, dispersed
spread, scatter, diffuse, unleash, fling, dissipate

dissipate
scatter, strew, unleash, fling, disperse

dither, dithering
falter, hesitate, vacillate, waver, stumble, stammer, oscillate, waffle, seesaw, fluctuate

dodge
balk, hedge, waver, wince, cringe, retract, quiver, flinch, swerve, bolt, lunge

dogged
tenacious, unflagging, determined, unyielding, persistent, firm, stubborn, hard nosed, persevering

douse
submerge, wash, lather, drench, bathe, deluge, drown, dunk, swab, inundate, saturate, scrub, rinse, cleanse, splash

drag
tug, haul, heave, lug, yank, hitch, pull, tow

drain
ooze, drip, leach, seep, trickle, exude, emanate, emit, surge, siphon

drape
dangle, flap, flaunt, droop, flutter, unfold, toss, cloak, cover, wrap, swathe, adorn

drench
saturate, awash, cover, flood, overflow, submerge, bathe, deluge, douse, drown, dunk, imbue, infuse, inundate

dribble
percolate, gurgle, seep, trickle, drip, leak, sprinkle, ooze, squirt, spout

drift
float, waft, buoy, hover, sail, skim, glide, flit, dart, flutter, dance, flicker, flurry, skate, flap, soar

drip
ooze, drain, effuse, trickle, exude, emanate, emit, leach, secrete, dribble, leak, percolate, sprinkle, seep

droop
dangle, flap, drape, wag, slump, sag, crumple, wilt, flop, wither, shrivel, dwindle, shrink

drown
dunk, infuse, drench, deluge, douse, inundate, saturate, submerge

drub
pummel, bang, flail, flap, hammer, lash, patter, pound, thump, wallop

drudgery
toil, labor, monotony, sweat, chore, grind, struggle

drum
pulsate, flutter, hammer, patter, throb, thump, vibrate

dunk
douse, drown, drench, bathe, deluge, inundate, saturate, submerge

dwindle
wilt, wither, shrivel, shrink, droop, taper, wane, ebb, subside

effervesce
simmer, swish, fizzle, bubble, burble, rustle, froth, foam, lather

effuse
exude, emanate, emit, ooze, seep, discharge, gush, radiate, flow

elongate
stretch, strain, pull, lengthen, extend, elastic, spring, protract

emanate
exude, effuse, emit, leach, ooze, secrete, spread, radiate

embody
merge, breathe, encircle, embrace, meld, express, integrate

embolden
invigorate, spur, energize, rouse, stimulate, inspire

embrace
cling, encompass, cradle, cuddle, grip, caress, nuzzle, stroke, touch, encircle, clutch

embroil
ensnare, trap, bait, entangle, enmesh, snare, entrap, snag

emergent
appearing, surfacing, developing, fledgling, budding, emanating, nascent, rising

emulsify
churn, blend, ferment, ripple, stew, whisk, soften

encompass
enclose, encircle, surround, corral, beset, envelop, cling, clutch, grip, confine

encumber
impede, hobble, restrain, fetter, bind, bridle, entangle, saddle, tie, tether, burden, strain

engrave
chisel, carve, mold, sculpt, shave, chip

enlarge
swell, expand, inflate, burst, bloat, balloon, distend

enmesh
trap, bait, entangle, ensnare, embroil, snare, entrap, snag

ensnare
enmesh, embroil, trap, entrap, bait, entangle, snare, snag

entangle
tether, tie, ensnare, trap, bait, enmesh, snag, fetter, bind, bridle, encumber, impede, embroil, snare, entrap, hobble, restrain, saddle

entrap
entangle, enmesh, snare, snag, ensnare, trap, bait, embroil

envelop
enclose, encircle, engulf, swathe, encompass, shroud

etch
imprint, impress, stamp, mark, trace, emboss, inscribe, brand

erode
crumble, crush, grind, pulverize, chafe, rub, scrape, abrade, graze

erupt
spew, burst, cascade, eject, flare-up, outbreak, heave, pour, spit, surge, squirt, spurt, explode

expand
swell, inflate, burst, bloat, balloon, enlarge, distend

explode, explosive
burst, shatter, blast, erupt, detonate, rupture, volatile, incendiary, fiery, combustible, charged, escalating

extract
> unravel, disengage, plumb, uncoil, unearth, extricate, untangle

extricate
> disentangle, extract, liberate, disengage, release

exude
> effuse, emanate, emit, leach, ooze, secrete, radiate, flow

evoke
> excite, stimulate, arouse, elicit, awaken, rouse, provoke

facile
> effortless, deft, flowing, smooth, proficient, dexterous

falter
> stumble, hesitate, reel, hedge, waver, shudder, vacillate, swerve, fluctuate, wobble, stammer

ferment
> churn, agitate, stew, fester, foam, brew, bubble, foment, froth, simmer, provoke

fetter
> bind, bridle, encumber, entangle, impede, restrain, saddle, tether, tie, shackle, constrain, hem in, hinder, leash, muzzle, yoke, hamper

fiddle
> tinker, dabble, fidget, finger, meddle, manipulate, twiddle

fidget
> fiddle, fret, twitch, jitter, wiggle, squirm, shuffle, wriggle, spasm

fish
> rummage, hunt, root, sift, cast, troll, bait, grope, fumble, ferret

fizz, fizzing
> bubbling, burbling, effervesce, simmering, swishing, frothing

flag

gesture, beckon, wave, mime, signal, undulate, flap, salute, motion, hail, warn

flail, flailing

wave, thrash, pummel, drub, flap, lash, thump, wallop, twist, flog, writhe

flap, flapping

twirl, whirl, flick, shimmy, twist, dangle, bobble, drape, droop, flutter, unfold, toss, wag, sway

flaunt

dangle, parade, flourish, flap, drape, flutter, broadcast, boast

flick

twirl, swish, flap, jerk, pluck, whisk, snap, tap

flicker

flit, dart, flutter, dance, float, flurry, skate, hover, shimmer

flinch

crouch, recoil, shrink, wince, cringe, reel, retract, shudder, retreat, quiver, tremble, squirm, writhe, contort, twitch, grimace

fling

cast, heave, lob, sling, hurl, pitch, scatter, strew, unleash, disperse, catapult, launch

flit

dart, flutter, dance, flicker, flurry, flap, wag, hover, whiz, hover, dash

float

waft, hover, sail, skim, soar, buoy, drift, glide, flit, dart, flutter, dance, flicker, flurry, skate

flood, flooded

drenched, awash, overflowing, submerged, teeming, soaked

flop
> slump, droop, sag, crumple, dangle, flutter, tumble, flap

flounce
> stomp, march, stamp, barge, clomp, clop, lurch, tramp, trudge, bounce

flounder
> fumble, blunder, bungle, grabble, stagger, stumble, grope, thrash, struggle, muddle

flow, flowing
> surge, cascade, stream, exude, gurgle, ebb, gush, rush, ooze, seep, course, trickle, rush, spring, flood

fluctuate
> shake, agitate, vibrate, oscillate, seesaw, veer, waver, undulate, vacillate, sway

flurry
> flit, flutter, dance, flicker, float, skate, burst, whirl, swirl

flutter
> flit, waft, buoy, drift, hover, sail, soar, glide, dart, dance, flicker, float, dangle, bobble, flap, unfold, toss, wag

fly
> glide, soar, sail, breeze, hover, flutter, flap, wave, circle, drift, float, swoop, zip, zoom, whoosh

fondle
> pet, cuddle, caress, grope, nuzzle, nestle, stroke, snuggle, paw

frolic
> dance, twirl, whirl, flap, shimmy, gyrate, twist, trot, sashay, saunter, prance, rollick

fry
> scorch, sear, scald, singe, seethe, burn, broil, flare, parch, smolder

fumble, fumbling
blunder, bungle, grabble, stagger, stumble, grope, flounder, botch

fuse
coalesce, unite, merge, blend, mingle, weld

gallop
scurry, hasten, bolt, burst, scuttle, hustle, scramble, dash, rush, scamper, scoot, sprint, trot

gesture
beckon, flag, mime, nudge, wave, motion, nod, signal, bow, shrug, wink, sign

glance, glancing
ricochet, rebound, deflect, graze, skim, brush, scrape, sideswipe

glide
coast, drift, hover, sail, skate, soar, skim, float, waft, buoy, flit, dart, flutter, dance, flurry, fly

glom
stick, adhere, attach, grip, clinch, hook, snatch

goad
incite, provoke, prod, badger, tease, arouse, needle, spur

gouge
lacerate, scoop, chisel, dig, scrape, gash, burrow, claw

grab
capture, grasp, grip, seize, snatch, snag, yank, pluck, wrest

grapple
wrestle, struggle, tackle, confront, grab, grasp, clash, tackle, seize

grasp
grab, capture, grip, seize, snatch, snag, wrestle, clasp, hook, seize

grate
> scrape, shred, chisel, scour, scratch, scuff, lacerate, file, chafe, rub, abrade, grind, graze

graze
> chafe, scrape, scratch, brush, abrade, shave, scuff, skim, glance, rub

grimace
> flinch, cringe, shrink, reel, retract, tremble, twinge, pang, wince, writhe, contort, recoil, twitch, blanch, shudder, retreat, quiver, squirm

grind
> crumble, crush, erode, squash, pulverize, abrade, scratch, scrape, mince, smash, grate, pound

grip
> clamp, anchor, brace, clasp, clench, clutch, grasp, vise, embrace, snag, snatch

grope
> fumble, blunder, bungle, grabble, stagger, stumble, flounder, poke, pry, fish, finger

grovel, groveling
> kneel, crawl, cower, snivel, cringe, stoop, slither, skulk, wriggle, crouch, creep

gyrate
> dance, twirl, whirl, flap, flick, frolic, shimmy, twist, trot, sashay, saunter, spin, spiral, pirouette

hammer
> pummel, drum, thump, pound, drub, bang, strike, trounce, whack

hamper
> shackle, fetter, constrain, hem in, hinder, muzzle, strap, impede, hobble, cripple, saddle, leash

harness
mobilize, tame, yoke, channel, curb

harpoon
snare, capture, entrap, lasso, lure, rope, hook, ensnare, trap, bait, entangle, enmesh, embroil, snag

haul
drag, heave, lug, hitch, tow, load, hoist

headlong
steep, precipitous, hasty, abrupt, breakneck, rushing, heedless

heave
lug, haul, fling, surge, lob, hurl, hoist, drag, yank, hitch, cast, sling, pitch

hedge
dodge, shield, cushion, sidestep, waffle, shuffle, stall, vacillate, quibble

hem in
yoke, impede, hobble, hamper, shackle, fetter, constrain, tether, hinder, leash, muzzle, strap

hew
chop, sculpt, chisel, knead, carve, shape, engrave, mold, cleave, hack, weld

hinder
impede, hobble, hamper, shackle, fetter, anchor, tether, constrain, hem in, leash, muzzle, strap, cripple, thwart

hitch
tow, drag, tug, haul, lug, tether, harness, fasten, moor, chain, yoke

hobble
fetter, bind, bridle, encumber, entangle, restrain, saddle, shackle, tether, constrain, hinder, impede, hamper, cripple

hoist
> boost, hike, lob, lift, heave, elevate

hook
> lasso, lure, rope, harpoon, ensnare, bait, entangle, enmesh, snag, embroil, entrap, snare, capture

hover
> float, waft, buoy, drift, sail, skim, glide, flit, dart, flutter, dance, flurry, skate, flicker, soar

hurl
> fling, cast, heave, lob, sling, pitch, propel

impale
> skewer, pierce, puncture, stab, spear, spike

impede
> fetter, bind, bridle, encumber, entangle, hobble, restrain, saddle, shackle, tether, constrain, hinder, muzzle, hamper, cripple

impinge
> intrude, encroach, invade, infringe, trespass, meddle, invade

imprint
> impression, stamp, mark, trace, emboss, etch, brand, emblem

improvise
> invent, concoct, ad-lib, unscripted, makeshift

incinerate
> burn, scorch, torch, cremate, destroy, ignite, combust

inert
> stagnant, dormant, still, motionless, immobile

inexorable
> relentless, incessant, unrelenting, unremitting, persistent, ceaseless, implacable, inflexible

inundate
drench, deluge, douse, drown, saturate, flood, engulf, overwhelm

jab
smack, slap, swat, thump, whack, bat, wallop, drub, poke, lunge, nudge, thrust

jerk
tug, jolt, heave, yank, wrest, shake, lurch, jolt

jiggle
shake, agitate, vibrate, fluctuate, rattle, sway, shimmy, twitch, bob, bounce

jittery
trembling, quivering, quaking, convulsing, fidgety, shaking, twitchy, flinching, wincing

joggle
waver, wobble, bobble, jerk, shake, twitch, squirm, jiggle, jostle, rattle, jolt

jolt, jolting
tremor, shiver, tremble, quiver, shudder, quake, quaver, shock, twitch, rattle, agitate, electrify

jostle
rattle, shake, joggle, scramble, elbow, jab, press, push, nudge, knock

kindle
arouse, stimulate, stir, enliven, excite, ignite, stoke, torch, fan

knead
sculpt, squeeze, weld, twist, press, shape, ply, mold, rub

knock
whack, thump, bang, bash, clash, clobber, punch, wallop

lacerate
> mangle, disfigure, shred, tear, scrape, slash, gash, lance, stab, cut, puncture, rip

lap, lapping
> splashing, swishing, sloshing, licking, swallowing, rolling, rippling, slapping

lash
> pummel, drub, flail, flap, hammer, pound, thump, wallop, whip, thrash

lasso
> snare, capture, entrap, lure, rope, trap, hook, harpoon, ensnare, bait, entangle, enmesh, snag

lather
> froth, foam, soap, scrub, douse, swab, cleanse

leach
> exude, effuse, emanate, emit, ooze, secrete, infuse, drain, seep, percolate

leak
> trickle, dribble, drip, percolate, seep, sprinkle

leash
> shackle, fetter, anchor, tether, constrain, hem in, muzzle, strap, yoke, rein, restrain, bridle

limp
> amble, crawl, stagger, totter, trudge, hobble, stumble, teeter

lob
> fling, cast, heave, sling, hurl, pitch, flip, propel, launch

lug
> drag, tug, haul, heave, yank, hitch, pull, tow, strain

lumber, lumbering
 stumble, fumble, trudge, slog, plod, shuffle, lurch, tromp, stomp, plod

lunge
 pounce, spring, swoop, dive, descend, sweep, nosedive, thrust, jab, charge, surge

lurch
 stumble, stagger, totter, pitch, careen, fumble, bumble, heave, seesaw, wobble, slide, sway

lure
 bait, entangle, enmesh, embroil, snag, snare, capture, entrap, lasso, rope, trap, hook, harpoon, ensnare

maneuver
 navigate, guide, finagle, jockey, pilot, wield, steer

mangle, mangled
 cripple, disfigure, shred, rip, twist, contort, warp, wring, wrench, writhe, tear

maraud, marauding
 loot, pillage, plunder, ransack, ravage, raid

maunder, maundering
 roam, drift, stray, wander, amble, meander

meander, meandering
 saunter, amble, idle, mosey, sidle, toddle, frolic, maunder, stroll, ramble, drift, traipse

meddle, meddling
 pry, encroach, impose, intrude, invade, snoop, tamper

meld
 merge, encircle, embrace, fuse, blend, mix, integrate, mingle

merge
meld, mingle, fuse, embrace, embody, encircle, unite, converge

mesh
tangle, knit, connect, engage, harmonize, lock

mime
beckon, flag, gesture, nudge, wave, mimic, imitate

mired
entangled, embroiled, ensnared, tangled, floundering, impeded, trapped

misstep
gaffe, blunder, stumble, miscue, topple, slip, bungle, faux pas

mold
chisel, carve, engrave, sculpt, knead, press, cast

muss
ruffle, crinkle, crumple, tousle, tangle, dishevel, rumple, churn, jumble, muddle

mutilate
shred, grind, mangle, pulverize, shave, split, tear, lacerate, maim, disfigure, rip

muzzle
shackle, fetter, anchor, tether, constrain, stifle, hinder, leash, strap, yoke, gag

needle
goad, badger, irk, taunt, bait, pester, nettle

nestle
burrow, cuddle, nuzzle, snuggle

nettle
rankle, vex, irk, provoke, gall, goad, pester, ruffle, rile

nimble
adept, agile, deft, dexterous, lithe, deft, limber, graceful

nudge
gesture, nag, press, prod, touch, elbow, flag, nestle, jab

nuzzle
caress, embrace, stroke, burrow, cuddle, snuggle

obliterate
destroy, decimate, shatter, explode, annihilate, eradicate, expunge

onslaught
brunt, impact, force, shock, clash, attack

oscillate
pulsate, drum, fluctuate, seesaw, teeter, throb, thump, vibrate

outstretched
spreading, radiating, lengthened, extended, expanded, reaching

overflow, overflowing
drenched, awash, flooded, submerged, teeming, swarming, spilling

pang
throb, tremble, twinge, grimace, vibrate, thump, ache, stab

pantomime
charade, imitate, gesture, mime, nod, salute, signal, shrug, wink

paralyze
startle, alarm, cripple, frighten, perturb, stun, unnerve, demolish, incapacitate, petrify

patter
scurry, flutter, tiptoe, tap, scuttle, trip, scamper

pell-mell
rushed, headlong, swirling, recklessly, haphazardly, hastily, chaotic

penetrate
   pierce, stab, probe, puncture, spike, prick, suffuse, perforate

percolate
   bubble, dribble, gurgle, leach, seep, trickle, drip, ooze, leak

perfunctory
   mechanical, cursory, offhand, slipshod, indifferent, disengaged, halfhearted, automatic, superficial

permeate
   soak, diffuse, drench, infuse, inundate, saturate, immerse, pervade, steep, penetrate

pervade
   imbue, permeate, drench, steep, instill, infuse, inundate, saturate

pierce
   puncture, stab, skewer, impale, penetrate, spike, perforate, cut

pitch
   fling, cast, heave, lob, sling, hurl, toss, launch, propel

pivot
   twist, twirl, wring, swivel, spin, wriggle, dance, whirl, revolve

plod, plodding
   slog, amble, trample, trudge, drag, lumber, stomp, tread

pluck
   flick, grab, joggle, wrest, yank, snatch, capture, seize, clutch, grip, grasp, snag

plunge
   swoop, dive, descend, sweep, nosedive, lunge, plummet, tumble, hurtle, sink

poke
   prod, prick, probe, pry, stab, jab, dig, nudge, thrust

pounce
  lunge, leap, dive, attack, strike, surge, spring

pound
  pummel, bang, drub, hammer, lash, patter, thump, wallop, bash

press
  nudge, nag, prod, knead, push, squeeze, squash, jam, crush, clasp

prick
  poke, pierce, probe, pry, stab, pierce, puncture, drill, perforate

probe
  poke, prick, pry, penetrate, pierce, dig, prod, sift

prod
  press, push, nudge, nag, jab, rouse, goad, poke, dig, elbow, butt

propel
  catapult, fling, launch, blast, spur, cast, shoot, thrust, throw, hurl,
  project, spur

pry
  delve, dig, poke, wedge, twist, wrench, wring, squeeze, extract,
  wrest

prying
  invasive, snooping, intrusive, meddling, pushy, nosy, snooping

pulsate
  quiver, fluctuate, heave, oscillate, throb, thump, vibrate, pulse,
  drum, beat, heave, surge

pulse
  throb, tremble, twinge, bang, vibrate, thump, quiver, twitch, surge,
  thud, pound

pulverize
  smash, grind, shatter, crush, crumble, pound, pulp, mash, mince

pummel
  bang, drub, hammer, lash, pound, thump, wallop, batter, thrash, flog, pelt, trounce

punch
  whack, thump, bang, bash, clobber, knock, wallop, blast, bonk, smash, strike, trounce

puncture
  claw, rip, stab, tear, poke, skewer, pierce, deflate, prick, rupture, lance, nick, perforate, slit

purge
  cleanse, expel, freshen, scrub, spruce, purify, eradicate, expunge, oust

purify
  cleanse, distill, filter, refine, clarify, purge

pushy
  prying, intrusive, meddling, aggressive, bumptious, forceful, offensive, overbearing, domineering

quail
  flinch, recoil, cower, cringe, tremble, shake, shrink, shudder, wince, quake

quake
  bobble, convulse, fidget, quiver, shake, tremble, twitch, tremor, shiver, shudder, sway, wobble, recoil

quaver
  tremble, quiver, shudder, quake, tremor, twitch, rattle, oscillate, wobble, sway, shake

quicken
  arouse, excite, awaken, kindle, enliven, electrify, invigorate, revive, stimulate, stir

quiver
shiver, shudder, quaver, tremor, quake, shake, tremble, twitch

rankle
vex, irk, annoy, provoke, gall, harass, inflame, nettle

rattle
unnerve, fluster, agitate, ruffle, unsettle, befuddle, bewilder, roil, disquiet, shake, spasm, sway, shudder, vibrate, shiver, jiggle

recoil
balk, dodge, retreat, tremble, waver, wince, repulse, cringe, retract, shudder, quiver, flinch, swerve, squirm, reel

reel
cringe, recoil, retract, retreat, quiver, flinch, wince, swerve, squirm, tremble, shudder

restrain
fetter, bind, bridle, encumber, impede, hobble, saddle, tether, tie, subdue, stifle, shackle

retract
retreat, recede, shrink, recoil, ebb, withdraw, wane

retreat
recoil, shrink, retract, reel, recoil, relinquish, recede, vacate

ricochet
boomerang, backfire, backlash, recoil, rebound, deflect, bounce, glance

rip
shred, tear, wring, claw, poke, puncture, stab, split, claw, wrench

ripple
churn, flutter, swirl, roll, blend, ruffle, whisk, wrinkle, splash, sway, swell, surge, undulate, wave

rock
sway, pitch, reel, totter, wobble, lurch, careen, falter, jiggle, seesaw, shake

roil
rattle, unsettle, agitate, ruffle, shake, vex, disturb

roll
ripple, churn, flutter, swirl, ruffle, whisk, revolve, circle, rock, spin, unfold, undulate

rollick, rollicking
prance, caper, frolic, romp, lively, spirited, exuberant, playful

rummage
root, fish, hunt, sift, rifle, poke, comb, scour, delve, ferret, ransack

rush
scurry, hasten, burst, scuttle, gallop, hustle, scramble, dash, sprint, bolt, trot, surge

sabotage
cripple, debilitate, wreck, ruin, hamper, torpedo, subvert

saddle
fetter, bind, bridle, encumber, entangle, impede, hobble, restrain, tether, tie

sail
float, waft, buoy, drift, hover, skim, soar, glide, dart, flutter, dance, flurry, skate, fly, breeze, flap, wave

salvage
recover, rescue, reclaim, preserve, recoup

sashay
dance, twirl, whirl, frolic, shimmy, gyrate, twist, saunter, sway, glide, prance

saunter
> amble, meander, mosey, sidle, toddle, whirl, shimmy, gyrate, trot, sashay, stroll

scamper
> bolt, burst, scuttle, gallop, scurry, hasten, hustle, scramble, dash, rush, trot, scoot, sprint

scatter
> strew, unleash, fling, disperse, dissipate, spread, disband, scramble

scoot
> bolt, gallop, dash, scuttle, scramble, rush, scamper, scurry, hasten, hustle, burst, sprint, trot

scour
> rub, scrape, buff, polish, rummage, root, comb, ransack, rummage, ferret out

scramble
> bolt, hustle, scoot, burst, rush, scamper, scuttle, gallop, scurry, hasten, sprint, dash

scrape
> grate, chisel, scour, file, scuff, abrade, scratch, grind, chafe, rub, graze

scratch
> gouge, scuff, scrape, chafe, graze, abrade, grind, corrode, rub

scrawl
> scribble, doodle, scratch, squiggle, jot

scribble
> scratch, squiggle, scrawl, doodle

scrub
> wash, bathe, refresh, lather, douse, rinse, cleanse, wipe, freshen, purge, spruce, swab

scuff
scratch, grind, rub, graze, chip, scrape, grate, chisel, scour, file, chafe, abrade

sculpt
chisel, knead, weld, hew, carve, shape, engrave, mold, shave, cast

scurry
gallop, hustle, scramble, hasten, burst, scuttle, dash, rush, scamper, scoot, sprint, trot, bolt

scuttle
scoot, sprint, scurry, hasten, bolt, burst, gallop, hustle, scramble, dash, rush, scamper

seep
ooze, leach, trickle, effuse, secrete, dribble, bleed, drip, sweat, soak, bubble

seize
grab, grasp, snatch, pounce, clutch, nab, grip, clasp, pluck

shackle
fetter, anchor, tether, constrain, hinder, leash, muzzle, hobble, hamper, cripple, yoke, chain

shake
agitate, vibrate, fluctuate, jiggle, shiver, shudder, rattle, sway, rock

shave
chisel, carve, engrave, mold, sculpt, trim, shear, graze, strip

shelter
cradle, shield, harbor, enclose, guard, screen, cushion, insulate, ward

shimmy
dance, twirl, whirl, gyrate, twist, amble, sashay, saunter, wobble

shower
splatter, splash, dapple, slosh, sprinkle, inundate, pour, spray, mist, swamp, deluge, flood

shred
grind, mangle, rip, pulverize, shave, split, tear, mutilate, lacerate, fray, strip, tatter

shudder
shiver, tremble, quiver, quake, quaver, tremor, twitch, cringe, reel, recoil, retract, flinch, wince, swerve, squirm

shuffle
amble, clop, hobble, lumber, lurch, scuffle, stagger, trudge, scrape, jumble

sidle
saunter, creep, sneak, slink, inch, edge, amble

sift
root, strain, rummage, comb, probe, winnow, sieve, trawl, filter, fish

skate
flit, dart, flutter, dance, float, flurry, glide, coast, drift, hover, sail, soar, skim

skewer
pierce, puncture, impale, stab, prick, cut, bore, slash

skim
float, waft, buoy, drift, hover, soar, glide, flit, dart, flutter, flicker, flurry, skate, sail

skulk, skulking
creep, prowl, slink, snoop, crouch, lurk, roam, sneak

slap
whack, bat, wallop, smack, swat, thump, jab, drub

slather
    smear, spread, daub, rub, wipe, smooth, coat

slump
    flop, droop, sag, crumple, shrink, plummet, slide, slouch, tumble, topple, collapse, wilt

smack
    slap, swat, thump, whack, bat, wallop, jab, drub, swipe

smash
    clobber, bang, bash, blast, bonk, punch, strike, trounce, whack

snag
    rip, entangle, enmesh, ensnare, trap, bait, embroil, snare, entrap, hook, tear

snare
    entrap, lasso, lure, rope, trap, hook, harpoon, ensnare, bait, snag, entangle, capture, enmesh, embroil

snatch
    capture, grab, seize, clutch, pluck, grasp, grip, snag, wrest, yank, nab

snuggle
    nestle, burrow, cuddle, nuzzle, caress

soar, soaring
    float, waft, buoy, drift, hover, skim, glide, flutter, dance, skate, sail, spiral

spatter
    spray, splash, splatter, slosh, sprinkle, flick, douse

spasm
    shudder, twitch, tremor, outburst, frenzy, convulsion, eruption, shiver, shake

spew, spewing
burst, cascade, eject, erupt, flare-up, outbreak, heave, pour, spit, surge, squirt, spurt

spill
flood, overflow, swarm, stream, teem, drip, splash, slosh, dribble, pour, splatter, squirt

spin
twist, wring, swivel, pivot, whirl, twirl, whorl, whisk, flutter

splash
dapple, shower, speckle, sprinkle, splatter, flick, douse, spatter, slosh, strew, slosh

splatter
splash, dapple, shower, speckle, sprinkle, flick, spatter, douse, spray, slosh

sprinkle
splatter, splash, dapple, shower, speckle, slosh, flick, pepper, spray, strew, mist, scatter

sprint
scurry, hasten, bolt, burst, scuttle, gallop, hustle, scramble, dash, rush, scamper, scoot, trot

spruce
cleanse, clean, freshen, purge, scrub, tidy, primp

spurt
surge, squirt, spew, burst, cascade, eject, erupt, heave, pour, spit

squiggle
scrawl, scribble, doodle, scratch, wiggle, curl

squirm
cringe, reel, recoil, retract, shudder, retreat, quiver, flinch, wince, swerve, tremble, uneasy

stab
   puncture, poke, claw, chip, pierce, jab, prick, spike, spear

stagger
   fumble, careen, lurch, stumble, teeter, sway, zigzag, waver, wobble, totter

startle
   alarm, arouse, paralyze, frighten, perturb, stun, unnerve, shock, jolt

stave
   avoid, avert, fend off, prevent, foil, thwart, ward, hinder, stymie, forestall

steady
   brace, quell, subdue, balance, secure, bolster, buttress, gird, prop

steep
   infuse, inundate, saturate, permeate, imbue, pervade, instill, douse, diffuse, drench, absorb, immerse, soak

stew
   churn, agitate, blend, emulsify, ferment, ripple, whisk

still
   dormant, fixed, undisturbed, immobile

stimulate
   excite, kindle, arouse, stir, enliven, provoke, thrill, spark, trigger, electrify

sting
   tingle, jab, prick, bite, pierce, stab, poke, burn

stir
   arouse, stimulate, enliven, excite, kindle, provoke, thrill, vex, rustle, agitate, spur, propel

stomp
> amble, barge, clump, clop, flounce, scuffle, shuffle, stagger, tramp, trudge

strap
> shackle, fetter, anchor, tether, leash, muzzle, harness, yoke

strew, strewn
> scatter, unleash, fling, disperse, dissipate, litter, toss, sprinkle

strike
> clobber, bang, punch, smash, trounce, whack, lash, collide, knock, pummel, hammer, pound

stroke
> caress, embrace, nuzzle, soothe, pet, comfort, brush, paw, fondle

struggle
> grapple, fiddle, wrestle, tackle, fumble, blunder, bungle, flounder, botch

stumble
> bungle, stagger, flounder, wrestle, grapple, fiddle, tackle, blunder, botch, fumble

stun
> startle, alarm, arouse, frighten, perturb, unnerve, shock, paralyze, daze, overpower

stunt, stunted
> hamper, hinder, restrict, impede, curb, thwart, bridle, constrain

stupor
> trance, rapture, musing, reverie, daze, bewilderment, swoon

stymie
> obstruct, hinder, hamper, thwart, crimp, confound, foil, constrain, restrain

submerge
drench, bathe, deluge, douse, drown, inundate, saturate, cover, flood, dunk

surge
erupt, spew, burst, cascade, eject, flare-up, outbreak, heave, pour, spurt, rush

swaddle, swaddled
swathe, cover, wrap, sheathe, bind

swat
smack, slap, thump, whack, bat, wallop, jab, drub, slug, knock, paw, crush

swathe, swathed
swaddle, wrap, cover, bind, drape, sheathe

sway
shake, swing, vibrate, fluctuate, jiggle, shiver, shudder, rattle, roll, wobble, lurch

swell
expand, inflate, burst, bloat, balloon, enlarge, distend, bulge, surge, fatten, billow, intensify, puff

swerve
veer, lurch, weave, careen, totter, stray, sidestep, zigzag

swirl
ripple, churn, flutter, blend, whisk, eddy, billow, spiral, revolve, flow, spin, twirl, whirl, snake

swish
effervesce, rustle, bubble, burble, hiss, whistle, rush

swivel
twist, contort, twirl, wring, spin, pivot, wiggle, whirl, flail, revolve, swing

swoon
faint, tremble, quiver, collapse, weaken, fade

swoop
plunge, dive, descend, sweep, nosedive, lunge, pitch, slide

tackle
grapple, wrestle, grab, seize, block, halt

tamp
ram, cram, wedge, jam, shove, squeeze, crush, squash

tear
claw, puncture, rip, stab, mangle, lacerate, shred, sever, mangle, slash, cut, claw

teem, teeming
abound, bristle, bustle, flood, overflow, swarm, stream, spill

teeter, teetering
shaky, flapping, quivering, jittery, tottering, wobbly, twitchy

tether
anchor, bridle, chain, harness, leash, restrain, shackle, yoke, fetter, bind, saddle, tie

thrash
pound, thump, hammer, writhe, jerk, flail, trounce, pummel, batter

thump
pulsate, drum, hammer, oscillate, patter, throb, vibrate, pound, thrash

thwart
obstruct, hinder, hamper, stymie, dodge, impede, curb

toddle
saunter, amble, idle, meander, mosey, sidle, teeter, totter

toss
dangle, bobble, flap, flaunt, drape, droop, flutter, unfold, wag, fling, lob, pitch

totter, tottering
limp, amble, stagger, trudge, teeter, lurch, careen, stammer, sway, zigzag, weave

tousle
ruffle, crinkle, crumple, muss, tangle, dishevel, rumple

traipse
amble, stroll, roam, trudge, trek, plod, wander, shuffle

trammel
barricade, impede, shackle, fetter, obstruct, constrain, hamper, bridle, entrap

trap
enmesh, embroil, ensnare, bait, entangle, snare, entrap, snag, hook, ambush, entangle

trickle
dribble, drip, leak, percolate, seep, sprinkle, ooze

trigger
provoke, activate, precipitate, launch, instigate, stir

trot
frolic, shimmy, gyrate, twist, sashay, saunter, scamper, scurry, scuttle

trounce
clobber, bang, bash, blast, bonk, punch, smash, strike, whack, drub, whip, thrash

trudge
limp, amble, crawl, stagger, totter, prod, slog, stumble, tromp, wade

twiddle
doodle, fiddle, twist, jiggle, twirl, fidget, putter, tinker

twirl
gyrate, twist, swirl, whirl, wind, wring, swivel, spin, pivot, wriggle, squirm, dance, flap, flail

twist
contort, mangle, twirl, warp, wring, swivel, spin, pivot, wriggle, squirm, wrench, whirl, flail, writhe

upsurge
gush, outpouring, surge, groundswell, escalation, upswing, torrent, cascade, burst, rush

unfaltering
unswerving, steady, undivided, unbroken, unflagging, focused, intent, determined, unwavering, tireless, unfailing

unflagging
unbroken, unswerving, unbending, direct, focused, inexhaustible, unceasing, unrelenting, tireless

unfold
flap, flutter, spread, unfurl, unravel, uncurl, unwind, fan out

unfurl
unfold, unravel, unwind, flap, spread

unleash
scatter, strew, fling, disperse, dissipate, vent, discharge, unchain

unnerve
cripple, debilitate, sabotage, shackle, rattle, startle, arouse, flinch, perturb, stun

unravel
disengage, extract, plumb, uncoil, unearth, untangle, unwind, disentangle, unsnarl

unswerving
>   undivided, unbroken, unflagging, focused, intent, determined, unfaltering, steady, unwavering

untangle
>   extricate, extract, unravel, disengage, untwist, disentangle, unknot, uncoil, untie

unwavering
>   unswerving, unfaltering, unshaken, steadfast, unflappable, sustained, unyielding, constant

vibrate
>   pulsate, drum, flutter, hammer, oscillate, throb, thump, tremble, twinge, pulse

vise
>   clamp, anchor, clasp, clench, clutch, grasp, grip

waffle
>   waver, dither, falter, wobble, vacillate, oscillate, hem and haw

waft
>   flutter, flit, drift, hover, sail, skim, puff, glide, dance, flicker, float, flap

wag
>   dangle, flap, drape, flutter, unfold, toss, fly, jangle, whirl, flop

wallop
>   hammer, pummel, bang, drub, pound, thump, punch, belt, slam

wandering
>   meandering, roving, nomadic, winding, roaming, drifting, wayfaring, vagabond, straying, vagrant

warp, warped
>   twist, contort, mangle, wring, wrench, writhe, distort, deform

waver, wavering
> quake, fidget, falter, quiver, shake, tremble, twitch, wobble, waffle, vacillate, hedge, teeter

wayfaring
> meandering, roving, nomadic, winding, drifting

whack
> thump, bang, bash, clash, clobber, knock, punch, wallop

whip
> lash, thrash, goad, provoke, flog, rouse, agitate, provoke

whir, whirring
> hum, fly, buzz, revolve, flutter, swish, vibrate

whirl, whirling
> twirl, spin, flap, ripple, dart, whorl, whisk, flutter, swirl, pivot, revolve, circle, surge, whir, bustle

whirlwind
> tornado, hurricane, vortex, cyclone, twister, lightning, whirlwind, eddy

whisk
> churn, dart, whip, flick, sweep, hurtle, snatch, pluck, bolt, race, gallop, zoom, scuttle, scurry, zip

wiggle
> squirm, twitch, twist, writhe, wriggle, jiggle, flail

wince
> writhe, contort, twitch, blanch, grimace, flinch, crouch, cringe, recoil, shrink, retract, shudder, retreat, quiver, tremble, squirm, reel

wobble
> shake, flop, teeter, sway, totter, rock, sway, seesaw, quiver, careen, tremble, waver

wrench
twist, wring, jerk, tug, yank, rip, wrest, dislodge, twist, heave

wrestle
grapple, fiddle, struggle, tackle, fumble, scuffle, tangle, stumble, tussle, grab

wriggle
twist, twirl, wring, swivel, pivot, squirm, wiggle, writhe, flail, slither

wring
twist, tear, claw, rip, wrench, squeeze, scrunch, knead, wrest

writhe
contort, recoil, twitch, wince, blanch, grimace, flinch, cringe, reel, retract, shudder, retreat, quiver, tremble, squirm

yank
pluck, flick, grab, joggle, wrest, snatch, wrench, seize

yoke
shackle, fetter, anchor, tether, constrain, hem in, hinder, leash, muzzle, strap

TASTE

An apple is an excellent thing — until you have tried a peach.
—George du Maurier, illustrator and novelist

FLAVORS - MOUTHFEEL *and* TEXTURE -
EATING, CHEWING, *and* FOOD

Taste is strongly connected to our instincts and emotions—
our innermost pleasures, desires, and dislikes. Taste words,
such as *bittersweet, spicy, sour, juicy*, can describe our experiences
and memories in flavorful terms. We may find some situations
unpalatable or *distasteful*, or they leave a *bad taste* in our mouths,
or have a peculiar *aftertaste*, while we find other experiences
delicious or intoxicating. We may hunger for excitement or relish
adventure—and salivate in anticipation.

Taste is a blend of flavors, textures, temperatures, smells, and
even ambiance. This explains why some things taste better with
the right mood or tempting aroma. The five basic tastes—*sweet,
sour, salty, bitter, savory*—combine into an astonishing array of
flavors of varying intensity, from *floral* to *acrid* to *tangy*, to entice
our palates. The texture and mouthfeel of food—whether

something is *creamy*, *rubbery*, *runny*, or *crispy*—profoundly affect our taste and enjoyment of food. Smell also intensifies and colors our experience of taste, so much so that taste is inextricably tied to smell.

Curiously, sense of taste is also connected to personal aesthetics and decorum. We call some things *tasteful*, when we find them pleasing and stylish, or *tasteless*, *unsavory*, or *in bad taste* when they insult our sensibilities. We may think someone has *good taste* in selecting cars or belt buckles, or *poor taste* in their choice of lampshades or lawn ornaments—a highly subjective assessment or perhaps an *acquired taste*.

The taste words in this book are divided into subcategories to help readers reflect on different facets of this intriguing sense: the range and subtleties of flavors; the mouthfeel and textures of foods; and the many words to describe eating, drinking, and chewing. Bon appétit!

FLAVORS

acerbic
    sour, bitter, sharp, biting, caustic, astringent, tart, acrid

acidic
    sour, sharp, burning, caustic, vinegary

acrid
    acidic, bitter, sharp, tart, sour, biting, pungent, stinging, burning, harsh

aftertaste
    finish, sensation, impression, zing, punch

aged
mellow, rich, flavorful, softened, ripe, soft, rounded, smooth

almond
nutty, toasted, sweet, delicate

apple
fruity, sweet, tart, berry, plummy, bright, sour, mellow

astringent
harsh, sharp, acerbic, acid, dry, cutting, biting, bitter

banana
fruity, sweet, tropical, starchy, luscious

beefy
meaty, gamy, fleshy, savory, hearty, pungent, salty

berry
sweet, fruity, plummy, sugary, mellow, rich, tart

bitter
acerbic, pungent, sharp, harsh, acrid

bittersweet
bitter, rich, coffee, burnt, sweet, chocolate

blackened
seared, scalded, burnt, crispy, scorched

bland
flavorless, tasteless, flat, dull, insipid, mushy, weak, watery

bouquet
floral, perfumy, fruity, flowery, spicy

brackish
salty, briny, piquant, saline, salted

bright
lively, flavorful, zesty, sparkling, effervescent, bubbly, intense

briny
salty, brackish, seaweed, saline, kelp, dulse

brisk
refreshing, fresh, crisp, lively, bracing, invigorating, stimulating

burnt
crispy, blackened, toasted, scorched, seared, charred, scalded, singed

butterscotch
buttery, creamy, sweet, caramel, toffee, candied, sugary, luscious

buttery
creamy, smooth, luscious, caramel, smooth, rich, milky, velvety, gooey, fluffy

candied
sweet, honey, syrupy, sugary, sticky, grainy, sugar-coated

caramel
candied, buttery, creamy, honey, syrupy, sweet, toffee, bonbon

caustic
acidic, biting, burning, scalding, cutting, pungent, tart, corrosive, acrid

cheesy
creamy, melting, sharp, rich, buttery, gooey, luscious, nutty, salty

cherry
berry, juicy, sweet, sour, perfumy, fruity

chocolaty
cocoa, sweet, rich, buttery, creamy, bitter, milky, bittersweet

cinnamon
  spicy, apple, sweet, allspice, aromatic

citrus, citrusy
  lemony, acidic, sour, citron, orange, bergamot, zesty, pungent, tangerine, lively, crisp

cloying
  sugary, syrupy, oversweet, nauseating, gooey, honey, sappy

cocoa
  sweet, rich, bitter, bittersweet, mocha

coffee
  bitter, burnt, toasted, mocha, chocolate, espresso

creamy
  buttery, smooth, silky, luscious, whipped, velvety, milky

crisp
  fresh, cool, refreshing, invigorating, bracing, brisk, citrus

delectable
  delicious, luscious, mouth-watering, tasty, succulent, scrumptious, sumptuous, toothsome

delicate
  soft, subtle, exquisite, silky, tender, mild, smooth

delicious
  delectable, flavorful, scrumptious, mouth-watering, lip-smacking, enticing, luscious, tempting

dirt
  sandy, muddy, gritty, grainy, earthy, clayey

dull
  bland, insipid, flat, stale, muddy, plain, flavorless

earthy
grassy, mineral, muddy, dirt, mossy, robust, rustic, savory

eggy
creamy, velvety, rich, buttery, fluffy

enticing
delicious, luscious, tempting, delectable, flavorful, scrumptious, mouth-watering, lip-smacking

exotic
spicy, flavorful, fiery, zesty, piquant, tangy, enticing

exquisite
delicate, luxurious, intense, rich, subtle

fatty
greasy, oily, buttery, slippery, gristly, lardy, unctuous

fermented
sour, alcoholic, fizzy, hoppy, salty, briny, overripe

fetid
rotten, rancid, rank, putrid, stinking, fusty, repulsive, revolting, rotting, foul

fiery
spicy, hot, burning, scorching, biting, sharp, piercing

fishy
meaty, gamy, fleshy, seaweed, kelp

flat
dull, bland, flavorless, stale, weak

flavorful, flavorous
lively, zesty, zingy, spicy, rich, tasty, savory, delectable, luscious, tempting, pleasing, pungent

flavorless
dull, flat, bland, insipid, tasteless

fleshy
meaty, gamy, plump, beefy, savory

floral
flowery, perfumy, grassy, bouquet

flowery
floral, perfumy, fruity, bouquet

fresh
cool, crisp, brisk, invigorating, raw, lively, ripened, flavorful

fruity
sweet, tropical, berry, plum, citrus, apple, cherry

full-bodied
rich, robust, flavorful, hearty, concentrated, heady, heavy, potent, bold

fusty
musty, stale, dusty, moldy, damp, mildewy, fetid

gamy
meaty, beefy, fleshy, pungent, strong, tainted

garlicky
oniony, savory, pungent, sharp

gingery
peppery, candied, sugary, bold, sharp

glazed
candied, sugary, syrupy, gooey, honey, confectionery

grassy
herbal, oniony, mossy, earthy, botanical

gristle, gristly
  fatty, oily, fleshy, meaty, fibrous, sinewy, tough

heady
  intoxicating, stimulating, alcoholic, potent, powerful, robust

hearty
  robust, rich, flavorful, satisfying, filling

herbal, herbaceous
  zesty, spicy, peppery, tangy, grassy, floral

honey, honeyed
  sweet, candied, syrupy, sugary, toffee, caramel

hot
  fiery, spicy, scalding, scorching, burning, zesty, seasoned

insipid
  bland, dull, flavorless, flat, tasteless, stale, watery

intoxicating
  heady, potent, alcoholic, strong, bracing

invigorating
  crisp, fresh, refreshing, quench, lively, sparkling

jammy
  fruity, floral, bouquet, plummy, berry, sweet

jejune
  dry, unnourishing, dull, insipid, meager, bland

juicy, juiciness
  mouth-watering, succulent, ripe, moist, syrupy, pulpy

lemony
  sour, citrus, citron, piquant, sharp

licorice
> anise, fennel, spicy, aromatic, candied

lip-smacking
> delectable, flavorful, scrumptious, mouth-watering, delicious, sumptuous, enticing

liquor
> stiff, bracing, smooth, alcoholic, malty, whiskey, elixir

lively
> bright, sparkling, refreshing, crisp, bracing, fresh, invigorating, zesty

luscious
> creamy, buttery, silky, smooth, delectable, sumptuous, toothsome, succulent, appetizing

malty
> alcoholic, fizzy, hoppy, yeasty, sudsy, foamy

meaty
> fleshy, thick, plump, robust, savory, hearty, beefy, pungent

medicinal
> menthol, metallic, plastic, off-flavor, aftertaste, bitter, artificial

mellow
> rich, smooth, soft, soothing, aged, full, round

melting
> creamy, smooth, velvety, silky, buttery

menthol
> cool, minty, crisp, invigorating, wintergreen, peppermint, fresh

metallic
> metal, copper, mineral, medicinal

mildewy
stale, damp, dusty, moldy, musty, funky, rotten, fusty

milky
creamy, thick, buttery, rich, velvety

mineral
complex, salty, earthy, coppery, rich, smooth

minty
cool, crisp, invigorating, menthol, wintergreen, peppermint

mocha
coffee, bitter, burnt, toasted, chocolate, espresso, cocoa

moldy
mildewy, musty, stale, damp

mouth-watering
delectable, juicy, scrumptious, succulent, luscious, savory, tempting

muddy
earthy, gritty, sandy, dirty, grainy, soggy, swampy

mushroom
rich, earthy, muddy, savory, umami, pungent, meaty

mustard
pungent, sharp, spicy, oniony, garlicky, sour, bitter, zippy

musty
stale, fusty, damp, moldy, skunky, dusty, mildewy

nectar
sap, honey, tonic, juice, elixir, ambrosia

nutty
crunchy, almondy, toasted, buttery, crispy, sweet

Taste: Flavors

oaky
woodsy, woody, smoky, complex, rich, bitter

off-flavor
stale, contaminated, rotten, funky, unpleasant, tainted, musty

oily
greasy, fatty, unctuous, buttery, creamy

oniony
garlicky, savory, pungent, sour

overpowering
pungent, spicy, intense, acrid, robust, potent

overripe
astringent, rotten, spoiled, rotting, sour, rancid

oyster
briny, salty, savory, umami, meaty, clam, shrimp, seaweed, fishy

palatable
tasty, flavorful, pleasing, agreeable, appetizing, enticing, tempting

penetrating
stiff, sharp, biting, piercing, potent, intense, bracing

peppermint
menthol, cool, minty, crisp, invigorating, wintergreen, fresh

peppery
spicy, savory, fiery, gingery, pungent, zesty, hot, stinging

perfumed, perfumy
floral, bouquet, flowery, fragrant

pickled
salty, spicy, fermented, cured, vinegary, briny

piney
wintergreen, grassy, floral, perfumy, rosemary, sharp

piquant
spicy, tangy, savory, zesty, rich, sharp, peppery

plummy
fruity, floral, raisiny, wine, bouquet, jammy

potent
heady, intoxicating, pungent, intense, penetrating

pungent
bitter, piquant, sharp, spicy, overpowering, peppery, stinging, tangy, zesty

putrefied
rotten, decayed, decomposed, stinking, festering, spoiled

putrid
rotten, rancid, rank, fetid, foul, rotting

rancid
fetid, spoiled, putrid, rank, moldy, rotting, curdled, sour

rank
rotten, rancid, putrid, fetid, noxious, sour, tainted, foul

raw
fresh, uncooked, unrefined, natural, lively, energizing, robust

refreshing
lively, brisk, bracing, invigorating, quenching, sharp, sparkling, bright, crisp

rich
flavorful, velvety, robust, juicy, savory, succulent, full-bodied, nourishing

ripe
  sweet, succulent, luscious, moist, tender, juicy

robust
  bold, flavorful, rich, full-bodied, potent

rotten
  putrid, rancid, rank, fetid, rotting, moldy, foul, sour

saccharine
  sugary, cloying, oversweet, artificial, medicinal, syrupy

salty
  piquant, spicy, savory, zesty, briny, pungent

sapid
  delectable, ambrosial, pleasing, engaging, tasty, zesty, palatable, enticing

sapor
  flavor, taste, essence, zest, extract, savor, tang, zing

savory
  piquant, succulent, zingy, tangy, umami, pleasing, pungent, spicy, zesty, enticing

scrumptious
  delicious, luscious, mouth-watering, tasty, succulent, delectable, tempting, enticing

seared
  burnt, charred, crispy, blackened, toasted, scorched

seasoned
  flavorful, rich, zesty, spicy, savory, tasty

seaweed
  fishy, piscine, briny, kelp, salty, saline

sharp
tart, tangy, astringent, sour, pungent, intense

silky
creamy, smooth, velvety, buttery, delicate, silken

skunky
musty, swampy, bitter, mossy, moldy, dank, musty, perfumy, tainted

soapy
sudsy, bubbly, tallow, waxy, foamy, frothy

soft
chewy, delicate, doughy, buttery, fluffy, velvety, mellow

sour
acerbic, lemony, vinegary, tart, sharp, puckering, rotten

sparkling
effervescent, lively, bright, invigorating, refreshing, crisp

spicy
fiery, hot, exotic, tangy, rich, pungent, peppery, savory, piquant
zesty, stinging, seasoned

stale
dry, musty, rancid, fusty, flat, moldy, sour

succulent
tender, delectable, delicious, luscious, mouth-watering, toothsome,
appetizing, juicy

sugary
sweet, syrupy, candied, honey, gooey, sticky, grainy, toffee, caramel,
oversweet, confectionery

sulfur
rotten egg, metallic, skunky, rubber

TASTE: FLAVORS

sumptuous
luscious, delectable, succulent, rich, appetizing, exquisite

swampy
mossy, spongy, damp, marshy, muddy, skunky, moldy

sweet
sugary, syrupy, honey, gooey, candied, caramel, toffee

syrupy
sugary, sweet, sticky, gooey, honey, gummy, sappy

tallow
waxy, soapy, sudsy, fatty

tangy
spicy, piquant, rich, sharp, pungent, peppery, zesty, salty, seasoned, tart

tart
sharp, lemony, vinegary, sour, biting, acidic, caustic

tasteless
flavorless, flat, dull, insipid, bland, weak, watery, stale

tasty
delicious, luscious, mouth-watering, delectable, succulent, flavorful, enticing, tempting

tempting
enticing, delicious, luscious, delectable, flavorful, scrumptious, mouth-watering, tasty, lip-smacking

tender
succulent, ripe, juicy, moist, delicate, soft

toasted, toasty
buttery, crusty, yeasty, crispy, nutty, roasted

toffee
buttery, creamy, sweet, caramel, butterscotch

tonic
refreshing, restorative, soothing, juice, nectar, stimulant, elixir, remedy, nourishing

toothsome
succulent, delectable, delicious, luscious, mouth-watering, savory, palatable, rich, scrumptious, tempting

turpentine
lacquer, metallic, synthetic, pungent, sharp

umami
savory, salty, piquant, tangy, mushroom, pungent

unappetizing
unappealing, undesirable, insipid, unpalatable, vapid, unsavory, repulsive

vanilla
sweet, fragrant, creamy, buttery, toffee, caramel

vapid
insipid, jejune, tasteless, flavorless, flat, dull, bland, weak

velvety
creamy, smooth, buttery, silky, luscious, whipped, rich, silken

vinegary
sour, acidic, sharp, briny, pickled, fermented

wine
sweet, dry, fruity, liquor, alcoholic, bouquet, oaky, intoxicating

wintergreen
cool, minty, crisp, invigorating, menthol, peppermint, piney

woody
  grassy, earthy, mossy, stringy, oaky

yeasty
  hoppy, fermented, frothy, fizzy

zesty
  zingy, tangy, spicy, pungent, flavorful, peppery, fiery, zippy

zingy
  zesty, flavorful, rich, tangy, spicy, peppery, lively

zippy
  flavorful, tangy, spicy, bright, flavorful

MOUTHFEEL *and* TEXTURE

astringent
  dry, drying, sharp, bitter, acrid, biting, harsh

baked
  soft, doughy, roasted, crusty, stewed

biting
  acerbic, stinging, caustic, acidic, cutting, fiery, sharp

boiling
  scorching, scalding, burning, hot, seared, sizzling, stinging

bracing
  cold, icy, refreshing, biting, frosty, invigorating, crisp, lively

bubbly
  frothy, effervescent, fizzy, sudsy, sparkling, lathery

burning
  scorching, scalding, boiling, acidic, caustic, fiery, tingling, searing

caustic
acidic, biting, burning, scalding, abrasive, pungent, acrid

chalky
gritty, powdery, granular, grainy, mealy, sandy

chewy
doughy, soft, crusty, crispy, crumbly, fibrous

chilled
cool, cold, frosty, icy, frosted

coarse
crunchy, scratchy, rough, grainy, lumpy, bumpy, rough

cold
icy, bracing, chilled, frosty, crisp, cool

congealed
lumpy, curled, thick, bumpy, clotted, gelled, glob, coagulated

cool
crisp, minty, chilled, icy, numbing, menthol, refreshing, stimulating

creamy
buttery, smooth, silky, luscious, whipped, velvety, milky, silken

crisp
fresh, cool, refreshing, invigorating, bracing, tart, tangy

crispy
crunchy, crusty, flaky, brittle, crumbly, dry

crumbly
crispy, flaky, brittle, crusty, powdery, crunchy

crunchy
crispy, crusty, nutty, crumbly, brittle

crusty
> flaky, crispy, brittle, dry, crunchy

curled
> congealed, lumpy, thick, bumpy, clotted, blobby, gelled

delicate
> soft, subtle, exquisite, silky, tender

desiccated
> dry, parched, baked, scorched, dusty, shriveled

dry
> desiccated, parched, gritty, chalky, astringent, crumbly

effervescent
> frothy, bubbly, sparkling, fizzy, foamy, carbonated

fatty
> greasy, oily, heavy, gristly, blubbery, unctuous

fizzy
> bubbly, effervescent, frothy, foamy, sudsy, sparkling, lathery

flaky
> crispy, crusty, pastry, crumbly, brittle

fleshy
> meaty, gamy, beefy, plump, blobby

foamy
> frothy, whipped, sudsy, whisked, fizzy, bubbly, lathery

frothy
> foamy, fizzy, whipped, bubbly, effervescent, sudsy, lathery

full
> satisfying, round, thick, rich, smooth, full-bodied, robust

gelatinous
> jellied, congealed, sticky, viscous, glutinous, clotted, gelled

gooey
> sticky, gummy, syrupy, tacky, sugary, slimy, gluey

greasy
> oily, fatty, slimy, buttery, slimy, gristly

gristle, gristly
> fatty, oily, fleshy, greasy, fibrous, tough, chewy

gritty
> sandy, chalky, mealy, powdery, grainy, granular

gummy
> sticky, gooey, syrupy, tacky, gluey

heady
> potent, alcoholic, exhilarating, intense, strong, intoxicating

heavy
> fatty, greasy, oily, full, ample, laden

hot
> fiery, spicy, scalding, scorching, burning, biting, peppery, stinging

icy
> cold, bracing, frosty, frozen, crisp, numbing

juicy
> mouth-watering, succulent, ripe, moist, watery

lukewarm
> tepid, cool, flat, dull

lumpy
> congealed, curled, thick, bumpy, mushy, clotted, gelled, blobby

mashed
creamy, soft, pureed, smooth, pulpy, pasty, crushed, minced

mealy
dry, powdery, gritty, chalky, crumbly, grainy

meaty
fleshy, thick, gamy, beefy, rich, full, savory

mellow
rich, smooth, soft, delicate

melting
creamy, smooth, velvety, silky, buttery, silken

milky
creamy, thick, buttery, silky, velvety

minced
mashed, pureed, diced, ground, crushed

moist
juicy, succulent, tender, watery

muddy
earthy, gritty, sandy, mealy, grainy, spongy, swampy

mushy
sloppy, lumpy, runny, soft, squishy, pulpy, mashed, slushy, spongy, doughy

nourishing
refreshing, restorative, soothing, stimulating, energizing, tonic

numbing
icy, biting, bracing, cool, frozen

oily
greasy, fatty, unctuous, buttery, slippery, smeary, slimy, creamy

parched
desiccated, dry, baked, scorched, shriveled, dried

pasty
gummy, gluey, chalky, sticky, doughy, gooey, starchy

powdery
chalky, mealy, gritty, grainy, sandy, granular, crumbly

plump
meaty, round, full, fleshy, beefy

prickly, prickling
stinging, tingling, burning, piercing, tickling

puckering
sour, acidic, vinegar, astringent, tart

pulpy
mushy, stringy, sloppy, lumpy, runny, slushy

quenching
invigorating, refreshing, satiating, moistening, cooling, appeasing, satisfying

refreshing
lively, brisk, bracing, invigorating, quenching, sparkling, satisfying, crisp

rubbery
chewy, tough, leathery, spongy, squishy, pulpy

runny
watery, thin, soupy, slurpy, slushy, soggy, tasteless, weak, sloppy, dripping

sandy
gritty, crumbly, powdery, grainy, powdery

scalding
> boiling, burning, scorching, blistering, piping, steaming, sizzling, fiery, stinging

scorched
> seared, blackened, charred, scalded, singed, burnt

scorching
> boiling, scalding, blistering, sizzling, burning, stinging, charred, fiery

silky
> creamy, smooth, velvety, buttery, melted, silken

slimy
> slobbery, slippery, greasy, gooey, slick, oozy, mucous

slippery
> slimy, greasy, oily, gooey, slick, smooth

slobbery
> slimy, slippery, slurpy, salivating, frothy, dribbling, drooling, runny

sloppy
> slushy, slurpy, runny, watery, messy, sludgy, oozy, muddy

slurpy
> slushy, sloppy, runny, watery

smooth
> creamy, velvety, silky, mellow, rich, buttery, soothing

soapy
> sudsy, bubbly, tallow, waxy, foamy, lathery, frothy

soft
> chewy, delicate, doughy, buttery, tender, squishy, fluffy, spongy, mushy

soggy
mushy, pulpy, sloppy, squishy, runny

soupy
watery, thin, runny, slurpy, soppy

sparkling
effervescent, lively, bright, invigorating, refreshing, bubbly, fizzy

stale
hard, dry, musty, rancid, fusty, flat, moldy

starchy
glutinous, doughy, bready, heavy

steamy, steaming
moist, hot, juicy, baked, succulent, piping hot

sticky
gooey, gummy, syrupy, tacky, sugary, gluey

stinging
biting, burning, scorching, piercing, tingling, prickling

stringy
pulpy, rough, woody, fibrous, stalky

succulent
tender, delectable, delicious, luscious, mouth-watering, juicy,
toothsome, enticing

sudsy
bubbly, soapy, foamy, lathery, frothy, hoppy

sumptuous
luscious, delectable, lavish, juicy, succulent, savory, tempting

supple
creamy, velvety, silky, mellow, rich, buttery, smooth, soft

Taste: Mouthfeel *and* Texture

tallow
waxy, soapy, sudsy, fatty, smeary

tender
succulent, ripe, juicy, moist, delicate, soft, supple

tepid
cool, lukewarm, flat, dull, lifeless

thick
full, rich, smooth, plump, meaty, hearty, bulky, chunky, heavy

tingling
prickling, stinging, bubbling, itchy, biting

toasted, toasty
crusty, crispy, dry, roasted

velvety
creamy, smooth, buttery, silky, luscious, whipped, rich

watery
runny, thin, soupy, weak, slurpy

waxy
soapy, tallow, sudsy, foamy, sticky

whipped
creamy, foamy, frothy, whisked, sudsy, smooth, bubbly

whisked
whipped, creamy, frothy, sudsy, bubbly, foamy

woody
tough, rough, stringy, pulpy, fibrous, stalky

zingy
zesty, flavorful, rich, tangy, spicy, peppery, lively

zippy
  flavorful, tangy, spicy, bright, flavorful

EATING, CHEWING, *and* FOOD

appetite
  hunger, craving, thirst, yearning, desire, famished, ravenous

belch
  burp, vomit, spew, spit, sputter, gush, disgorge, hiccup, erupt

binge
  gorge, guzzle, devour, gulp, gobble, scarf

bite
  chew, gnaw, chomp, munch, morsel, nibble, maul, gobble, tear, crunch

blend
  concoction, soup, brew, tonic, extract, infusion, potion, tincture, remedy, elixir

brew
  concoction, soup, blend, tonic, extract, elixir, infusion, potion, tincture, remedy

burp
  belch, vomit, spew, spit, sputter, hiccup, erupt

chew
  bite, gnaw, grind, munch, crunch, chomp, nibble, gobble

chomp
  bite, gnaw, grind, munch, crunch, chew, nibble, gulp

clench
  grit, grind, gnash, grate

Taste: Eating, Chewing, *and* Food

concoction
> brew, soup, blend, tonic, extract, elixir, infusion, medley, potion, tincture, remedy

connoisseur
> epicure, gourmet, foodie, aficionado

crave
> desire, appetite, hunger, thirst, yearn, pine, lust, hanker

crumb
> soupçon, bite, nibble, morsel, dollop, tidbit, pinch, dab, sliver

crunch
> munch, chew, bite, chomp, grind, gobble, bite, gnaw

delicacy
> gourmet, treat, luxury, nectar, tidbit, feast

devour
> gobble, gulp, wolf, voracious, ravenous, gnaw, maul, gorge, relish, swallow

distaste
> aversion, disgust, repellent, repulsion, revulsion

dollop
> bite, nibble, spoonful, morsel, tidbit, glob, soupçon

drool
> salivate, slobber, dribble, spit, spittle, drivel

elixir
> extract, infusion, potion, concoction, tincture, remedy, tonic, brew, blend

epicure
> gourmet, foodie, connoisseur, aficionado

extract
> elixir, infusion, potion, concoction, tincture, tonic, brew, juice

famished
> ravenous, hunger, hungry, starving, voracious

feast
> delight, treat, banquet, spread, delicacy, indulgence, gorge, gobble, gulp, devour, binge, maul

gag
> burp, belch, vomit, purge, spew, spit, sputter, gasp, choke, retch

glutton, gluttonous
> ravenous, voracious, greedy, insatiable, starved, wolfish

gnash
> grind, grate, chew, gnaw, crush, chomp, mince

gnaw
> chew, bite, chomp, munch, nibble, devour, maul

gobble
> devour, gulp, gorge, nibble, munch, maul, scarf, bite, chew, gnaw

gorge
> gobble, gulp, devour, binge, maul, scarf, guzzle, wolf

gourmand
> epicure, gorging, glutton, gourmet, guzzler, binge

grate
> grind, gnash, mince, crumble, crush

grind
> gnash, chew, crumble, pulverize, grate, crush

grit
> grind, gnash, clench, grate, mince

gulp
　　devour, gobble, slurp, wolf, guzzle, swallow, swig, slosh, chug

gusto
　　zest, vigor, relish, appetite, delight, brio

gut
　　visceral, instinctive, deep-seated, inherent, ingrained

guzzle
　　gulp, swill, slurp, swig, gorge, bolt, slosh

hanker
　　crave, desire, appetite, hunger, thirst, yearn, lust, pine

hunger, hungry
　　ravenous, voracious, craving, lusting, yearning, longing, thirsty,
　　desiring, famished, greedy

indulge, indulgence
　　feast, treat, luxury, delicacy, extravagance, excess

infusion
　　concoction, brew, blend, tonic, extract, elixir, potion, tincture,
　　remedy, immersion, soup

insatiable
　　unquenchable, ravenous, voracious, gluttonous, wolfish, yearning,
　　greedy, unappeasable

juice
　　tonic, sap, nectar, liquor, extract, milk, essence, spirit

lick
　　suck, lap, tongue, slurp, sip

mince
　　grind, cut, chop, grate, crush, pulverize

morsel
    bite, nibble, dollop, tidbit, soupçon, taste

mouthful
    bite, nibble, spoonful, morsel, tidbit, chunk, gulp

nibble
    chew, bite, gnaw, grind, munch, crunch, chomp, tidbit

nourish, nourishing
    sustain, nurture, satiate, satisfy

palate
    appetite, flavor, taste, zest, gusto

potion
    concoction, blend, tonic, extract, elixir, infusion, brew, tincture, remedy, soup

pucker, puckering
    purse, tighten, smack, crinkle

purge
    vomit, burp, belch, gag, spew, spit, sputter, cleanse, expel, heave

quench
    satiate, indulge, assuage, appease, gratify, relieve, satisfy

ravenous
    famished, hungry, starving, insatiable, voracious, wolfish

retch
    vomit, purge, spew, spit, burp, belch, sputter, gag, gasp, choke

salivate
    drool, slobber, dribble, relish, spit, spittle

satiate, satiating
    fill, satisfy, quench, fulfill, indulge

satisfy
nourish, quench, satiate, appease, indulge, fulfill

savor
relish, delight, revel, sip, enjoy

scarf
gobble, devour, gulp, gorge, nibble, munch, guzzle

sip
slurp, suck, savor, swirl, swallow

slobber
salivate, slurp, dripping, dribble, slaver, drool

sloppy
slushy, slurpy, runny, watery, slimy, oozy

slurp
suck, sip, slosh, swirl, lick, guzzle, gargle, swig

smack
relish, lick, slurp, savor, suck

smorgasbord
buffet, variety, spread, medley

soupçon
bite, nibble, morsel, dollop, tidbit, crumb, pinch

spit
drool, slobber, dribble, spew, sputter, spittle, slaver

sputter
burp, belch, gag, spittle, spew, spit

starve, starving
ravenous, hungry, famished, voracious

suck
slurp, sip, drink, gulp, lick, lap, smack

sustenance
nourishment, refreshment, edibles

swig
gulp, gargle, guzzle, sip, swill

swill
gargle, swig, guzzle, gulp

thirst, thirsty, thirsting
unquenchable, parched, craving, burning, unfulfilled, yearning,
dry

tidbit
bite, nibble, spoonful, morsel, dollop

tincture
concoction, soup, blend, tonic, extract, elixir, infusion, potion,
brew, remedy

unquenchable
parched, insatiable, voracious, ravenous, yearning, unappeasable,
thirsty

vomit
burp, belch, gag, purge, spew, spit, sputter

voracious
devouring, ravenous, insatiable, gorging, unquenchable, greedy

wolfish
ravenous, voracious, gluttonous, greedy

yearning
thirsting, craving, burning, lusting, unfulfilled, desiring, wanting

SMELL

Even as I think of smells, my nose is full of scents that start awake sweet memories of summers gone and ripening grain fields far away.
—*Helen Keller, American author, lecturer, and activist*

AROMATIC *and* FRAGRANT - DISTINCT *or* INTENSE - REPULSIVE *or* NOXIOUS

Smells are histories. An invisible cloud of aftershave, pipe tobacco, and shoe polish signals a visitor was here. A scarf carries the scent of latte and spice cake. An old book smells damp and salty.

Smells are trails. Not the source itself but a trail of the source—a secret message billowing out along an unknown path. Follow the swirling trail back to the source. A sugary, vanilla-drenched, confectionery trail. A whiff of lilac with a long, seductive reach. The sudden sting of smoke from a fire smoldering somewhere. A repulsive stench. All leading you somewhere by the nose to itself.

Smells are memories. Of a childhood house, Grandma's kitchen, church incense at a funeral, a baby's delicate skin, a path in a pine forest. Precise, distinct gateways beckoning you back to the past.

Smells are assessments. *I smell a rat. That stinks. She's smelling like a rose.*

Smells are warnings. One sniff and we reject the milk. Gas leak danger. Skunk alert. *I'd turn back if I were you.*

Smells are reminders. To come alive, to experience, to rejoice (and perhaps to bathe). Uplifting, warm, sharp, revitalizing. Inviting us to engage, expand, and explore.

In this section, we examine the aromas and fragrances that delight us; the distinct, intense, and unmistakable odors that sharpen our senses; and the repulsive, noxious smells that revolt us and warn us of potential harm.

AROMATIC *and* FRAGRANT

airy
    light, fresh, breezy, brisk

allspice
    spicy, cinnamon, fragrant, aromatic

apple
    fruity, sweet, berry, aromatic

aroma
    whiff, scent, smell, odor, bouquet, perfume, fragrance, incense

aromatic
    perfumed, scented, fragrant, odoriferous, spicy, redolent

banana
    fruity, sweet, tropical, starchy

berry
> fruity, sweet, plum, apple, tart

botanical
> herbal, grassy, weedy, mossy, floral

bouquet
> flowery, floral, perfumed, scented, incense

buttery
> sweet, candied, honey, caramel, creamy

candied
> sweet, honey, syrupy, sugary, confectionery

caramel
> candied, buttery, creamy, honey, syrupy, sweet, toffee

cedar
> piney, woody, mossy, woodsy

chocolaty
> cocoa, sweet, rich, coffee, burnt, roasted, creamy

cinnamon
> spicy, apple, sweet, allspice

citrus
> lemony, fresh, clean, citron, sharp, orange

clean
> fresh, refreshing, crisp, bright, pure

cocoa
> chocolaty, sweet, rich, coffee, burnt, creamy

earthy
> rich, robust, woody, woodsy, herbal, muddy

evergreen
  piney, cedar, woody, weedy, mossy, grassy, rosemary

floral
  flowery, herbal, perfumed, bouquet, botanical, blossomy

flowery
  floral, herbal, perfumed, fragrant, blossomy

fragrant
  aromatic, perfumed, scented, floral, flowery, incense

fresh
  clean, minty, refreshing, pure, crisp, invigorating

fruity
  apple, berry, sweet, honey

grassy
  herbal, botanical, weedy, mossy, earthy

herbal, herbaceous
  botanical, grassy, weedy, floral, minty

honey, honeyed
  sweet, candied, syrupy, sugary

incense
  fragrant, smoky, spicy, exotic, perfumed

lemon, lemony
  citrus, clean, sharp, fresh, refreshing, invigorating

lilac
  floral, perfumy, bouquet, fragrant, flowery

lime
  citrusy, clean, lemony, sharp

menthol
sharp, minty, wintergreen, crisp, invigorating, refreshing

minty
sharp, fresh, herbal, crisp, invigorating, refreshing, menthol

mossy
herbal, woody, moist, grassy, damp

nectar
sap, honey, sweet, wine, ambrosia

odoriferous
scented, fragrant, aromatic, perfumy, pungent, spicy

odorous
flowery, aromatic, fragrant, scented, spicy, smelly

orange
citrus, clean, sweet, tangy

perfumed, perfumy
aromatic, scented, fragrant, herbal

piney
cedar, woody, mossy, grassy, evergreen, rosemary, earthy

powder
sweet, fragrant, soft, perfumy

redolent
rich, fragrant, sweet-smelling, reminiscent

rose, rosy
aromatic, perfumed, lilac, floral, flowery, sweet, blossomy

scent
aroma, whiff, smell, bouquet, odor, spice

spicy
    complex, piquant, exotic, rich, fragrant, tangy

sweet
    candied, cloying, honey, vanilla, fruity, buttery, berry, confectionery

sugary
    honey, vanilla, candied, confectionery, toffee

whiff
    aroma, scent, smell, odor, fume, puff, blast, waft, sniff, snuff

woodsy
    cedar, piney, mossy, grassy, earthy

woody
    cedar, piney, mossy, botanical, weedy, grassy, earthy

vanilla
    sweet, honey, sugary, candied

DISTINCT *or* INTENSE

acidic
    sour, citrus, burning, caustic, vinegary, sharp, biting

acrid
    pungent, rank, sour, vinegary, acidic, sharp

ammonia
    sharp, fumy, pungent, vaporous, bracing, piercing, burning

beefy
    meaty, gamy, fleshy, savory, pungent, salty

biting
    stinging, sharp, acrid, pungent, piercing, intense, burning

burnt
fiery, smoky, charred, blackened, scorched, seared

camphor
aromatic, mothball, sharp, intense, bracing, bitter

charred
burnt, scorched, smoky, blackened, seared, singed

cheesy
creamy, sharp, rich, buttery, milky, salty

coffee
bitter, burnt, roasted, chocolate, toasted, sweet

complex
spicy, rich, exotic

dank
damp, humid, musty, muggy, slimy, moldy

doggy
dank, sweaty, skunky, moist, musky

dusty
musty, sooty, stale, chalky, dirty, sandy, grubby

eggy
creamy, velvety, rich, buttery

exhaust
fumy, fuel, gas, gassy, vaporous

fiery
smoky, burnt, charred, seared, spicy, pungent

fishy
meaty, piscine, gamy, seaweed, briny, salty

fleshy
> meaty, gamy, beefy

fumy
> gassy, vapor, fuel, exhaust, gasoline

fusty
> stuffy, musty, stale, dusty, moldy, damp, mildewy

gamy
> meaty, rancid, fleshy, beefy

garlicky
> oniony, savory, pungent, sharp, sour

gassy
> fumy, vaporous, exhaust, fuel

gingery
> peppery, candied, sugary, aromatic

horsey
> sweaty, musty, barnyard, doggy

leather
> earthy, soft, musky

loamy
> earthy, woody, clayey, muddy

meadow
> grassy, herbal, earthy, mossy, muddy, blossomy

medicinal
> sharp. piercing, artificial, chemical, synthetic

metallic
> mineral, tinny, coppery

mildew, mildewy
  moldy, musty, damp, stale

moist
  wet, humid, dank, dewy, muggy

moldy
  musty, damp, stale, mildew, funky

muddy
  woody, sandy, clayey, earthy, loamy, grassy

mushroom
  rich, earthy, muddy, savory, mossy, damp, sandy, woody

musky
  sweaty, scented, perfumed, aromatic, skunky

mustard
  pungent, sharp, spicy, oniony, garlicky, sour, bitter

musty
  damp, stale, dusty, moldy, fusty

nutty
  almondy, toasted, hazelnut, buttery

oniony
  garlicky, savory, pungent, sour

penetrating
  stiff, sharp, biting, piercing, permeating, pungent, intense, stinging

peppery
  spicy, savory, fiery, gingery, pungent

pickled
  salty, spicy, fermented, cured, vinegary, briny, sour

plastic
synthetic, metallic, rubber, fumy, chemical

pungent
sharp, strong, ripe, caustic, acrid, spicy, tangy

rain
earthy, clean, fresh, mossy, sweet, dewy, moist, humid, muggy

ripe
strong, intense, pungent, sharp, rich, sour

rubber
plastic, burnt, charred, chemical

savory
pungent, piquant, succulent, zingy, tangy, mushroom, earthy

seared
burnt, charred, crispy, blackened, toasted, scorched

seaweed
fishy, piscine, briny, salty, grassy

sharp
pungent, penetrating, intense, biting, piercing

skunky
musky, swampy, doggy, dank, fragrant, musty, odorous

smell (n)
aroma, whiff, scent, stink, odor, perfume, essence

smell (v)
sniff, detect, whiff, discern, inhale, snuff

smoky
burnt, fiery, ash, woody, sooty, smoldering

sniff
    snort, whiff, snuff, inhale, snuff

soapy
    waxy, perfume, powdery, frothy, fragrant

sooty
    dusty, musty, chalky, powdery, moldy

sour
    acidic, lemony, vinegary, tart, sharp, citrus, stale, rank

spicy
    fiery, exotic, rich, pungent, sharp, salty

stale
    musty, rancid, fusty, flat, moldy, sour

stuffy
    fusty, musty, stale, dusty, airless

sugary
    sweet, syrupy, candied, honey, gooey, confectionery

swampy
    skunky, mossy, grassy, algal, dank, marshy, wet, humid

sweaty
    musky, skunky, ripe, horsey, rank, dank, humid, muggy

synthetic
    plastic, metallic, rubber, fumy, chemical

tart
    acidic, lemony, sour, biting, sharp, tangy

turpentine
    lacquer, metallic, synthetic, chemical

weedy
　　grassy, herbal, botanical, woody

yeasty
　　doughy, fermented, creamy, toasty

zesty
　　pungent, sharp, fresh, tangy

REPULSIVE *or* NOXIOUS

biting
　　stinging, sharp, acrid, pungent, piercing, intense, burning

cloying
　　sickening, nauseating, oversweet, overpowering, gooey

fetid
　　putrid, rank, rotting, stinky, stinking, foul, repulsive

foul
　　odorous, smelly, stinking, acrid, putrid, rank

miasma, miasmal
　　reeking, rank, rotten, stink, stenchful, odorous

nauseating
　　putrid, rank, sickening, repulsive, fetid, foul

noxious
　　repulsive, odious, putrid, foul, fetid

odorous
　　smelly, stinking, foul, acrid, putrid, rank

putrid
　　nauseating, rank, fetid, rotting, repulsive, repugnant, gagging

putrefied
rotten, decayed, decomposed, stinking, festering, spoiled

rancid
stale, spoiled, rank, putrid, stinking, rotten, sharp

rank
foul, repulsive, odorous, smelly, stinking, acrid, putrid, repugnant

reek
stink, smell, stench

repugnant
foul, repulsive, revolting, vile, nauseating

revolting
repugnant, foul, repulsive, abhorrent, appalling, vile

rotting, rotten
putrid, fetid, rank, moldy, tainted, decaying

smelly
odorous, stinking, foul, acrid, pungent, rank, rancid, putrid

spoiled
rotten, overripe, putrid, sour

stench, stenchful
reek, rank, odor, stink, miasma, foul

stinging
biting, sharp, acrid, pungent, piercing, burning

stink, stinky, stinking
stench, reek, rank, odor, odorous, smelly, foul, acrid, pungent

sulfur
rotten egg, metallic, skunky, burnt rubber

Resources

The following resources were helpful reference materials during the construction of *Thesaurus of the Senses*. See also the Notes section for references related to the senses.

Random House Word Menu, by Stephen Glazier; Random House: New York, 1997.

The DICT Development Group; http://www.dict.org.

The Synonym Finder, by J. I. Rodale; Warner Books: New York, 1978.

Thesaurus.com; Roget's 21st Century Thesaurus, 3rd ed.; Philip Lief Group: Princeton, NJ, 2009.

New Oxford American Dictionary, 3rd ed.; Oxford University Press: Oxford, 2010.

Oxford American Writer's Thesaurus, 3rd ed., by D. Auburn et al.; Oxford University Press: Oxford, 2012.

Roget's II Pocket Thesaurus; Houghton Mifflin Company: Boston, 1987.

20,000 Words; compiled by Louis A. Leslie; McGraw-Hill: New York, 1965.

A Dictionary of Synonyms and Antonyms, by Joseph Devlin; Popular Library Inc.: New York, 1961.

The New International Webster's Pocket Thesaurus of the English Language; Trident Press International: Naples, FL, 2002.

Notes

Connecting with the Senses: Exercises

Exercise 12: For advice on using all of your senses in connecting with nature, including how to expand your sight using "splatter vision," see *Tom Brown's Field Guide to Nature Observation and Tracking*, by Tom Brown, Jr.; Berkley Trade: New York, 1986.

Exercise 19: For a look at what people with synesthesia experience, see "Rare but Real: People Who Feel, Taste and Hear Color," by Ker Than, livescience.com, February 22, 2005; http://www.livescience.com/169-rare-real-people-feel-taste-hear-color.html.

Exercise 23: In her delightful book *A Natural History of the Senses* (Vintage Books, 1990), Diane Ackerman notes that we often describe smell based on what something "smells like" rather than its actual scent. See also "Why So Few English Words for Odors?" by Jessica Love, *The American Scholar*, January 16, 2014; https://theamericanscholar.org/why-so-few-english-words-for-odors/

Hear

For a fascinating discussion about what the Big Bang and early universe may have sounded like, based on research by astronomy professor Mark Whittle, see "Is This What the Big Bang Sounded Like?" by William Cocke, *National Geographic*

News, March 22, 2005, http://news.nationalgeographic.com/news/2004/09/0920_040920_big_bang.html.

Touch

In his book *Touch: The Science of Hand, Heart, and Mind* (Viking Press, 2015), neuroscientist David Linden explores the many unique dimensions of touch, including its compelling connection to language and emotion.

Taste

"How does our sense of taste work?" *Pubmed Health*, January 6, 2012; See http://www.ncbi.nlm.nih.gov/pubmedhealth/PMH0033701/

Smell

In Helen Keller's book *The World I Live In* (1908), she discusses her exquisite sense of smell that allowed her accurately perceive distances, coming storms, distinct places and their various rhythmic activities, plants and animals, and the individual scents of people. She writes, "In my experience smell is most important, and I find that there is high authority for the nobility of the sense which we have neglected and disparaged."

Acknowledgments

Writing is an inner journey fueled by persistence and inspiration. I am grateful for the kind support and encouragement of family and friends who have helped me in this journey. Special thanks to Don Hart, writer and word lover *par excellence*, for guidance and brilliant creative insight; Tonya Foreman for her artistic eye and invaluable collaboration; Mary Ann Hart for huge moral support and helpful feedback; Kerry George for inspiration and advice; Connee Draper for always delightful writing discussions at Zen Cha teahouse; and Susie, Gemma, Coo Coo, and Maggie of Four Cats Publishing LLC for helping make everything run so smoothly.

Word Index

Word Index

Word Index

Word Index

ropy, 64, 261
rose, 38, 349
rosy, 38, 349
rotten, 129, 325, 357
rotting, 357
rotund, 64
rough, 77, 261
rough-hewn, 64
rounded, 64
rousing, 129, 236
rubber, 354
rubbery, 64, 261, 334
ruby, 38
ruckus, 166
ruddy, 38
rueful, 92
ruffled, 261
rugged, 64, 77, 261
ruined, 140
ruinous, 140
rumble, 162
rumbling, 162
ruminating, 92
rummage, 297
rumpled, 77, 261
runny, 334
rush, 297
russet, 38
rust, 38
rusted, 77
rustic, 141
rustle, 176
rustling, 176
rusty, 38
rutted, 64

S

sable, 38
sabotage, 297
saccharine, 325

saddle, 297
saffron, 38
sagging, 261
saggy, 261
sail, 297
salacious, 236
salivate, 342
sallow, 39
salmon, 39
salty, 325
salubrious, 236
salutary, 236
salvage, 297
sandy, 39, 261, 334
sapid, 325
sapless, 262
sapor, 325
sappy, 262
sardonic, 92
sashay, 297
satiate, 342
satiating, 342
satin, 77
satiny, 77, 262
satisfy, 343
saturated, 262
saucy, 129
saunter, 298
savage, 92, 129
savor, 343
savory, 325, 354
scald, 236
scalding, 236, 335
scale, 170
scaly, 262
scamper, 298
scan, 152
scant, 47
scanty, 47
scar, 236
scarf, 343

scarlet, 39
scarred, 236, 262
scarring, 236
scathing, 236
scatter, 298
scenic, 141
scent, 349
schism, 51
scintillating, 129, 236
scoff, 195
scold, 195
scoot, 298
scorched, 236, 335
scorching, 236, 335
scorn, 195
scornful, 92
scour, 298
scowling, 92
scraggly, 64, 141
scramble, 298
scrape, 298
scratch, 298
scratchy, 262
scrawl, 77, 298
scrawled, 77
scrawny, 64
scream, 195
screech, screeching, 166, 176, 196
screen, 152
scribble, 77, 298
scrub, 298
scruffy, 141, 262
scrumptious, 325
scrupulous, 129
scrutinize, 152
scrutinizing, 152
scuff, 299
sculpt, 299
sculpted, 64
scurry, 299

Word Index

Word Index

Y

yank, 311
yawning, 48
yearn, 247
yearning, 98, 344
yeasty, 329, 356
yell, 202
yelp, 202
yodel, 179, 202
yoke, 311

Z

zesty, 329, 356
zingy, 329, 337
zippy, 329, 338

Subject Index

Made in the USA
Monee, IL
07 June 2023

35426397R00221